Worlds from Words

James Phelan

Worlds from Words
A Theory of Language in Fiction

The University of Chicago Press

Chicago and London

The University of Chicago Press, Chicago 60637
The University of Chicago Press, Ltd., London

Library of Congress Cataloging in Publication Data

Phelan, James, 1951–
  Worlds from words.

  Bibliography: p.
  Includes index.
  1. Fiction.   2. American fiction—History and
criticism.   3. English fiction—History and criticism.
4. Style, Literary.   I. Title.
PN3331.P5   801'.953   80–25844
ISBN 0–226–66690–5

JAMES PHELAN is assistant professor
of English at Ohio State University.

For Betty

Contents

Preface   ix

Part One   The Theory and Its Powers

1. Style and Theories of Style:
   The Problem and a Strategy
   for Solution   3

2. Deliberative Acts vs.
   Grammatical Closure:
   Stanley Fish and the Language of
   The Ambassadors   15

3. Literary Discourse,
   "Ordinary Discourse," and Intentions:
   David Lodge and the Language of
   Sister Carrie   67

4. Determinate and Interdeterminate Value in
   the Linguistic System:
   J. Hillis Miller and the Language of
   Persuasion   117

Part Two   Limits of the Theory

5. Verbal Artistry and
   Speech as Action:
   Elder Olson and the Language of
   Lolita   155

6. Design and Value in
   a World of Words:
   Umberto Eco and the Language of
   Willie Masters' Lonesome Wife   184

7. Multiple Questions, Multiple Answers,
and the Status of Our Theory:
Pluralism and the Language of Fiction   221

Notes   233
Selected Bibliography   245
Index   253

Preface

Like many another author, I have discovered that the book I have written is not the book I set out to write. I began with the idea of studying some elements of prose style—emphasis, focus, pace, balance, and rhythm, among others—and have ended by exploring various issues in literary theory—linguistic indeterminacy, reader response, authorial intention, and critical pluralism, among others. I did not write the original book because I found I had to write the theoretical one first. The value of the more restricted study, I assumed, would be that it could offer a more precise way to talk about style in fiction, and consequently, help us understand how a novelist's prose affected our pleasures in his or her novel. I found, however, that although it might be possible to refine our notion of a stylistic element such as pace, I could not evaluate the effectiveness of any one sentence's movement until I had a way of talking about it as part of a larger context. And any such context, it seemed, had to include some notion of a writer's intention. Once I got to the problem of intention, everything changed. The work of such important stylistic critics as Josephine Miles, Richard Ohmann, Samuel Levin, and Michael Riffaterre became less directly applicable to my problem, and that of the literary theorists I examine in the following pages (Stanley Fish, David Lodge, J. Hillis Miller, Elder Olson, and Umberto Eco) far more central. An approach to style concerned with its component elements and with characterizing an author's style as a whole gave way to one concerned with illuminating the specific effects of specific stylistic choices at specific points in a work; such an approach seemed more suitable for assessing how important stylistic effects were for the success of a particular novel. Some of my initial ideas about the elements of style did carry over into this book, but they are not presented here in any systematic way; the focus on the theoretical issues and on the relative importance of style from work to work required a different kind of organization.

The consequences of this mutation during gestation are not only that the original book is still to be written but also that this offspring lodges in the territory of various specialties without taking up permanent residence in any. It is an essay on style and an inquiry into hermeneutics, an analysis of five novels and an experiment in theory construction. Different readers, then, are likely to react to the book in different ways. Those primarily interested in practical stylistics may become impatient with the theoretical discussions, whereas those interested primarily in theory may find the specific analyses too detailed. I welcome readers not interested in theoretical argument to proceed directly to the practical criticism; if the analyses are at all compelling, I imagine that at least some will turn to the reasoning that underlies them. I invite those primarily interested in theory just to sample the practical analyses, which are necessarily detailed because they provide the basis for large claims about individual novels. My hope is that my readers' interests in superior fiction and excellent fictional prose (admittedly Dreiser's is an exception) will be sufficient inducement for them to read the analyses all the way through. Needless to say, my fonder hope is that all readers will want to read every word.

Like many another author, I owe thanks to more people than I can name in a brief space. Some, however, must be singled out. The Research Committee of the College of Humanities at The Ohio State University granted me a quarter's released time from teaching so that I might finish this book. My colleagues, James Battersby, Richard Finholt, Nicholas Guild, and Christian Zacher read all or parts of the manuscript and offered important encouragement and advice. Joseph Williams helped shape many of the ideas about style in the book and made valuable suggestions for revision of earlier drafts. Wayne Booth provided numerous useful recommendations and crucial support during the later stages of the writing; even more important, he asked the question that led to chapter 6. The late Sheldon Sacks profoundly influenced most of the arguments I advance here, and he taught me virtually everything I know about asking critical questions and reasoning to their answers. I deeply regret that he did not live to see this book completed, but the memory of his extraordinary intellect, astonishing energy, and unlimited generosity remains a source of wonder and inspiration for me. Finally, my wife, Elizabeth Menaghan, helped the most by always being there, by sharing in all the visions and revisions, all the questioning of whether it was worth it after all; for that—and so much else—I dedicate this book to her.

James Phelan

1

The Theory and Its Powers

1 Style and Theories of Style: The Problem and a Strategy for Solution

What is the role of the medium in the art of fiction? Consider for a moment the quite different language of Vladimir Nabokov and Theodore Dreiser.

> Lolita, light of my life, fire of my loins. My sin, my soul. Lo-lee-ta: the tip of the tongue taking a trip of three steps down the palate to tap at three on the teeth. Lo. Lee. Ta.
>
> *Lolita,* chapter 1

> The play was one of those drawing room concoctions in which charmingly overdressed ladies and gentlemen suffer the pangs of love and jealousy amid gilded surroundings. Such bon-mots are ever enticing to those who have all their days longed for such material surroundings and have never had them gratified.
>
> *Sister Carrie,* chapter 32

Each of these passages illustrates quite dramatically why its author has his particular reputation as a stylist. Nabokov's creation of Humbert Humbert's invocation to Lolita is the virtuoso performance of a verbal wizard: he exploits phonology, syntax, and semantics, sound, sense, and word order to provide a special trip for our tongues—and minds—as we watch Humbert celebrate the name of his beloved and explain what she means to him. Nabokov's passage is graceful, lyrical, beautiful.

On the other hand, Dreiser's description of the Broadway play Carrie Meeber attends with her more sophisticated friend, Mrs. Vance, is the inept performance of a verbal bumbler: not only is the language prosaic, but the sense and movement of the passage are disturbed by the false connective, "such bon-mots" (what bon-mots?), and the rudimentary grammatical mistake of the final phrase ("them" has no antecedent, Dreiser means "their longings"). Dreiser's passage is sloppy, awkward, clumsy.

Yet both *Lolita* and *Sister Carrie* are successful novels; both have earned the admiration and respect of countless readers, and both seem assured of permanently important places in our literary tradition. What do these facts reveal about the relation between language and fiction? Is style an important element of successful novels or a nonessential extra which occasionally provides an added fillip to our pleasure? Is style perhaps essential to the success of some novels and nonessential to that of others? More concretely, does *Sister Carrie* succeed in spite of its style, is the style somehow beside the point, or indeed, does Dreiser find a way to make his clumsiness a virtue? Does *Lolita* succeed only because of its brilliant style, would it succeed with a more workmanlike one, or indeed, does the stylistic brilliance detract from or compete with other elements of the work?

In order to decide among the various possibilities we must address fundamental questions about the nature of language, the nature of fiction, and the relation between the two. Is fiction a purely verbal art? Is paraphrase of literary language impossible? If so, then Dreiser most likely found a way to make a virtue of his clumsiness, and Nabokov probably needs his brilliant style. Are there elements of fiction, e.g., character and action, which are essentially nonlinguistic, and more important than language? Is there a limit to how much the stylistic revision of a novel can improve it? If so, then Dreiser's awkwardness may be beside the point, and Nabokov's stylistic brilliance may be unnecessary or disruptive.

It is not until we can satisfactorily answer such theoretical questions as these that we can confidently answer our specific questions about *Lolita* and *Sister Carrie*. But once we take this necessary trip into the often misty territory of literary theory, we extend the significance of our inquiry beyond the boundaries of two works. If we ask enough of the right questions and if we pursue their answers with sufficient rigor, we shall develop a comprehensive theory that will allow us to account for the language of any work in the entire realm of prose fiction. Such a theory is the proper answer to the question of our first sentence; such a theory is the ultimate goal of this essay.

II

Had we world enough and time, we could ensure that our theory would indeed be comprehensive by constructing it through the analysis of hundreds of novels and virtually every theory about the relation between language and literature. But lacking such leisure, we must build the theory from a more limited survey, and so can feel that the theory is truly comprehensive only if it meets some rigorous criteria: it must emerge out of a broad range of questions about language, about fiction, and about the relation between them; it must offer convincing accounts of the role language plays not only in at least one novel which initially seems to offer good evidence for the theory, but also in at least one which seems to present problematic evidence for it; the theory must be superior to alternative explanatory models that would dispute both its predictions and its assumptions. These criteria, though rigorous, initially simplify our task by guiding us to an appropriate method of inquiry.

If we were to examine several theories about the relation between language and fiction in connection with the same novel, we could discover the relative strengths and weaknesses of each theory, but we could not be sure that the resulting theory was truly comprehensive. We would be unable to test adequately the hypothesis that even our brief glance at *Lolita* and *Sister Carrie* suggests we ought to explore: language can play different roles in different works. If we were to sketch our theory and then test it against one competitor by comparing how well each explained the role of style in four or five different novels, we could reach some suggestive conclusions about language in fiction, but again we could not feel confident that these conclusions constituted a comprehensive theory. Since the differences among most theories of language in literature are ultimately the result of the different assumptions they make about language, we could not justifiably conclude that our theory was more powerful than a third or fourth competitor based on assumptions about language we have not examined. In short, this method would not allow us to confront a sufficiently broad range of questions about language.

Although each of these strategies has some advantages, we cannot simply glue the methods together; to analyze each of four or five different novels in connection with each of four or five different theories would make our inquiry extremely unwieldy, if not repetitious and mechanical as well. To meet the standards for comprehensiveness, we must select a diverse group of theories and a diverse group of novels and then match them in such a way that each novel helps illustrate the powers and limits of one theory, and each theory in connection with one novel raises different fruitful questions about language in literature. Furthermore, we must select theories and novels that not only allow us to explore a broad range of questions but also require us to challenge strongly the successive answers we arrive at after examining each pair of novels and theories. Our method, in short, will be radically inductive. We shall build the theory not from unquestioned assumptions but from the diverse questions raised by specific novels and specific competing approaches; we shall constantly test the theory's design, the strength of its foundation, and its explanatory capacity by considering the evidence offered by each new novel and by examining the alternative explanations offered by each new theory. The power of our theory can be measured in two ways: (1) whether for each novel considered it gives us a more satisfactory account of the language than the approach we are examining in connection with that novel; and (2) whether in its full elaboration, after the cumulative exposition and demonstration of it over the course of the entire essay, it is compelling enough to convince us that it can yield a satisfactory account of the language of any novel—or failing that ultimate success, that it is the closest we can come to such a theory.

Before considering which novels and theories to choose, I want to specify the way I shall use the terms "language" and "style." The relation between them here is roughly analogous to that between "rhythm" and "meter." "Language" is the general term, used to refer to the system which unites sounds and meanings, and used especially to refer to that system as the medium of fiction. "Style" is the specific term, used to refer to particular uses of that system. "Style" also has another sense, which I shall develop more fully later: those elements of a sentence or passage that would be lost in a paraphrase. For much of the theoretical discussion of the essay I shall use the general term, a choice largely dictated by the other positions I consider. Many of those theorists maintain that the particular language of a text is the all-important determinant of our response to the text, and hence, for them, there is no style apart from content, or to put it another way, language is style.

Nevertheless, my questions about the medium of fiction shall not lead out toward questions about the similarities and differences among language and other representational media, but shall lead in toward questions about style. Although I believe that this essay will have implications for an investigation into what can be represented in fiction as opposed to, say, sculpture and painting, or even the drama and film, it is focused more on the diverse uses novelists have made of their language. It asks, to restate the central problem in slightly different terms, the following question: given that the form (or forms) we call the novel includes works that seem to use the medium as differently as *Sister Carrie* and *Lolita,* what conclusions can we draw about the relative importance of that medium in creating successful works of art?

III

In one sense there are really only two theoretical positions: (1) fiction is a purely verbal art, and every response we make to it can be explained as a response to language; or (2) fiction is an art that is created through language but whose effects must be explained not only by reference to that language but also by reference to nonlinguistic elements such as character, action, and plot. (Strict logic tells us that a third position is possible, i.e., that language is unimportant, that it is merely the neutral vehicle through which the all-important content is communicated; however, in practice no theorist argues that the medium of an art form is unimportant.) My initial hypothesis is a variation of the second position: language is never all-important in fiction, but the degree of importance it has may vary a great deal from novel to novel, or indeed, from one passage in a novel to another. This hypothesis is based in large part on the tentative assumption that individual works embody the determinate intentions of their authors; this assumption makes it possible to speak about *the* role that language plays in a work. The hypothesis is also based on the related assumption that different intentions require different functions from the language that embodies them. As indicated above, both the hypothesis and its underlying assumptions will be developed and seriously tested in the course of this essay; and because they represent beginning rather than concluding positions, there can be no guarantee that they will emerge from the scrutiny intact.

The contrast between the two basic theoretical positions is clearly illustrated by the work of "organicist-idealist" critics on the one hand and that of neo-Aristotelian critics on the other. The organicist-idealists believe that the special properties of literary language make a novel a self-contained world of meaning; for them, paraphrasing the language of a novel would always significantly alter that world since the paraphrase would inevitably alter the meaning. For them, the essential element of construction in a novel is language; elements such as character and plot in their view are only convenient abstractions from language.

In contrast, the neo-Aristotelians view language as the least important of the elements that affect our response to fiction. These critics view all the elements of construction—the objects imitated, the manner and order of imitation, the particular language of the imitation—as means to an end, not ends in themselves. The single end all these elements contribute to is the complex intellectual or emotional effect a work produces in us, and this effect results from the particular synthesis an author makes out of all the elements of the work. The synthesizing principle of most novels, in the neo-Aristotelian view, is the author's representation of a particular action. Thus for them, the world of a novel is the world of a represented action; paraphrasing the language of a novel would only alter that world slightly, since the paraphrase by definition would still represent the same action.

In scrutinizing these two theories, then, we shall directly confront the major issue of whether fiction is essentially a verbal art, and the secondary issue of whether language can vary in importance from one work to the next. Although each position has various prominent representatives (Murray Krieger, William Wimsatt, David Lodge to name just a few from the first group; R. S. Crane, Wayne Booth, Elder Olson, a few from the second),[1] the specific work done by some individuals makes them especially suitable for our purposes. Lodge's book, *Language of Fiction,* sets out to answer a question very much like the one I am addressing here, and his conclusion that language is all presents a clear challenge to our initial hypothesis. Elder Olson has given the most extended direct treatment of language in literature of any neo-Aristotelian; consequently, his work provides the most difficult test for our hypothesis that the role of language varies from work to work.

In order to explore the limits of Lodge's theory, we should examine it in connection with a "badly written great novel"; to test Olson's, we need a novel of great stylistic beauty. Again we can choose among several representatives: in addition to Dreiser's novels, something by Walter Scott or Thomas Hardy could be matched with Lodge's approach, and in addition to Nabokov's works, something by James Joyce or Virginia Woolf (among others) could be matched with Olson's. But since Dreiser is probably the most egregiously deficient stylist among novelists of the first rank, it makes sense to match Lodge's theory with *Sister Carrie*. And since Humbert Humbert's monstrous actions present such a sharp contrast to his marvelous prose, it makes sense to match Olson's with *Lolita*.

Despite their differences, both organicist-idealist and neo-Aristotelian critics offer theories based on the reliability of the text, i.e., on the assumption that an author creates a determinate meaning which resides in the language of the text, and hence, which we all can share. Other theorists argue that this assumption is itself based on an illusion, and consequently offer quite different ways of accounting for language in fiction, although in one sense they are saying that language is all-important. Some theorists maintain that literature is not in the text but in the reader. For these reader-response critics, the language of a text is not important for what it is but for what it makes us do. Furthermore, since what we do is not strictly controlled by the grammar of the text, meaning cannot be properly determined by examining the syntax and semantics of a text but only by examining the series of mental operations we perform as we read the text. One advantage of the reader-response approach is that it enables us to avoid such problems as we seem to have with *Sister Carrie*. A reader-response critic can say that Dreiser's language is not sloppy and clumsy, that indeed it is not anything in itself except the stimulus for our mental operations. This critic could then explain why the novel still continues to please by referring to what readers learn from those operations.

In examining the reader-response approach, then, we shall face the large question of the relative importance of authors, readers, and texts in interpretation. We shall also raise an important question about the relation of parts to wholes. Reader-critics often assume that the basic experience of a whole work is contained in each of its parts, that every part is, in a sense, a microcosm of the whole. If this assumption can be well substantiated, it would be strong evidence that the language of individual sentences and paragraphs would indeed be the most important elements of a work's construction.

Although reader-response criticism probably now has more proponents than either the organicist-idealist or the neo-Aristotelean approach, one figure stands out as the most prominent and provocative of them: Stanley Fish.[2] Since Fish has most fully articulated the assumptions, purposes, and values of the reader-response approach and has done extensive practical criticism employing it, his work will provide a strong test for our hypothesis. Again there are numerous novels we might match against Fish's theory, but our choices are narrowed in part by our hypothesis and by what we have already chosen. If we only wanted to test Fish's theory, we might choose a Hemingway novel where the language appears to be more important for what it is than for what it makes us do. But since we want to explore the hypothesis that language plays different roles in different works, we want to be sure that we choose a work where the style seems to have a different role from the one it has in either *Sister Carrie* or *Lolita*. And since we want to challenge the ideas that language is never all-important and that authorial intentions not readers' mental operations create meaning, it makes sense to select a novel which seems compatible with Fish's theory. Thus, we might choose something by George Meredith, Henry James, or perhaps William Faulkner. Because James's language seems to stimulate the most intricate mental operations, and because how he expresses something often seems more important than what he expresses (though his style does not achieve the self-conscious beauty of Nabokov's), it makes sense to work with one of his later novels. Thus, we shall match Fish's approach with *The Ambassadors*.

A fourth group of theorists locates meaning in the text but argues that textual meaning is radically unstable and open because language is an unreliable medium. These deconstructionist critics begin with Saussure's insight that language is a system in which individual signs have meanings not on the basis of any positive relationship between signifiers and signifieds but only on the basis of the differences between signs. These critics then maintain that because there is no center or ground to the linguistic system, it is an illusion to think that linguistic texts have a

center or ground which enables them to establish a positive relationship between their signs and a determinate meaning. What
texts do instead, the deconstructionists suggest, is dramatically
present on a smaller scale the play of difference operating in the
whole linguistic system. Thus, in their view, the critic's job is to
open up that play of difference, to show how it introduces into any
text so many meanings that we are forced to recognize the text's
indeterminacy.

In considering the deconstructionist approach, therefore, we
shall confront the fundamental questions of whether and how
language can be regarded as a reliable medium, whether and how,
that is, we can view it as capable of embodying and preserving an
author's determinate intention. Of the most prominent deconstructionists, Jacques Derrida, Paul de Man, Geoffrey
Hartman, and J. Hillis Miller, the best representatives for our
purposes are Derrida and Miller.[3] Derrida's work provides the
philosophical foundation for the entire movement, and Miller's
work expresses a view of language and interpretation most
strongly antithetical to the view on which our initial hypothesis is
based. The deconstructionist approach provides such a radical
challenge to our hypothesis that we could match it with virtually
any work we thought had a determinate meaning, but two considerations lead us to Jane Austen's *Persuasion.* First, Austen's last
novel is one whose value seems to depend in large part on her
ability to accomplish an enormously difficult task of determinate communication. Austen chooses to show her heorine, Anne
Elliot, suffering throughout much of the action because of the
way she is treated by the man who is to be her eventual husband, Frederick Wentworth. For the novel to succeed, Austen must represent Anne's suffering without making us judge
Wentworth negatively or feel that she would be anything less
than supremely happy with him. Second, *Persuasion,* like novels
by Henry Fielding, Joseph Conrad, and Ernest Hemingway
among others, is a work whose success also seems to depend
on both the events it represents and the language in which it
represents them. Our description of Austen's task suggests that
her style must play an important role in her success; at the same
time, Anne must become engaged to and marry Wentworth, and
the very fact that they do come together will have a significant

impact on our response regardless of the particular language in which it is represented. *Persuasion,* then, seems to represent a fourth possible role of language in fiction, one in which style is important but yet not clearly more important for the work's success than other elements of construction.

An approach which raises still further questions about language in fiction is taken by semioticians who argue for the self-referentiality of the text. These critics would agree with Fish, Lodge, and Miller that everything in an "aesthetic" text can be explained by language, but would go further than any of them in emphasizing the importance of the medium in these texts: language is not only the medium of communication but also, through the inventive way in which it is used, the subject of communication. Thus, for example, although the apparent content of a text may be observations about the weather, the author's rich and ingenious use of language may focus our attention on his medium, and we shall regard the subject of the weather merely as a means for achieving his end of revealing properties of language. The semiotic critics would not claim that this process happens in every fictional text; they do not equate the class "aesthetic texts" with the class "prose fictions."

Nevertheless, in examining this semiotic approach, we must consider whether language ever does operate this way in fiction; if we find it does, we shall at the very least be required to modify our initial hypothesis. Of the two most prominent semioticians, Roland Barthes and Umberto Eco, the one whose work most directly tests our hypothesis is Eco.[4] He provides both a systematic method for focusing on the phonology and connotations of a text and a theoretical account of the value of such analysis. And the challenge to our hypothesis will be greater if we consider Eco's approach in connection with some recent experimental fiction that seeks to eliminate such traditional elements as character, action, and plot. We can find good examples among works by John Barth, Donald Barthelme, Robert Coover, and William Gass among others, but Gass has written a work which seems especially suitable. *Willie Masters' Lonesome Wife* offers us split texts, mirror pages, an exploded narrator, and a great range of tones and styles; furthermore, it takes language itself as one of its explicit subjects. Gass's work, in addition to challenging our hypothesis that the medium never becomes all-important, presents us with questions about the value of some experimental fiction, and indeed, about the nature of fiction itself.

IV

The theorists, then, will sometimes be considered with novels that seem quite compatible with their theories (Fish with *The Ambassadors*, Eco with *Willie Masters' Lonesome Wife*), and at others with novels that seem to present difficult challenges to their theories (Lodge with *Sister Carrie,* Olson with *Lolita,* Miller with *Persuasion*). The reason for this variation is the inductive strategy of the essay: as we test our initial hypothesis and develop our theory, we need to raise different challenges to it at different points, and we are better able to do that by varying the way novels and theories are matched. Our initial hypothesis also determines the order in which we shall consider our matched pairs of theories and novels. In part one, in order to test the idea that language is not all-important in fiction, we shall consider the three comprehensive theories that claim it is, those of Fish, Lodge, and Miller, and the three novels that intuitively seem to represent three distinct kinds of subordination, *The Ambassadors, Sister Carrie,* and *Persuasion.* We shall begin with the apparently compatible match between Fish and *The Ambassadors* because that match immediately challenges our hypothesis and because it allows us to explore the fundamental issue of the relation between grammatical meaning and "experienced" or "actual" meaning in a way that will lay the foundation for further theoretical discussion. In chapter 3, we shall examine Lodge's approach because his arguments about the distinction between literary and nonliterary language allow us to consider in some detail both the status of character and action in relation to language and the crucial concept of intention. By the end of chapter 3, then, we shall have analyzed the roles of both text (how important is grammatical structure?) and context (how important is intention?) in our understanding of a work, and thus shall have laid the basic foundation of our theory. In chapter 4, we shall consider the radical challenge to that position posed by the deconstructionists, and in so doing, shall make more explicit the view of language as an abstract system, i.e., the relation of words to one another, and to the community that uses them, upon which the theory is based. At the same time, we shall be testing and demonstrating the explanatory power of the theory by analyzing the styles of James, Dreiser, and Austen.

In part two, we shall challenge the theory from a somewhat different direction: more from the evidence of the novels than from the explanations of the other theories. In chapter 5, we shall first contrast our approach with the language-is-least-important position of Olson, then try to see how well it can explain our experience of *Lolita*. In chapter 6, we shall test the adequacy of our theory for dealing with Gass's experimental work, especially when compared to the explanation offered by Eco's semiotic approach. Finally, in chapter 7, we shall assess the status of our theory and discuss its relation to the five other theories we have examined.

This essay, then, will not only be an analysis of the role language plays in five different novels, but also an investigation into general properties of language and literature. As we develop our theory, we must also consider such questions as the relation of parts to wholes in literary works, the relation of "ordinary" to "literary" language, the relation between indeterminate language and determinate communication, the relation between the grammar of a text and its meaning, and the relation between the meaning of a text and its author's intention. Our investigation, therefore, while firmly grounded in the attempt to answer a single question and while devoted in large part to the close analysis of passages from individual works, will also treat numerous issues fundamental to any theory of literature or literary experience.

2 Deliberative Acts vs. Grammatical Closure: Stanley Fish and the Language of *The Ambassadors*

I

Among the numerous methods critics have offered for investigating the relation between language and literature, Stanley Fish has put forth one of the most influential, provocative, and idiosyncratic. I call his approach "idiosyncratic" because it is based on a number of personally developed strategies of interpretation rather than on any fully formulated theory of literature. Yet his approach deserves to be examined in a study of language in literature precisely because of the provocative—and brilliant—nature of his idiosyncrasy: anyone who does intelligent criticism while agreeing both with structuralist theorists that the literary text is an illusion and with neo-Aristotelian theorists that the critic's job is to account for our common experience of a work must also present a case that raises interesting questions about the relation of language and literature, and about the nature of literary experience.

I should like to formulate those questions in this chapter by examining Fish's reader-response strategy in the context of investigating the language of *The Ambassadors*. I choose James's novel because it is the kind of text Fish likes to work with, one that "does not allow a reader the security of his normal patterns of thought and belief,"[1] and because it invites some fruitful questions about the role of its language, particularly the extent to which the success of the book is a result of James's famously complex style. By applying Fish's method to *The Ambassadors*, and then reexamining my findings in the light of the questions the analysis raises, I hope to obtain a greater understanding of the strengths and weaknesses of Fish's approach, an answer to my question about the role of language in *The Ambassadors*, and most importantly, some initial insight into the relation between language and fiction.

Although I shall eventually take sharp exception to much of what Fish says, I shall, in order to be fair, withhold my disagreements until I have presented the major points of his position and shown it in operation. And although I believe my representation of Fish is accurate, I must admit that he might not be willing to accept fully my account of his position. Because I am primarily interested in the general questions his approach raises, particularly whether the meaning of literary works is created by authors and texts or by readers, I have found it necessary to trace his descriptions of his interpretive strategy and his practical analyses of texts back to their underlying theoretical assumptions, and to extract a coherent theory from them. In short, I may have made him appear to be more of a systematic theorist than he actually is—he himself has said that his "theory" is "full of holes"[2]—and hence I may have committed him to positions he would deny holding. But even if this is the case, since I am concerned with those theoretical positions and not Fish himself, it will not seriously affect any of my conclusions.

II

At the heart of Fish's approach are two related ideas: (1) that reading is a temporal process and (2) that the meaning of a sentence is the reader's experience of that process. His method, therefore, proceeds by "the rigorous and disinterested asking of the question, what does this word, phrase, sentence, paragraph, chapter, novel, play, poem, *do?*"[3] The actual execution of the method "involves an analysis of the developing responses of the reader in relation to the words as they succeed one another in time."[4] More specifically, "the category of response includes any and all of the activities provoked by a string of words: the projection of syntactical and/or lexical probabilities; their subsequent occurrence or nonoccurrence; attitudes toward persons or things, or ideas referred to; the reversal or questioning of those attitudes; and much more."[5]

That readers sometimes perform such activities almost everyone will acknowledge; what is distinctive about Fish is that he claims these activities are always going on, and that they are the most important thing that goes on. As I indicated above, in his system the activities a reader performs while experiencing a sentence are the real meaning of that sentence. What he says about one sentence by Walter Pater, he would say about any sentence: "It is an experience; it occurs; it does something; it makes us do something. Indeed, I would go so far as to say, in direct contradiction of Wimsatt-Beardsley [and their notion of the affective fallacy] that what it does is what it means."[6] Or in other more provocative words, "there is no direct relationship between the meaning of a sentence (paragraph, novel, poem) and what its words mean."[7]

Fish is perhaps even more exceptional because he claims that there is no specifiable relationship between a reader's activities and the grammar of a sentence. Thus, his unit of analysis is not the sentence, the clause, the phrase, or the word, but rather what he calls "the deliberative act":[8]

My unit of analysis is formed (or forms itself) at the moment when the reader hazards interpretive closure, when he enters into a relationship of belief, desire, approval, disapproval, wonder, irritation, puzzlement, relief with a proposition...; and that moment, while it may occur only once in the experience of a particular sentence, may just as well occur twice or three times or as many times as the preceding acts of closure and interpretation are modified or revised. There is no way to predict just how many times and in what ways this will occur by scanning the physical features of a text because there is no regular invariant relationship between these features... and the deliberative acts readers perform.[9]

With these two moves—postulating that the meaning of a sentence is not the meaning of its words, but rather the reader's experience of it, and postulating that the reader's experience cannot be determined from an examination of syntax, word order, or other physical features—Fish makes the text disappear. Neither syntax nor semantics is the key to meaning; about the best that can be claimed for the text is that its semantic component, what Fish calls its "message or point" is one of the constituents of its meaning. But the thrust of Fish's theoretical argument is that this semantic component is a much less important constituent than the deliberative acts. As we shall soon see, he will go so far as to say that a sentence can mean the opposite of what it says.

Although the text disappears under Fish's scrutiny, he insists that there is a certain uniformity of response to any given text.[10] The responses he describes are those made by any "informed reader," by anyone who has the historical and semantic knowledge as well as the linguistic and literary competence necessary to experience a text fully.[11] For example, to experience *Paradise Lost* fully we need at least the literary competence to understand epic conventions, the linguistic competence to understand Milton's syntax, as well as the semantic knowledge of such things as his allusions, and the historical knowledge of his theology. Everyone who shares this knowledge and this competence, Fish says, will perform essentially the same deliberative acts, or in other words, will have essentially the same experience of the work.

Let us look briefly at Fish's method in operation, before suggesting how he might approach *The Ambassadors*. One of Fish's own selected illustrations of the method will serve us well. He takes two sentences which, he says, at one level of abstraction are equivalent in meaning, and applies his experiential analysis to show that their meanings are actually radically different. The first is by Alfred North Whitehead, "This fact is concealed by the influence of language, moulded by science which foists on us exact concepts as though they represented the immediate deliverances of experience"; the second by Walter Pater, "And if we continue to dwell in thought on this world not of objects in the solidity with which language invests them but of impressions, unstable, flickering, inconsistent, which burn and are extinguished with our consciousness of them, it contracts still further."[12]

About the Whitehead sentence, Fish comments that it "doesn't mean what it says," because the reader experiences not the inexactness which the sentence is ostensibly about but rather the tidiness which it seems to deny. The reader sees the "inexactness" reduced to the easily graspable "this fact," and he sees the clauses of the sentence follow one another in logical fashion. Fish concludes that "the sentence, in its action upon us, declares the tidy well-ordered character of actual experience, and that is its meaning."[13]

In contrast, Fish says, the Pater sentence means what it says. It starts out presenting the reader with a "world of fixed and 'solid' objects" but once the reader reaches the word "impressions," that fixed and solid world begins to "melt under [his] feet."

The words following "impressions"—"unstable, flickering, inconsistent"—"only accentuate the [world's] instability." As the sentence moves closer to its end, it becomes more and more inexact, and finally, "when the corporeality of 'this world' has wasted away to 'it' ('it contracts still further'), the reader is left with nothing at all."[14]

Fish's analysis of the Pater sentence illustrates, as he himself says, his method's "independence of linguistic logic."[15] Although the syntax of the sentence never leads us to believe in the existence of the fixed and solid world—"not" governs the phrase "of objects in the solidity with which language invests them"—Fish argues that the words in this phrase are more forceful and, therefore, work against and overwhelm our attention to and memory of "not." Thus, on Fish's account, although the syntax consistently denies the existence of the solid world, Pater can still let us experience that solidity before he takes it away.

Both examples also demonstrate more clearly than his theoretical discussion the relationship between the deliberative acts and the semantic content of the sentence. Ralph Rader has criticized Fish for finding the same kind of subversive syntax distinctly expressive of numerous different works.[16] Fish replies that the contradiction is only apparent because his argument is never about syntax but always about deliberative acts, and these acts "are always reasoning about something."[17] The reader does not assume or approve in a vacuum, but rather "he does these things with reference to the concerns to which the text has directed him, for example, the question of the responsibility for the Fall,"[18] or in this case, the question about the inexactness of the world.

From this remark, we might conclude that Fish is backing away from his more radical position—that the deliberative acts are a sentence's real meaning—to settle into the more comfortable position of saying that the deliberative acts help shape our final interpretation of the semantic and syntactic meaning. But this is not the case. What he is doing is acknowledging more fully than he has before that the semantic content of a sentence is a part of its meaning. This then allows him to argue that the same series of abstract deliberative acts—say, the formation of an initial hypothesis and the subsequent rejection of it—means one thing in this sentence by Pater, quite another in *Paradise Lost,* and still another in Donne's sermon, *Death's Duell.*[19] In all cases, however, Fish will finally be less concerned with the actual information the reader is processing than he will with how the reader processes it and what this processing does to him.

Before analyzing a passage from *The Ambassadors*, we have a final important part of the theory to consider. For Fish, any passage in a work will be a microcosm of the whole work; or as he puts it, "the basic experience of a work... occurs at every level."[20] This assumption governs all of his analyses, and again his own example will serve as a good illustration of what this point means. In *The Pilgrim's Progress*, Christian asks a shepherd, "Is this the way to the Celestial City?" and receives the reply "you are just in your way." Fish comments that "the inescapability of the pun reflects backward on the question and the world view it supports, and it gestures toward another world view in which spatial configurations have moral and inner meanings, and being in the way is independent of the way you happen to be in."[21] Furthermore, because the reader takes Christian's question seriously, that is, without questioning it, the shepherd's reply is a comment on him as well as Christian. Fish concludes; "What has happened to the reader in this brief space is the basic experience of *The Pilgrim's Progress.* Again and again he settles into temporal-spatial forms of thought only to be brought up short when they prove unable to contain the insights of Christian faith."[22]

Given this assumption that any passage is a microcosm of the whole, we should be able to pick any passage from *The Ambassadors* for our analysis. I have chosen the opening paragraph of book 8, chapter 3, partly at random, partly because it has not attracted any critical attention, and partly because it marks a significant step in Strether's internal drama. I do not claim that Fish himself would analyze the passage exactly as I do here, but I do insist that my analysis is based on his principles and his practice.

   [1]As the door of Mrs. Pocock's salon was pushed open for him, the next day, well before noon, he was reached by a voice with a charming sound that made him falter just before crossing the threshold. [2]Madame de Vionnet was already on the field, and

this gave the drama a quicker pace than he felt it as yet—though his suspense had increased—in the power of any act of his own to do. [3]He had spent the previous evening with all his old friends together; yet he would still have described himself as quite in the dark in respect to a forecast of their influence on his situation. [4]It was strange, none the less, that in the light of this unexpected note of her presence he felt Madame de Vionnet a part of that situation as she hadn't yet been. [5]She was alone, he found himself assuming, with Sarah, and there was a bearing in that—somehow beyond his control—on his personal fate. [6]Yet she was only saying something quite easy and independent— the thing she had come, as a good friend of Chad's, on purpose to say.[23]

At this point in the novel, the Pococks, the second wave of ambassadors from Woollett, have just arrived in Paris. What James describes here is the beginning of Strether's first visit to Sarah, the most influential of these ambassadors. We recognize with Strether that this meeting is extremely important because his engagement to Mrs. Newsome, indeed, his whole future, depends upon his ability to convince Sarah that he has not bungled his job as Mrs. Newsome's ambassador by not having already brought Chad home. And his ability to convince her will depend in large part on the outcome of this first visit.

The first sentence of the passage begins rather curiously, locating Strether in space—"at the door of Mrs. Pocock's salon"—rather than time. Although we know where Strether is, and although we begin to look forward to the simultaneous action promised by "as," we are slightly disoriented because we do not know when the action is occurring. Are we to assume that this action follows immediately upon the heels of the action in the preceding chapter—the arrival of the Pococks and Strether's cab ride with Jim—or that it is much later? This slight disorientation is soon corrected; in fact we locate Strether in time—"the next day"—and then relocate him—"well before noon"; and with this precise specification, we are settled comfortably in the discourse and move on to the main clause.

What we find there—"he was reached by a voice with a charming sound"—is welcome information. Because it is Sarah's room, because it is well before noon, because we have not previously heard Sarah's voice described, we assume that this voice is hers and because of the positive connotations of "charming" we take it for an auspicious omen. As informed readers of James, we do not equate a charming voice with moral greatness, but we now expect that Strether's present meeting with Sarah will be more pleasant than we had first anticipated.

For these reasons, we are taken up short when we reach the end of the sentence—"that made him falter just before crossing the threshold." All our expectations have been frustrated; we must go back and reevaluate the information we have just processed. The charming voice now seems ominous rather than auspicious. The adverbials of time now take on a new significance: it is especially startling for Strether to hear this voice in this place at this time. We know now that the voice cannot be Sarah's and begin to wonder about the identity of its apparently threatening owner. Finally, this new ominous note is reinforced when the sentence ends by locating Strether in space. Because he falters "before crossing the threshold," we wonder how well he will be able to handle what awaits him on its other side; that is, this faltering before the threshold seems to prefigure even graver falterings once he crosses it.

At the beginning of the next sentence we again get a firm footing in the discourse as we continue to trace the growing ominousness of Strether's situation. We learn that the owner of the charming voice is Madame de Vionnet, but we do not immediately get an explanation of why the sound of her voice made Strether falter. We assume for the moment that it is her presence, pure and simple, that Strether finds unexpected and disconcerting. Meanwhile we learn that she "was already on the field," and we realize that Sarah's salon has now become a battle or a playing field on which Strether and Madame de Vionnet will fight for their futures against Sarah.

But almost immediately we must make another adjustment: Madame de Vionnet's presence "gave the drama a quicker pace than he felt it as yet." Her maneuver, then, is a part of a drama, and consequently, the ominous note we had been following has been muted to some degree. With this addition of the dramatic metaphor, we conclude that this encounter between Strether and Madame de Vionnet is not one stage of a war or a very serious game, but rather one scene in the drama Strether and company are enacting. And while the drama is one of genuine actions and emotions, with serious consequences for the participants, it does not imply the inevitable waste and desolation of war, the inevitable sifting of winners from losers in a game. While the ominous note does not entirely disappear, it is definitely much softer.

Because of this softening, and because we can read this clause as the reason for Strether's faltering, we reinterpret the significance of that faltering: we see it now not as a warning of danger but rather as a pause where he switched gears—awkwardly perhaps, but in relative safety—in order to keep up with Madame de Vionnet's "quicker pace." By this point in the sentence, the danger of Strether's situation appears to be receding.

We have been able to make such revisions and reinterpretations because of certain assumptions we make about this this part of the sentence: we assume that "it" is a pronoun, referring to "drama," and we assume that the comparative "than he felt it as yet" will end, regardless of what comes between the dashes, with "had." That is, we expect the main clause here to read, "Madame de Vionnet gave the drama a quicker pace than he felt it as yet had." But once again our expectations are frustrated. When we read "in the power of any act of his own to do," we understand that "it" is not being used as a pronoun, but rather as an expletive to introduce the understood clause "it was in the power [etc.]." Once again we must drastically reinterpret the sentence. We are not learning about Strether's relative safety but rather about his powerlessness relative to Madame de Vionnet. Strether's faltering again seems to indicate his danger; it is an implicit recognition of her greater power. We are back with the ominous note.

Furthermore, this unexpected sentence ending makes us revise our interpretation of what comes between the dashes; it makes us experience this clause ("though his suspense had increased") ambiguously. While we are still expecting it to be followed by "had," we understand it to mean simply that in spite of the quickened pace Strether now felt, Strether's suspense about the outcome of the drama and especially about the present interview had increased. Then, once we read the end of the sentence, we understand the increase in suspense as a kind of compensation for Strether's own inability to quicken the pace of the drama:

although he has not been able to increase the pace, he has been able to feel more suspense. Because we experience both meanings in the course of the reading process, we do not have to choose between them; both meanings are the meaning of the clause. In either reading, however, our main impression is one of Strether's powerlessness—he is in suspense because he does not have control over the events of the drama—and the ominousness of the situation is emphasized.

The reader's experience of these two sentences, then, mirrors Strether's experience in the book. We begin, like Strether, thinking that we know where we are and what we can expect. And like him, we are quickly thrown into doubt: we find we must reject our initial hypotheses and take up new ones. But these, too, turn out to be misleading, and we must revise again. Eventually, we become aware of the tentative nature of our assumptions, but this does not prevent us from making them; instead, we continue this very active process of modifying our conclusions and expectations in the light of the next deliberative act we make as we read. Like Strether, we become active searchers after the real truth of the situation in Paris; and the book's meaning is not just the realization of the final complex truth, but also the process by which we arrive at that truth.

The beginning of sentence 3 again provides the reader with welcome information in a rather straightforward manner: "He had spent the previous evening with all his old friends." We expect to find some antidote to the present danger, if only in the knowledge that Strether should acquire in such an evening. However, when the clause doesn't end at "friends" but continues to "together," our expectations are slightly upset. Again we revise our impression: Strether spent the previous evening *not* "together with his old friends" but rather "with his old friends together"—and himself not quite part of their group. The ambiguity of "old friends" suddenly becomes prominent: are these "long-time" friends or "former" ones?

Nevertheless, the experience of this clause is only a slight jolt to our expectations. The statement is still offered as a positive one (there is no qualifying "although"), and we conclude that if Strether did not receive an emotional benefit from the previous evening, he at least should have received a cognitive one. But again we are frustrated; we learn that "yet he would still have described himself as quite in the dark in respect to a forecast of their influence on his situation." We not only revise our assumption about the benefits of the previous evening, we experience how utterly useless it had been to him. When we reach "quite in the dark," we expect the rest of the sentence to read something like "about how those friends would influence his situation." But once we reach "forecast" we must reassess the degree of his darkness; at this point, he cannot even guess how they will influence him.

Thus, by the end of the sentence we are thinking exactly the opposite of what we did at the beginning: we have seen the sentence apparently offer an antidote and then take it away. We are back more than ever with the ominous note: Sarah remains a potentially dangerous unknown, while Madame de Vionnet's presence seemingly compounds the danger.

The first half of sentence 4—"It was strange now, none the less, that in the light of this unexpected note of her presence"—again offers us the hope of an antidote. We assume that James is setting up an explicit reversal: "now" not only brings us clearly back to the present, but it also suggests that "now there is a difference"; it is "strange" that in spite of ("none the less") his previously unsuccessful efforts at forecasting the influence of his old friends, he is suddenly no longer "in the dark" but "in the light"—and though we realize that he is not completely in the light, we also realize that he can at least see something. We are also expecting the reversal because Strether's new-found light is provided by the same surprising and quite literal note—the one hit by Madame de Vionnet's voice—that initially caused him to falter. What we expect him to see in this light (what we expect the reversal to consist of) is precisely what we are denied at the end of the last sentence: some clue to the influence of his old friends on his situation.

Once again we learn that we have expected the wrong thing. What is illuminated is not the influence of the ambassadors from Woollett but his situation, or more precisely, the influence of Madame de Vionnet on his situation—"he felt Madame de Vionnet to be a part of that situation as she hadn't yet been."

Our focus now shifts to Madame de Vionnet and her effect on Strether's situation. In sentence 5, we retain that focus and build on the information we have just processed. Here we do not have our expectations thwarted, but rather experience the sentence making its expected point in distinct increments: "she was alone" "he found himself assuming" "with Sarah" "and there was a bearing in that" "somehow beyond his control" "on his personal fate."

Our experience is striking because it shows to what extent we have learned our lesson: because we have seen Strether and ourselves make so many modifications and revisions up to this point, when we read "he found himself assuming," we conclude that he is assuming incorrectly—we know that Madame de Vionnet will not be alone with Sarah. Yet we do not respond to the consequence of that assumption—"that there was a bearing in that—somehow beyond his control—on his personal fate"—as if it were irrelevant. Instead, we recognize the general truth this thought contains: Madame de Vionnet has become such a part of Strether's situation that if she were alone with Sarah, there would be a real bearing on his personal fate. And the incremental experience, especially the juxtaposed contrast between "beyond his control" and "on his personal fate" emphasizes the danger of his position. It is as if Madame de Vionnet has become an uncontrollable part of himself: he cannot know what she will do next, but he will still be responsible for her actions.

But our experience of the final sentence calls this conclusion into doubt. What we experience here is Madame de Vionnet's clear independence of Strether. She is speaking of things that have nothing to do with him, and to his (as well as to our own) surprise, she is speaking of them with ease: "Yet she was only saying something quite easy and independent." Furthermore, the end of the sentence reminds us that she has not come because of any connection with Strether, but rather has come "on purpose" because she is "a good friend of Chad's." Thus by the sentence's end, the ominous note once again has receded into the background.

What, then, are we to conclude about Strether's situation here? Is he in danger or isn't he? Should we fear for him or feel confident? What the reading experience has taught us is precisely that we should not ask such "either/or" questions. No sooner do we conclude his situation is dangerous than our next deliberative act forces us to conclude it is not. And so we go, back and forth, up and down, until we realize that the search for the certainty of a simple answer is a futile one and that the desire for a simple answer must be overcome if we are to find the truth.

Our basic experience here occurs at every level. Strether must learn the same lesson. He starts by believing that Madame de Vionnet is "base, venal—out of the streets," then completely reverses his opinion and believes that her relationship with Chad is the most virtuous of "virtuous attachments." Finally, once he realizes that the relationship is also a sexual one, he must overcome the impulse to revert to the values of Woollett and believe once again that she is base and venal. Strether's victory is that he is able to come to terms with the complexity of the real situation; he is able to cease either idealizing or condemning Madame de Vionnet and Chad, and can recognize instead that as complex human beings they have their peculiar strengths and weaknesses, their moral obligations and emotional needs, their fond hopes and strong desires. Strether can finally recognize, too, that although they are a part of his situation, they are also independent and distinct, and they must act, for better or worse, according to their own lights.

James's victory in the book is that he does not simply show us Strether's drama, but rather that he literally re-creates it in us. As we have seen in this one passage of six sentences, we too are forced to revise our assumptions over and over again, until we stop searching for the simple truth. We must become suspicious of our easy judgments of the characters; we must learn to live with the uncertainty and doubt the reading experience constantly creates in us, because that is the way to genuine truth. We must learn, finally, as *The Ambassadors* teaches us in almost every sentence, that the truth—about people, about "living" (in Strether's sense), about any human experience—is not at all simple but rather is many sided, complex, and extraordinarily difficult to grasp.

This, then, is the way Fish might analyze the passage. I do not doubt that he could improve the analysis by altering some of my statements and including others I do not make, but I do believe that what I have done fairly represents the kind of analysis Fish himself would do. And, I think, the analysis is quite attractive. Using Fish's approach, I was able to explain the significance of units as small as the word and as large as the sentence; I was also able to explain the movement of individual sentences and of the whole passage. Furthermore, the deliberative acts I isolated led to statements about the book as a whole which were both plausible and original: we probably did not think about *The Ambassadors* in this way before, but in light of this argument, we see certain things about the book, especially the way it educates us, for the first time. Finally, the analysis based on Fish's system has the attraction of being able to give a more comprehensive account of James's famous complexity than we have previously seen: *The Ambassadors* is complex not just because its syntax is complex, but because it is always asking us to make revisions—even in places such as sentence 6 of our passage, where the syntax is relatively straightforward. Fish's method, in short, is able to do just about everything we could want a stylistic analysis to do.

However, before embracing his system wholeheartedly, we need to reexamine the validity of Fish's assumptions in order to determine with greater certainty just how attractive his system is. How well can it meet the challenge of a competing theory of how we read? Is it more compelling, less valid, or simply different? It makes sense to begin with the fundamentals of his analysis, the deliberative acts, and to ask two simple but essential questions about them: Do they exist? And do they deserve the status Fish gives them?

I have said earlier that almost everyone will agree that readers sometimes make the deliberative acts that Fish describes. We could point to utterances as far apart as a sentence from Fielding's *Jonathan Wild* and a pair of sentences from a recent newspaper ad, both of which depend upon a reversal of our initial expectations for their effects:

> He [Fireblood] in a few minutes ravished this fair creature [Laetitia], or at least would have ravished her, if she had not, by a timely compliance, prevented him.[24]
> There is not one reason why your dog should eat Recipe. There are four of them.

Even without doing a detailed analysis, we can still see that with Fish's approach we would be able to account for the effects of these examples quite convincingly.

However, the effect of these sentences can also be explained by a strong competing explanation of what happens when we read. According to this theory, we remain open to all the possibilities the syntax and semantics allow until we see which possibility is actually employed, and then we give the sentence a meaning. Or to put it in Fish's language, we do not have interpretive closure until we have syntactic and semantic closure, and thus the meaning of a sentence has a close correspondence to what Fish calls its "message or point." Proponents of this theory would look at the two examples I have just cited and point out that the alleged deliberative acts are not made until after we have at least partial grammatical closure, or until after the statement of propositions ("he ravished this fair creature," "there is not one reason why your dog should eat Recipe") which can or do form complete grammatical units by themselves. In this case, then, we have two different theories of how we read explaining the same effect.

In more complicated cases, however, adopting Fish's approach will cause us to ascribe one set of effects to a given sentence, while adopting the grammatical closure theory will cause to ascribe a quite different set of effects to the same sentence. In analyzing a sentence like "There was a nervousness in his movements that George could detect as his friend came through the door," Fish would find this by now familiar pattern: because "George" is the noun closest to "his" we initially assume that George is the one who is nervous, but then at the end of the sentence, we must revise this hypothesis when we learn that it is George's friend who is nervous. And this unsettling experience, Fish would probably argue, increases our own anxiety about the situation. A proponent of the grammatical closure theory, however, would reject this interpretation because in his view we do not understand the sentence at all until the semantic closure tells us that George's friend is nervous, and the syntactic closure tells us the relationships between George, his friend, and their actions. For a grammatical closure theorist, the sentence means what it says.

A better example of the different theories leading to different conclusions about the same sentence is the dispute between Fish and Ralph Rader over how we read certain similes from *Paradise Lost*. Rader also provides an interesting contrast to Fish because he too wants to account for the reader's experience. It will be instructive to examine their respective arguments about one of these similes; we may then be able to adjudicate their dispute and make some determination about the validity of Fish's method.

The simile at issue describes Satan's spear:

> His spear, to equal which the tallest Pine
> Hewn on Norwegian Hills to be the Mast
> Of some great Ammiral, were but a wand.
>   [1:292–94]

Fish argues that from the first line we tentatively assume that the spear and the pine are equal, that the next line and a half reinforce this image of the two side by side, and then this equivalence relationship is overturned by the final phrase, "were but a wand." In the ensuing confusion, "the reader loses his hold on the visual focal points, and is unable to associate firmly the wand with either of them. The result is the momentary diminution of Satan's spear as well as the pine, although a second, and more wary reading, will correct this; but corrected the impression remains...."[25]

Rader replies that he does not read the lines this way—or rather Fish's own analysis having made him lose the freshness of his first impression, he does not reread them this way; he rereads them, instead, as "an unconfusing but surprising evocation of a sense of the spear as much, but indefinitely, larger than the visualized pine."[26] (The fact that this is a rereading does not cloud the issue; Fish argues, a few pages later, that if you are really reading and not just remembering the message, you will have the same experience every time.[27]) In even greater contrast to Fish's reading is Rader's general claim about the simile: "until the words yield this meaning they cannot be said to have made sense at all."[28]

Both critics insist that their reading is the correct one and both are basing their readings on the belief that "a mind asked to order a succession of rapidly given bits of detail (mental or physical) seizes on the simplest scheme of organization which offers itself."[29] For Fish this simplest scheme is the succession of deliberative acts he describes; for Rader it is seeing the bits of detail as parts of a syntactically complete and semantically coherent statement, a statement that should also have "pragmatic significance within the communicative situation."[30] For Rader, this communicative situation in a literary work is the perceived formal intention of the work, an intention which the reader intuits and which thereby governs his interpretation of individual sentences.

I shall have more to say about this account of the reader's experience later; for now I shall focus only on his position in favor of grammatical closure.

The danger in trying to resolve this dispute is to become involved in arguments over what happens in our minds as we read. Fish claims to know, but Rader, while refusing to offer a different description of the process, replies that Fish's account contradicts his final understanding of the simile. The temptation is to find out what really happens and prove that one or the other is correct. But of course we cannot really know what happens,[31] and it is not absolutely certain that whatever happens should be equated with meaning.

At this level of analysis, then, we cannot finally decide about the validity of Fish's method. Because we cannot get inside the mind, we cannot be sure that we make deliberative acts of the kind that he suggests, and, more importantly, we cannot know whether they deserve the status he gives them. But on the other hand, we cannot be sure that they do not exist as he describes them. We have seemingly reached an impasse: Fish's guess is as good (or as bad) as Rader's. One way out of this impasse is to move from a consideration of *how* we read to one of what we must know in order to read, that is, to shift our focus from the steps of the reading process to those conclusions about its outcome everyone can agree on.

Despite their differences, both Fish and Rader would agree that we have not understood the simile unless we recognize that at least part of its meaning is that the spear is much, though indefinitely, larger than the pine.[32] In order to have understood the simile, then, we must somehow have "seen" (all descriptions unavoidably become metaphorical at this point) that it was describing that *relationship* between the pine and the spear. Although we do not know *how* we "see" that relationship, we do know *what* we must possess in order to see it: linguistic competence (in Chomsky's sense)[33] in English. This rather obvious point, which Fish himself would readily agree with, has implications that will call his method seriously into question.

Part of what Chomsky means by linguistic competence is a speaker's ability to interpret correctly utterances he has not previously encountered. A competent speaker can do this because he intuitively knows the finite number of rules that govern the potentially infinite number of sentences in his language. For a competent speaker, there are no new sentence types (there are no new syntactic relationships),[34] only new sentences, and as a metaphorical description of competence, not a literal one of performance, we can say that a speaker has understood a sentence when he has "seen" how it makes particular use of the general rules. And he cannot see that until he knows all the rules that are being employed in that sentence; or in other words, a statement cannot be properly understood until there is syntactic and semantic closure.

At this point Fish might justifiably reply that I still have not proven him wrong; that all I've done is to show what we must know in order to understand a sentence's "message or point." But this account of what we must know in order to read can also deal with his deliberative acts. Because we are using a finite number of rules to generate a potentially infinite number of sentences, all utterances are potentially ambiguous in numerous ways until they have grammatical closure: the rules are necessarily flexible, and we can envision many possible relationships among sentence elements until the syntactic and semantic closure enables us to see which one of these potential relationships is actualized.[35] What this means is that there are many possible deliberative acts that can be made at any given unclosed point in a sentence. And, in fact, these deliberative acts are not only numerous, they can also be contradictory.

Moreover, Fish's principle of the "informed reader" will not exclude any of these deliberative acts. For example, in Milton's simile describing the spear, we may conclude after two and a half lines (as Fish does) that the simile is describing equivalent objects, and will end with a phrase like "were just that size" that summarizes this equivalence. But we could also assume that since Milton has just described Satan's enormous shield, this simile is describing the spear as much larger than the pine, and will end, therefore, much as it does. Finally, we could also assume that Milton wants to emphasize Satan's finiteness as well as his genuinely prodigious size, and that therefore, the simile is describing the pine as larger than the spear, and will end in a phrase like "need be cut in twain." (These latter two readings become more likely if we take "equal," as Rader suggests, in its sense of "compare.") Notice that not only our linguistic competence in Chomsky's sense, but also Fish's own principle of the "informed reader" make each of these readings plausible. If we admit one as part of the simile's meaning, we have to admit them all.

Before trying to determine whether all these deliberative acts should be considered as part of the simile's meaning, I would like to note in passing one practical consequence of Fish's approach. If two different critics isolated two different deliberative acts, they could "prove" quite different theses about a work. If in the simile from *Paradise Lost* the first critic isolated the deliberative act Fish describes, he could begin to prove Fish's fallen reader interpretation. If the second isolated the deliberative act in which we assume from the start that the spear is larger than the pine, he could begin to prove that we are always in collusion with Milton, looking down upon the action. The point is that because the number of possible deliberative acts one can make at any one point in a sentence is quite numerous, we can, if we are clever enough, use Fish's method to prove almost any thesis about any text. And if someone tells us that he does not read the text the way we do, we can reply that he is not a fully informed reader. We already have reason to be suspicious of Fish's approach.

The crucial question about the method, however, is whether it is legitimate to assign meaning to deliberative acts. It may be a mis-application of the method to assign meaning to only one de-liberative act, but that doesn't prove that the method itself is invalid. Let us look at the consequences of considering all the de-liberative acts as part of the meaning of a sentence. In the case of Milton's simile, accounting for all the deliberative acts—the spear and the pine are equivalent, the spear is much larger, the spear is much smaller—would lead us to conclude that we cannot prop-erly understand the relationship between the spear and the pine. But every competent speaker of English, Stanley Fish not least among them, will understand the simile as specifying a particular, comprehensible relationship between the two objects. Only one of the simile's several potential meanings is actualized, and the others become irrelevant. We must interpret only one of the meanings as relevant in order to read the simile as we do. Fish's description of *how* we read cannot be accepted because it con-tradicts *what* we know about what we read.

Perhaps I can clarify this point with an analogy. Suppose we hear the phrase, "illegal alien crackdown" on a news broadcast. Our linguistic competence allows us to see that this phrase has at least four mutually exclusive meanings: (1) some unspecified agent is cracking down on illegal aliens; (2) some unspecified agent is cracking down on aliens in an illegal manner; (3) illegal aliens are cracking down on some unspecified thing or person; (4) aliens are cracking down on some unspecified thing or person in an illegal manner. In other words, our competence tells us that there are at least four possible syntactic and semantic relationships among the words of this phrase.

Suppose further that after listening to the broadcast for a short time we realize that the relationships between the words are those specified by meaning number one. This is analogous to our reaching the end of Milton's simile and seeing that the pine is "but a wand" in comparison to the spear. The important question now is whether the other possible meanings of the phrase are relevant to our understanding of it; and this is analogous to asking whether the deliberative acts we might make in reading the simile should be considered as part of its meaning. Our knowledge as competent speakers tells us that the other meanings are irrelevant. Once we "select" the particular semantic and syntactic relationships of meaning number one, we find it totally irrelevant to our understanding of the news broadcast that the phrase "illegal alien crackdown" might also mean someone is cracking down on aliens in an illegal manner. Similarly, once we understand the relationships specified by the semantics and syntax of the simile, the deliberative acts we might have made become irrelevant to our understanding of it.

In summary, then, we can see that Fish's approach is finally not attractive because the fundamental assumption on which it is based—that deliberative acts constitute the real meaning of an utterance—is poorly motivated. Our linguistic competence allows us to see that at any point in a sentence numerous deliberative acts are possible, and that there is no reason to say that some are more plausible than others. Consequently, including deliberative acts as part of a sentence's meaning will often lead us to conclude that the meaning of the sentence is that there is no comprehensible relationship between its elements; but this conclusion contradicts our knowledge that sentences do specify particular relationships.

III

The grammatical closure approach, then, seems to provide a sound basis for investigating linguistic effects. By expanding upon that approach, we can develop a working hypothesis about the way we understand the meaning of texts, a hypothesis which will also account for the role style plays in that understanding. In keeping with the grammatical closure approach, the hypothesis takes as a first principle the assumption that the meaning of any sentence is a result of the syntactic and semantic relationships our linguistic competence enables us to perceive among the elements of that sentence. In a sentence such as "John, the door is open," the meaning derives from the semantic content of the words and the relationships the syntax expresses between John and the speaker, between "the door" and "open" and between "John," and "the door is open." However, while these things are necessary conditions for meaning, they are not the only ones. The sentence, "John, the door is open" could be an assertion, two commands (for John to leave, or for him to close it), two requests, a warning, an explanation (of why John is cold), and probably many other things as well. Knowledge of the context includes all the variables that affect the communicative situation or "speech event": the intention of the speaker, his audience, his relationship to his audience, the occasion of the utterance, even things such as the time of day and the speaker's social class and education.

The second principle of our hypothesis, again related to the grammatical closure approach, is that synonymy exists. Since grammatical closure, not the temporal sequence of words in a sentence, determines meaning, different ways of expressing the same relationships among signifieds (the concepts associated with words) have roughly the same meaning. More generally, the assumption that synonymy exists is justified by such observable phenomena as our ability to recognize what we have said in someone else's paraphrase of it, and our ability to share knowledge—even with people who do not share our language. The term "synonymy" here refers not only to those cases where different linguistic forms have exactly the same meaning,[36] but also to cases where they have roughly the same meaning. In other words, we ought not deny that there are differences between two sentences that, say, describe the same event, but we should also insist that those differences are different in kind from those between either one of them and another sentence that describes a different event. For example, the differences between "The quick, red fox jumped over the lazy, tan dog" and "The swift, russet fox leaped over the listless, brown dog" are different in kind from those between either one of these sentences and "The cat sat on the mat."

With this example, the distinction between synonymous and nonsynonymous utterances is fairly obvious. The question that soon arises, however, is at what point differences in language become so great that two versions of the same event, thought, feeling, command, etc., no longer say the same thing. The mistake that is often made in trying to settle this question is to take some one sentence as the primary *Ur*-sentence, then to compare other versions with it, and finally to decide what the class of synonymous sentences is by some arbitrary judgment of closeness to or divergence from the *Ur*-sentence. The problem with this process is that it makes the *Ur*-sentence the true description of the referent, the idea, or act, and all other sentences merely approximations of the truth, when, in fact, the *Ur*-sentence is as much an approximation as any other one. By using language at all, we "interpret" the world to some degree (although of course some "interpretations" are more accurate than others). In our example pair of sentences, we can see this process of interpretation clearly: on the syntactic level, we choose to start with the fox and predicate something about his relation to the dog instead of vice versa, while on the semantic level, we use certain categories to describe the event rather than others, e.g., "russet" rather than "red."

Another reason that makes this question about where synonymy ends impossible to answer in any absolute way is that context influences meaning. Two sentences that would not be paraphrases of each other in one context may very well be paraphrases in another, and vice versa. Probably the most dramatic example of this phenomenon is the use of code words. When one of the country bumpkins in Thornton Wilder's *The Matchmaker* tells the other that he will exclaim "Pudding!" when they are in the middle of an adventure, and then proceeds to do so, his exclamation is a paraphrase of the sentence "This is an adventure!"

In most other contexts, of course, these two exclamations are nonsynonymous.

This example is also instructive because it demonstrates that the basis of synonymy is not the objects we describe with language, but rather the agreements we make about its meaning. As Frege pointed out in his famous example of the difference between "morning star" and "evening star," the referent can remain the same while various descriptions of it change considerably in their "sense." To put the point another way, the basis of synonymy, that which enables us to understand two different descriptions as having the same sense, is our linguistic competence. In the case of our example sentences, it is our knowledge of and participation in the linguistic community's agreements about the semantic content of the words and the significance of the syntactic structures that allow us to recognize that both of them—and in a context where we are describing an event we have just witnessed, numerous others such as "the tan dog was jumped over by the red fox" and "the fox went over the dog"—have something in common that they do not have in common with other sentences. Let us call what they have in common their "sense," which we shall specify by X, and let us define the class of synonymous sentences as all those that have X in common.

This description of synonymy provides a basis for us to talk about the effects the language of a sentence has on our understanding of its sense; in other words, it provides a basis for us to talk about style. We cannot specify which parts of a sentence are stylistic and which parts are pure content or sense—if we try, we fall back into the *Ur*-sentence trap—but when we look at any two synonymous sentences we can know that the differences between them are stylistic. Because any class of synonymous sentences is potentially quite numerous (we can always alter a sentence slightly) and will allow for large variation in the language of its sentences, we have offered a rather broad definition of style, one that will allow us to discuss both syntax and semantics. The best way to determine within the class of synonymous sentences whether certain syntactic and semantic choices are preferable to others is by reference to the context. If, for example, you are John's parent, and you want him to close the door he just left open as he entered the house, and you want to be gentle but firm with him, the sentence "John, the door is open" is preferable to the more sharp command implied in "John, you left that door open again!" If, however, this scenario has repeated itself several times, you may want to be more sharp than gentle, and so the second sentence will be preferable.

Having developed our working hypothesis to this extent, let us return to Fish's reader-response approach. In order to forestall objections that the previous critique of his method still boils down to an unresolvable argument over how we read, and in order to clarify and develop our hypothesis further, I shall look at Fish's approach from another point of view. Let us assume for now that we are again at an impasse, that as far as we can determine Fish's hypothesis and ours are equally valid. We shall try to choose between them by looking at the consequences of each, first, for our view of language as a means of communication, and second, for the way we regard the relation between language and literature. At the same time, this discussion will lead to positive statements about language in literature and to a different analysis of the passage from *The Ambassadors*.

Let us recall, for a moment, Fish's sample analysis of the Whitehead and Pater sentences. Although Fish acknowledges that on a general level the sentences have an equivalent meaning—"that language which pretends to precision operates to obscure the flux and disorder of actual experience"[37]—he would argue that because the Whitehead sentence does not actually mean what it says, it will always be an inferior means of communicating that apparently equivalent meaning. His argument here indicates how he would treat other pairs of sentences with the same general meaning. Suppose we have two sentences, "2 is greater than 1," and "Given any unit, which we shall call x, if we find another identical unit x, and add it to our first x, we shall say that the resulting sum will be greater than our initial x." Fish would always say that the first formulation is the superior means of communicating the equivalent general meaning because it relates the simple fact in a simple straightforward manner. He would also maintain that we cannot say such statements as "the world is absurd" or "the world is chaotic" without subverting our ostensible communication. In short, his theory of the way we read implies that we can communicate effectively only if we match the deliberative acts that we ask our audience to make with our ostensible subject.

On the other hand, our hypothesis implies that we determine the relative effectiveness of a pair of sentences with equivalent general meanings by reference to the contexts in which they are to be uttered. For example, although the two sentences are not closely synonymous, I think we can see that the Whitehead sentence is superior, say, for communicating the general meaning to an undergraduate linguistics class, while the Pater is superior, say, for communicating the same general meaning to a highly educated audience that would be reading his words. Similarly, ''2 is greater than 1'' is probably better for a grammar school arithmetic class, and the more complicated expression is better for a book on number theory.[38] And again, there is nothing special about the form of ''the world is absurd'' which subverts its point; it means precisely that (unless we know from the context that the speaker is being ironic), and in certain situations it will be more effective because it is concise and to the point. In short, our hypothesis maintains that language in communication is more flexible than Fish would have us believe; that we communicate best not when we match our subject with deliberative acts but when we choose the one statement from the numerous possible synonymous expressions that in its particular syntactic and semantic form is the most appropriate way to convey the ''message or point'' to the given audience.

I do not claim that this view of language as a means of communication is inherently ''truer'' than Fish's view—I cannot point to any theory of grammar which says this view is superior—but I do think it is more in line with our experience as communicators. Does not the rhetoric we all use—choosing this word rather than that, putting this clause ahead of that in order to make my point most effectively with this audience—support the more flexible view? When we hear someone say ''life is chaotic,'' don't we assume he means what he says (again unless we know from other signals that he is being ironic) rather than ''life is orderly''? When Fish says that the Whitehead sentence does not mean what it says, isn't he also saying that ''it does not mean what all you readers think it means''? Common sense, if nothing else, should make us question the validity of any method that can lead to such a conclusion.

Fish's theory also has important consequences for our view of the relation between language and literature. The first is that the language of a work plays the same role in all parts of a work, or as we have already seen him say, "the basic experience of a work ...occurs at every level." This is one of Fish's most curious positions because he is at one and the same time insisting on the fact that the experience of a sentence is a purely temporal process, and ignoring the fact that the experience of a whole work is also temporal. More important than the logical inconsistency, however, is what this assumption leads us to conclude about literature. If the basic experience occurs in every sentence—or at least in every paragraph—then the narrative or argumentative structure of a work becomes mere excrescence. It is true that according to Fish's theory the structure should also give us the basic experience, but this view reduces the function of structure to repeating what happens at the sentence level. In Fish's essay on *The Pilgrim's Progress,* for example, he does not acknowledge that Bunyan might have arranged the *order* of Christian's temptations for any artistic purpose, but rather he sees each temptation, regardless of where it occurs, as repeating the lesson of every other one. On Fish's account, the narrative or argumentative structure becomes merely the shell which an author uses to keep a reader's interest, while he repeats his real work at the sentence and paragraph level until he can be sure that the reader has got the point.

In Fish's system, not only does language play the same role in all parts of a work, but it plays the same role in all works. Because the language of any work always provides the occasion for the reader to make his deliberative acts, and because the deliberative acts are the meaning of that work, language has the same role in *Paradise Lost* as it does in *The Ambassadors,* as it does in *King Lear,* as it does in *Death's Duell,* and as it does in "Sailing to Byzantium." The only essential differences among these works—or between any two works—is the different deliberative acts they ask us to perform.

The final consequence of Fish's system I would like to point to is closely related to the first two. Because the series of deliberative acts a reader performs while he reads always teaches him something, and because the deliberative acts are a work's real meaning, all literature is primarily didactic. *Paradise Lost* teaches us an awareness of our fallen nature and of God's goodness; *The Pilgrim's Progress* teaches us what it means to be in the Way; even a lyric like Milton's twentieth sonnet, "Lawrence of virtuous father virtuous son," becomes a way to teach us—that the things of this world are neither good nor bad in themselves;[39] and extrapolating from these conclusions, I have said Fish would argue that *The Ambassadors* teaches us that the truth about human experience is always complex and difficult.

On the other hand, our position has quite different consequences. Because we assume that synonymy exists, and hence, that the particular language of a text is not the all-important determiner of its meaning, we can take more seriously the idea that the experience of a whole text is temporal. Since we assume that somewhat the same meaning could have been created in different language, we shall not regard individual linguistic effects as microcosms of the whole work. Instead, we can examine the influence of the effect on its immediate context and then the influence of that context on the next larger structure, and so on until we reach the level of the work as a whole. At the same time, we shall judge the appropriateness of the linguistic effect by reference to our sense of the whole context, or in other words, to our idea of the perceived formal intention of the work.

There is a paradox here but not a contradiction. When we select any one sentence to analyze, we shall see it in the context of all the other sentences we have read up to that point—and the resulting hypothesis, tacit or explicit, we have made about the form of the whole; in other words, our sense of the context will guide our interpretation of that sentence, will allow us to see it as appropriate or inappropriate, as effective or ineffective, and so on. At the same time, this new sentence, with its new information and new implications, will alter the context (either greatly or slightly), will refine our knowledge of the form, and thus affect our response to new sentences. We perceive the intention through sentences accumulating, but accumulating sentences are seen in light of the intention. It is this view of the reader's experience that Rader is adopting when he says that a sentence must have "pragmatic significance" within a work.[40]

In further contrast to Fish, our position leads us to argue that since the reading process is temporal and since we are always reading about "something," the language of a work can have varying degrees of importance, depending upon the something that is being described. Consider, for example, Sir Walter Scott's *The Heart of Midlothian*. In the middle of the book Jeanie Deans is faced with the difficult choice of either lying to save her sister or telling the truth and giving damaging testimony against her. Scott has made it clear that the ethically superior choice is for Jeanie to tell the truth, but he also wants to evoke the reader's sympathy for Jeanie when she decides to do so. Simply by directly representing the scene in the courtroom, and by being consistent in his characterization of Jeanie (a condition that means his language cannot undercut her action), Scott will accomplish his purpose regardless of whatever else his language does. That language does not need to be precise or to describe careful discriminations of feeling; Jeanie's act itself is sufficient to evoke the sympathy. However, later in the book, after traveling on foot to London, Jeanie beseeches Queen Caroline to grant a pardon to her sister. Everything else in the book has been building up to that speech, and Scott has made it clear that given the situation then existing between Scotland and England, Queen Caroline will not be favorably disposed to hear Jeanie's plea. So the speech itself must be magnificent. If it is not, Scott can still have Queen Caroline grant the pardon, but we won't find it plausible. The success of Scott's book depends to a large degree on how well he writes this speech.

For much the same reasons, our position implies that language may play different roles in different works: its importance depends to a large extent on the "something" that is being represented in its total context. If, for example, the things being represented are in themselves slight or insignificant, and the author wants to show how under certain conditions for certain characters they become extremely significant, he will probably rely on his language to convince us of the transformation. If, on the other hand, the thing being described is a typical pattern of action that the author can assume we shall recognize as typical, his language probably will be less important than the actions he describes. In fact, we may want to investigate the possibility that in such a work an author could be sloppy in his descriptions and still create a moving book. In general, because we assume that synonymy exists, we are also postulating that literature is more than just language, that it is character, action, and thought as well (the "somethings" that are described by language),[41] and we are suggesting further that the relationship among these elements need not be constant within a work or from one work to the next.

Finally, because our position insists that literary works have a content apart from the way we seem to process the information they give us, we do not conclude that all works are didactic. An author can represent a character in a given situation simply for the sake of that representation or in order to teach us something. In any one case, we shall know because of the way the content of the work, which includes the descriptions of the character, his actions and his situation, the narrator's comments on these things, and the organization of the work, directs our response: it will either direct us to generalize from the particular situations and formulate a general truth, or it will center our interest on this character in this situation. Furthermore, because the relationship among language, character, and action varies from work to work, our responses to two didactic works or two mimetic works can also differ greatly. The particulars of these differences are less important than seeing that our position admits them, while Fish's does not. In other words, his system will not allow us to account for the unique achievements of works as different as *Paradise Lost* and *The Ambassadors*—or indeed, for the quite different experiences we have in reading them. There is no guarantee that by adopting our position we shall be able to do these things, but by allowing the differences to exist we will have made an important first step.

Having looked at these consequences, I submit that Fish's system asks us to pay too high a price. It binds us to a rigid rule of effective communication—match the deliberative act with your subject—and a rather simplistic view of literature, where it plays the role of the Great Leveler: what started out as a way of accounting for the complexity of a reader's response has ended by denying that complexity—because all works are complex in the same way. Though in need of further testing and development, our working hypothesis about the way we understand the meaning of texts, with its principles of grammatical closure, synonymy, and contextual influence, can more satisfactorily explain the rich diversity of our experience with language in both daily communication and literature.[42]

IV

In order to answer our question about the role of language in *The Ambassadors*, then, we cannot remain satisfied with our Fishean analysis, but must examine James's language according to the principles of our position. I shall analyze the passage from

book 8 once again, and then shall test my conclusions by analyzing another passage. In order to answer fully the question of the
relative importance of the language, we would have to analyze
most of the book. Instead, I shall consider these two passages as
"characteristic" of the role language plays in the whole book, and
thereby indicate the kind of answer we would get if we did a full
analysis. I want to be careful here to distinguish my use of
"characteristic" from Fish's idea that the basic experience of a
work occurs at every level. By "characteristic," I mean that the
language generally has the same relationship to character and
action that it does at these two points. I do not mean that either
passage is a microcosm of the whole, but rather that each is one
more small step in the developing experience. Each happens to be
similar to other steps in the way its language works (unlike *The
Heart of Midlothian*, *The Ambassadors* seems to maintain a fairly
consistent relationship among its elements), but each is also quite
different in the information it gives us and the judgments it asks us
to make. Therefore, in doing my analysis I shall consider why
James should desire the effects he creates at those points in the
book. And in order to do that, I need to define the formal intention of the novel.

   The Ambassadors is designed to represent Strether's moral and
cognitive growth throughout his experience in Paris; it traces his
development from his initial position as a fifty-five-year-old New
England Puritan with a secure and comfortable, though funda-
mentally unsatisfying, future to his final position as an in-
tellectually and morally mature man with no plans or expectations
for the future beyond his knowledge that he must always act in
accordance with his often uncomfortable sense of what is right.
Although James does not clearly indicate early in the novel what
the endpoint of Strether's growth will be, he does reassure us that
Strether's development is in a positive direction and that he will
reach a desirable end.

   A glance at some of James's narrative techniques will further
clarify this characterization of the novel. From the very first sentence of the novel, where he tells us that Strether "was not
wholly disconcerted" to find that Waymarsh had not yet arrived
at the hotel, the narrator almost never reports an event or tells us
a fact without also telling us Strether's internal response to it. At
the same time, because the narration is almost exclusively limited
to Strether's consciousness, we measure the importance of facts

and events according to their impact upon his internal state. Because the narration is limited to Strether's consciousness, we never discover (although we may have our suspicions) anything about the situation in Paris before Strether himself does, so we never feel superior to him even when he is making his greatest mistakes. Moreover, the narrator's own obvious sympathy for Strether combines with Strether's admirable qualities to make us sympathize with him and desire his positive growth.

Furthermore, although we see that the obstacles to his growth are not to be taken lightly—at the outset of the novel, Strether is strongly influenced by Woollett values, is not able to take decisive action on his own, and is not able to see things and people as they are—he also displays characteristics that make us expect he will achieve that growth. His reluctance to meet Waymarsh and his forwardness in making Maria Gostrey's acquaintance make us see that he will be open to the experience of Europe, and hence, able to go beyond his Woollett values. His friendship with Maria, who knows both Europe and human nature very well, is a further reassurance that he will not go too far astray until he is able to act for himself. And finally, his own active consciousness, which, though often mistaken, is constantly seeking after the truth, provides another assurance that he will eventually achieve his desirable internal alteration.

It is in light of this account of James's intention that I shall analyze the passage from book 8, chapter 3; in the course of the analysis we should be able to gain further insight into the specifics of James's intention, as well as into the role language plays in his achievement of that intention.

The kind of analysis I will do is an analytic procedure, not one of discovery. It depends on a knowledge of the whole of *The Ambassadors*, not just on a knowledge of it up to this point. Although our knowledge of what has gone before and our intuition of the formal intention of the whole guides our reading of every part, we cannot fully account for the effects of any part until after we have read the whole. We could not, for instance, account for "appropriate surprise" in a work—such as Strether's discovery of the sexual nature of Chad and Madame de Vionnet's relationship— because we could not adequately characterize the significance of the small hints or minor details that make our later surprise appropriate.

In one sense I shall be "idealizing" a reader as I analyze. I do not claim that my analysis is equivalent to the literal reading process, that readers are always aware of the effects I point to, just as I would not claim that readers of *King Lear* are actively aware of all the ways in which the subplot interacts with the main plot to affect our response to the whole. However, just as most critics would claim that the interactions between the two plots do exist (they can be recognized when pointed out), I would claim that the linguistic effects I point to also exist. Like the interactions between the plots, they exist as part of our intuitive experience of the work. What this analysis aims to do, then, is to give us cognitive knowledge of that part of our intuitive experience.

Because I am interested in the relative importance of language, I shall compare the original with the following paraphrase in which the language works quite differently. The principle governing the paraphrase is that the passage should be as simple and direct as possible; therefore it eliminates most of the embeddings, the metaphors, the periphrastic phrases and whatever else seems to slow down the reading process.

[1]Early the next day, as someone pushed the door open for him, crossing the threshold of Sarah's salon, he faltered because he heard a charming voice. [2]Madame de Vionnet was there before him, and this made the action seem quicker than anything he had done—although his suspense had increased. [3]Although he had spent the previous evening with his old friends, he still couldn't forecast how they would influence his situation. [4]Nevertheless, it was strange that Madame de Vionnet's presence now made him feel that she was more a part of his situation than ever. [5]He assumed that she was alone with Sarah, and that bore on his personal fate in a way that he couldn't control. [6]Yet she was only saying what, as a good friend of Chad's, she had come to say.

In the original, James uses both his syntax and his vocabulary to describe a new and complex relationship between Strether and Madame de Vionnet, a relationship which has an important impact on the way we respond to their interview with Sarah. In that interview, Strether takes a major step in the working out of his internal fate, because he takes a major one in the working out of his external fate. During the interview, Madame de Vionnet "publicly drew him into her boat," and Strether, after some trepidation, "took up an oar and since he is to have the credit of pulling, pulled." By aligning himself so clearly with Madame de Vionnet here, Strether virtually seals his fate with Mrs. Newsome: having seen him in Madame de Vionnet's boat, Sarah will probably make sure that he will never again be in Mrs. Newsome's. We shall see what this means for Strether's internal state as we analyze the passage.

Sentence 1: "As the door of Mrs. Pocock's salon was pushed open for him, the next day, well before noon, he was reached by a voice with a charming sound that made him falter just before crossing the threshold."

Paraphrase: Early the next day, as someone pushed the door open for him, crossing the threshold of Sarah's salon, he faltered because he heard a charming voice.

In this sentence, James strikes the keynote of the passage as he describes Strether's faltering. The chief effect of his description is to give us a vivid sense of that faltering. Because James begins to describe the action in the passive ("the door was opened for him"), and because he then directs us to locate him in time, thereby introducing a stasis in the action, we develop an image of Strether motionless before the open door. He remains in that position while we learn "he was reached by a voice with a charming sound." Strether has yet to do anything active himself; it is as if he is under a spell. The voice finally breaks that spell—and Strether falters. Because we see this so vividly and because it comes at the end of the sentence, it receives a strong emphasis. Furthermore, because it is the sound of the voice and not any physical obstacle (such as the threshold) that makes Strether falter, we understand the physical action as a sign of his mental misgivings upon hearing the voice.

"Falter" is the first of many words in the passage that indicate Strether's precarious position as he approaches the interview. Stronger than "hesitate" and without the sense of the ridiculous associated with "stumble," it rather nicely conveys the idea that there is something dangerous, but not necessarily destructive, about the owner of the charming voice.

The main weakness of the paraphrase is that it directs our attention away from the faltering (which is also expressed more concisely, "he faltered") to the reason for it—"because he heard a charming voice." In this version, we are more concerned with the identity of the speaker than we are with what that speaker's presence means for Strether. And as we see in the next sentence, where "Madame de Vionnet" is named right away, James is not concerned with perpetuating the mystery of the speaker's identity, but with the influence of her presence on Strether's internal state. Strether knows Madame de Vionnet is there as soon as he hears her voice, and James wants us to follow Strether's internal reaction to things as they happen. The reason he does not name Madame de Vionnet in the first sentence is that he wants to make us participate in Strether's faltering as much as possible so that we will fully appreciate the danger of his situation. Even though the syntax and word order would still convey the image of him motionless before the door, we would not be as involved in Strether's faltering if we knew that the voice was Madame de Vionnet's.

There are other important effects of the original that are lost in the paraphrase. The original makes it more clear than the paraphrase that it is the mere presence of the owner of the voice that upsets Strether: when we read the periphrastic "a voice with a charming sound," we are sure it is the voice itself and not anything the voice is saying that upsets him. The original also emphasizes the unexpectedness of the voice to a much greater degree. The reference to Strether's "old friend" as Mrs. Pocock rather than "Sarah" is a reminder of the distance between them, and hence, of the even greater distance between Sarah and anyone else from Chad's circle, especially Madame de Vionnet. The employment of the two adverbials of time after the first clause instead of just one in the more common initial position makes us pay greater attention to them: we see that Strether's surprise results not just from hearing the voice, but from hearing it on this day (the day after the arrival of the Pococks) at this time ("well before noon"). By emphasizing the unexpectedness of the voice in this way, James allows us to infer the extreme boldness—in Strether's eyes at least—of Madame de Vionnet's move. This "base woman" who has "corrupted" Chad has now dared to enter the sanctuary of the New England Puritan.

By the end of the first sentence, then, we are aware of the importance of this unexpected note for Strether, and we regard his faltering as a sign of the precarious position he is now in. He, of course, no longer believes that she is a "base woman"—indeed he has promised to save her—but he is not ready to make a complete break with Mrs. Newsome over her, and he does not know what the consequences of her presence will be.

Sentence 2: "Madame de Vionnet was already on the field, and this gave the drama a quicker pace than he felt it as yet—though his suspense had increased—in the power of any act of his own to do."

Paraphrase: Madame de Vionnet was there before him, and this made the action seem quicker than anything he had done before—although his suspense had increased.

In this sentence, we begin to get more specific information about Strether's internal state. In the first clause, "Madame de Vionnet was already on the field," we learn who owns the voice—in fact, we shift our focus to her, as we should in order to keep pace with Strether. More importantly, we see that the room which James describes rather formally as a "salon" in sentence 1 has now for Strether and Madame de Vionnet become a playing field or perhaps a battlefield. The differences between the two metaphors are only differences in degree. Each is infinitely more revealing than the literal paraphrase, "Madame de Vionnet was there before him," each tells us Strether's psychological state—he is preparing for combat or competition, not conversation—and each reminds us of the importance of the outcome: we know from what we have read so far that the stakes of the battle or the game are the futures of Chad, Madame de Vionnet, and Strether. In short, this brief metaphor, whichever way we take it, gives us a revealing glimpse into the struggle that will be going on beneath the surface conversation of the interview.

In the rest of the sentence, James describes the immediate consequence of Madame de Vionnet's presence, and makes a comparison between her and Strether. Again the difference between the original and the paraphrase is instructive. In the paraphrase we learn the facts but little about Strether's internal state: Madame de Vionnet's presence "made the action seem quicker than anything he had done—although his suspense had increased." In the original, however, James's representation of Strether's thought also lets us see more deeply into the psychological state that is giving rise to the thought. The switch from the battle or playing field metaphor to the dramatic metaphor ("and this gave the drama a quicker pace") throws a new light upon how

Strether views his situation. For the moment, he looks upon the interview as a battle or a sports competition, but he also looks upon the whole experience in Paris as a play which he is helping to enact, even though he has not read the script. And now Madame de Vionnet, another actor, has suddenly increased the pace of the action and he must do his best to get in step. The dramatic metaphor also governs the comparison between Madame de Vionnet and Strether.

In that comparison, the syntax creates a distinct sense of Strether groping to find his way in this drama, which has now definitely gone out of his control. Because James expresses the negative effects of Strether's actions in positive language—"he felt it as yet . . . in the power of any act of his own to do"—he creates the greatest sense of Strether's powerlessness. It is clear from James's sentence that Strether has exercised his "power" and felt it to have no effect. It is as if he has thrown his best punch, looked for its effect, and found that his opponent did not even notice it. Furthermore, by explicitly focusing our attention on the "power" of a personal "act," James is making questions of power and control relevant to the outcome of the interview. We see clearly that for now Madame de Vionnet has significantly more power than Strether.

The "though" clause, "though his suspense had increased," which is embedded in order that James may emphasize the more important information of Strether's failure, is further evidence of Strether's lack of control. James does not specify any reason for or agent of the increased suspense; instead, it is something that *happens to* Strether, even while he fails to quicken the pace. This clause is yet another element of the passage that both makes us recognize the importance of the interview and fear for Strether's performance in it.

Sentence 3: "He had spent the previous evening with all his old friends together; yet he would still have described himself as quite in the dark in respect to a forecast of their influence on his situation."

Paraphrase: Although he had spend the previous evening with his old friends, he still couldn't forecast how they would influence his situation.

Although the dramatic metaphor is dropped and the subject is apparently changed, sentence 3 adds further information about Strether's relative control of the drama as he approaches the interview. Our focus shifts clearly back to Strether as James presents us with a fact—"he had spent the previous evening with all his old friends together"—and then the psychological importance of the fact—"yet he would still have described himself as quite in the dark in respect to a forecast of their influence on his situation." The ambiguity in the description of that fact is at once unsettling and reassuring. By placing "together" at the end of the clause, James indicates that Strether happened to be with his old friends while they were "together" with each other, rather than that he was "together" with them. His "old friends" then may be his "former" friends rather than his "longtime" ones. Viewed in this way, the clause is a reminder of how alone Strether now is. But then when we remember that James has made us aware of the serious deficiencies of Woollett society, we see the clause as a positive reminder of how far Strether has traveled—mentally and morally—since he left it.

The difference between the original sentence as a whole and the paraphrase, where the "although" qualifies the fact from the start, is one of emphasis. We do not have to agree with a Fishean critic that the first clause definitely sets up expectations for a reversal of the theme of powerlessness; it is enough to see that after the grammatical closure of the first clause such a possibility—even with the unsettling ambiguity—does exist. Then, when the second clause tells us that Strether is still in the dark, his lack of control is emphasized. In other words, because we have seen the possibility of a reversal, we are more struck by the information that denies the reversal. The information itself is another note in the chorus proclaiming Strether's difficult situation: James's language is emphatic—Strether is "quite in the dark."

Furthermore, the syntax of this part of the sentence emphasizes how much in the dark Strether really is. James's nominalizations—"in respect to a forecast of their influence on his situation"—remove the explicit agents of the action, and hence produce an effect that is totally absent from the more direct paraphrase, "couldn't forecast how they would influence his situation." Because there is no agent for the act of forecasting, we see not only that Strether himself is unable to predict what would happen, but also that he could not recognize a true forecast if someone else gave it to him.

The passage so far has, as we expected from our description of James's intention, focused primarily on Strether's internal state. And the facts about his state—his powerlessness relative to Madame de Vionnet, his uncertainty about both what to expect from the Pococks, and just what his connection to them now is, and his general lack of control over his situation—emphasize the difficulty of his situation when Madame de Vionnet draws him into her boat. We see that her maneuver is a part of her larger pattern of action toward Strether, but that this time there is a difference. Previously she has very subtly committed him to her cause of convincing Chad to stay in Paris, so subtly in fact that Strether becomes committed before he is fully aware of what he is doing. On these occasions (their conversation at Chad's dinner party, their talk over lunch after meeting at Notre-Dame), he feels that she has driven in an attractive but painful "golden nail," binding him more and more closely to her cause. The difference here is that Strether is now more aware of what she is asking him to do. Once he has been drawn into the boat, he has a clear choice to make. Although he will not be acting from a position of strength, he must act and must take responsibility for his action. From what we have seen in this passage so far, we realize that Strether's decision to take up an oar and pull is neither an act of foolish bravado nor of romantic idealism. What his decision means *positively* we can better appreciate after looking at the rest of the passage.

Sentence 4: "It was strange, none the less, that in the light of this unexpected note of her presence he felt Madame de Vionnet a part of that situation as she hadn't yet been."

Paraphrase: Nevertheless, it was strange that Madame de Vionnet's presence now made him feel that she was more a part of his situation than ever.

In this sentence, we finally see Strether gain some positive information: he sees Madame de Vionnet as "a part of his situation as she hadn't yet been." Again James builds carefully to the important information. In the first part of the sentence, he calls our attention to the information by calling it "strange," he places it in a contrasting relation to the information of sentence 3 by saying "none the less," and he further contrasts it by saying "in the light," which of course recalls "in the dark" of the previous sentence. It is important to see, however, that James is not about to work a complete reversal: where Strether himself was "quite in the dark," he is now only looking at his situation in the light of "the unexpected note" of Madame de Vionnet's presence. And this mention of the physical fact of her presence completes the preparation for its psychological importance, which again is given at the end of the sentence.

The precision of James's language is perhaps most clear here where the last half of the paraphrase—"Madame de Vionnet's presence now made him feel that she was more a part of his situation than ever"—is quite close to the original. Although the same information is emphasized and although the semantic content is quite similar, we can only understand the description in the paraphrase, "she was more a part of his situation than ever" to mean that Madame de Vionnet is now more than ever a subordinate part of Strether's situation. However, in the less specific wording of the original, "a part of that situation as she hadn't yet been," we can not be so sure who is in control. On the one hand, we can see Madame de Vionnet simply as subordinated to Strether, as under his wing, and therefore quite as vulnerable to Sarah as he is. On the other, the suggestiveness of "as she hadn't yet been" and our memory of her greater power in controlling the pace of the drama allow us to see Strether as the real subordinate, to see that if she is under his wing, she still controls their flight. Thus, even here where Strether does gain positive information, we see that the information limits rather than increases his sense of control.

Sentence 5: "She was alone, he found himself assuming, with Sarah, and there was a bearing in that—somehow beyond his control—on his personal fate."

Paraphrase: He assumed that she was alone with Sarah, and that bore on his fate in a way that he couldn't control.

This sentence shows what this new realization of his relation to Madame de Vionnet means for Strether. And here everything is Strether's own thought; he is not reacting to physical facts but to imaginary ones. As we saw in the Fishean analysis, James presents the thought in small increments. He focuses not as the paraphrase does on Strether's mental action, but rather on

Strether's main interest, Madame de Vionnet. We learn first that "she was alone," and then James interpolates "he found himself assuming," before completing the thought, "with Sarah."

There are several noteworthy effects here. By breaking the thought at "alone," James gives that word a special emphasis, and in light of the previous sentence, it takes on a rather ominous meaning. This ominousness is reinforced by the short third increment, which emphasizes that she was alone with Strether's antagonist. Unlike the more straightforward paraphrase, "he assumed that she was alone with Sarah," James's version is able to emphasize both unpleasant aspects of the situation. We conclude that when Strether imagines Madame de Vionnet alone with Sarah he is imagining the worst. The second increment leaves open the possibility that Strether is assuming incorrectly, and it indicates that he is reflecting on his own mental process, that is, that he is thinking of himself thinking. Because he finds that he is thinking the worst, this phrase is a reminder of his active imagination and of his courage; he imagines the worst almost without trying and without resisting it once it appears; instead, he seems to accept it rather dispassionately.

The end of the sentence makes it clear why the situation Strether imagines is dangerous for him: "there was a bearing in that—somehow beyond his control—on his personal fate." James again saves the most important information for the end of the sentence, but by interpolating "somehow beyond his control," he is able to emphasize each of the three parts of the sentence. Moreover, "somehow beyond his control" is another suggestion of Strether's growing courage; it is a further reflection, and a rather grim one, on the fact that Madame de Vionnet will have a bearing on his fate regardless of his wishes, and yet he is able not only to admit this reflection, but to accept it as well. These small reminders of Strether's courage serve as assurances that in spite of his powerlessness the interview will not be disastrous for him.

Finally, the direct language of the juxtaposed contrast— "somehow beyond his control" and "on his personal fate"— clearly indicates the potential danger of Strether's situation: her actions will exert some control over his future. Again Strether has reached a firm conclusion that underlines rather than mitigates his danger. Although James gives us some assurance that the interview will not be disastrous for Strether, he never lets us underestimate its seriousness, including its potential danger, for the working out of Strether's fate.

Sentence 6: "Yet she was only saying something quite easy and independent—the thing she had come, as a good friend of Chad's, on purpose to say."

Paraphrase: Yet she was only saying what, as a good friend of Chad's, she had come to say.

In this sentence, James takes us back to the external scene as he tells us what the charming voice is saying. James's language apparently makes it clear that Strether has no immediate cause for alarm. By beginning with "yet," James clearly marks the change from the ominous note of the previous sentence, and by extending the description of what she was saying, he emphasizes Madame de Vionnet's independence of Strether. This extended description in the original is decidedly more emphatic than the more direct expression of the paraphrase, "she was only saying what . . . she had come to say." By stating first that she is saying "something quite easy and independent," James is making a literal assertion, which from the narrative manner we also recognize as Strether's, of Madame de Vionnet's independence, and then, by telling us somewhat more specifically what that something is—"the thing she had come, *as a good friend of Chad's, on purpose to say*" (emphasis mine)—he reminds us of Madame de Vionnet's closer ties, thereby reinforcing this sense of her independence of Strether.

This sentence, however, does not nullify the conclusions we have made in the previous ones, but complicates them. Madame de Vionnet may now be more a part of Strether's situation than ever, but she also has her own fate to work out. She is not just an uncontrollable extension of Strether but an independent human being with problems and concerns that have little to do with him. The sentence's final effect, then, is to make us more aware of Strether's danger: this powerful woman may very well use him to attain some of those independent aims.

Because we have seen Strether's powerlessness emphasized in this passage, we see the difficulty of his position in the interview. Because we see him realize how much a part of his situation Madame de Vionnet has become, we see his decision to take up an oar and pull as a strong, decisive moral choice. He does not want to make a clean break with Mrs. Newsome, but he knows that since Madame de Vionnet is already so much a part of his situation, acting as her good friend will greatly increase the likelihood of such a break. Madame de Vionnet puts him in a situation where he has only two alternatives, and they are both undesirable: he can repudiate her, thereby acting against his belief in her essential goodness, or he can settle comfortably into her boat, thereby closing off his chance of a reconciliation with Mrs. Newsome. It is a sign of Strether's growing moral courage that he sacrifices his own possible happiness for his belief in Madame de Vionnet.

Viewing Strether's choice in this way has important implications for the way we read much of the rest of the book. Having seen Strether's difficult but unflinching commitment to Madame de Vionnet here, we can better appreciate the force of his shock when he discovers that her relationship with Chad is not as virtuous as he had imagined. It appears then, if only for an instant, as if he has thrown his future away for nothing—or rather for a common, treacherous woman. And although we may initially be as shocked as Strether, our memory of Madame de Vionnet's manipulation of him is one of the reasons why we find his discovery plausible: if she were as wonderful, exquisite, and virtuous as Strether imagines, she would not use him as she does.

Having seen Strether experience his shock so severely, we can, in turn, better appreciate the moral strength that keeps him from reverting to the values of Woollett and simply condemning Madame de Vionnet. He is generous and honest enough to see that although she was not as wonderful as he thought, neither was she as base and "hideous" as Sarah believed her to be; that if she did use him for her own ends, it was because the desperateness of her situation drove her to it. This chain of effects ends finally in our admiration of the moral perception that allows Strether to see and to sympathize with Madame de Vionnet in both her genuinely exquisite personality and her almost pathetic dependence on Chad, and that also allows him to urge Chad to stay with her because she who has given him so much also needs him very much.

In general, then, we can see that the local effects of James's language in this passage contribute significantly to the intended representation of Strether's moral and cognitive growth. In fact, our discussion of the effects of the language has shown that his moral growth aids his cognitive growth and vice versa, so we might best characterize James's intention as the representation of Strether's growth in moral vision.

Perhaps the best way to generalize about the role James's language plays in the accomplishment of his intention is to consider the effects of the paraphrase. Although the paraphrase would make good expository prose—it is clear, direct, and fairly smooth—it is very bad prose for *The Ambassadors*. We have seen again and again that making the sentences flow more smoothly has also eliminated much of the complexity of the internal action. If we eliminate this complexity, Strether becomes a dull, cardboard character and *The Ambassadors* becomes a melodramatic book.

The material action James selects could quite easily be regarded as sentimental: a widower of fifty-five who feels that life has passed him by goes to Paris (of all places) to "save" a young man from a corrupt woman, only to discover that the young man is extraordinarily improved and is "living" life to the full; the older man then changes his advice to the younger one, thereby jeopardizing his position at home; then the older man discovers that his young friend is not quite as improved as he thought, and will not take his advice to remain with the woman anyway; finally, we are left feeling great pity for the old man who now has only the memories of his largely vicarious experience.

It is my contention that *The Ambassadors* does not affect us in such a sentimental way because of the complex responses James's language requires. The paraphrase does not change the thoughts Strether has or the things he does; it does not even change the emphasis on the internal action. What it does change, however, is the way those things are described, and consequently it changes the way we respond to them. We do not have the same understanding of Strether's lack of control over the situation or of his new and complex relation to Madame de Vionnet. Consequently, if the paraphrase replaced the original, we would not respond in the same way to Strether's choice during the interview, or to what he does when he discovers the sexual nature of Chad and Madame de Vionnet's relationship. Strether's moral judgments would not be as fine, nor would our expectations and desires for him be as strong. When we remember that the language creates similar complex responses throughout the book, that, in other words, *The Ambassadors* is built as a series of small steps like the one James describes in this passage, we can see that the language plays a decisive role in its success. It is the way James describes Strether's internal action at each of these steps that enables us to see and participate in the complex moral and psychological growth Strether experiences, and it is our participation in that experience that gives the book its greatest value.

V

In order to test and perhaps refine this conclusion about James's language, I now turn to the novel's final paragraphs because they have become the center of a critical controversy, and because attempting to provide a possible solution to that controversy by analyzing the language should clarify how important this element of the novel is.

At the end of the novel, Strether has forfeited his whole future—his marriage to Mrs. Newsome, his job as editor of the *Woollett Review,* his respectable position in the town—by casting his lot on the side of Madame de Vionnet. He has nothing to go home to, and nothing to stay in Paris for—until Maria Gostrey, in the final scene, offers to marry him. Strether is attracted by the offer, but refuses it because he feels that in order "to be right" he cannot "out of the whole affair" have got anything for himself.

Critics of the novel, as even a brief sampling will show, are sharply divided in their opinions about the success of this ending. F. O. Matthiessen argues that "the burden of *The Ambassadors* is that Strether has awakened to a whole new sense of life. Yet he does nothing at all to fulfill that sense. Therefore, fond as James is of him, we cannot help feeling his relative emptiness."[43] Robert Marks does not see how Strether could seriously entertain Maria's offer, and accuses him of hypocrisy in not telling her this immediately: "He doesn't return her love. It wouldn't be in accordance with the things that have come most to characterize him. But he *is* willing to go off with credit for this 'renouncement' also: he lets poor convenient, amusing, unforgettable, impossible Gostrey have as his reason his 'moral position' which he could more suitably address to Mme. de Vionnet—if to anybody at all."[44]

Frederick Crews and Ronald Wallace, on the other hand, endorse the interpretation James gives the ending in his Notebooks:[45] "He can't accept or assent. He won't.... He has come so far through his total little experience that he has come out on the other side—on the other side even, of a union with Miss Gostrey.''[46]

We have seen first of all—and our analysis of the language has confirmed this point—that *The Ambassadors* is an internal action in which Strether gradually attains mature moral vision. Therefore, we must judge how satisfactory the ending is according to how it represents Strether's internal state, and according to how well this representation is a plausible conclusion to the progression we have seen so far. We could not, for example, be satisfied with an ending in which Strether accepted an estate in the country and a substantial annual income from Mrs. Newsome, because such an ending would sacrifice Strether's moral integrity to his external comfort. His external circumstances really do not matter; Matthiessen is not justified in expecting Strether to *do* anything to fulfill his "new sense of life." What matters most is Strether's moral vision: he must be true to the fine moral sense we have seen him exercise when he chose to commit himself to Madame de Vionnet regardless of the personal consequences. It is by remaining true to this moral sense that Strether can be most happy because it is in this way that he can most respect himself.

By the time of his final conversation with Maria, we have already seen Strether exercise that moral sense in his final interviews with Madame de Vionnet and Chad. As I mentioned above, with Madame de Vionnet he is at last the stronger actor, but he does not use his strength to triumph over her by condemning her for her adultery; instead, he comes to understand it as a result of her weakness, her almost pathetic dependence on Chad. With Chad, Strether tries every argument he can think of to persuade him to remain with Madame de Vionnet, even though he realizes that all his arguments will be in vain. In spite of all Madame de Vionnet had done—"she had made him better, she had made him best"—Strether realizes that "he was nonetheless only Chad." But his moral sense tells him that Chad should be aware of what he is doing in abandoning Madame de Vionnet, so he goes on making his arguments.

Now with Maria's offer his moral vision faces its stiffest test: nothing he can go home to is quite so attractive, and no one else could offer him anything that seems so unobjectionable. Yet Strether's vision is so keen that he sees he cannot get anything out of the experience for himself without destroying the value of that experience. It is only in this sense that Strether has come out on the other side. It is not that he has left Maria behind in any way, but rather that he cannot feel he has acted without regard for his own benefit, if he comes away with so great a benefit as Maria.

But the mere act of Strether's refusal—even on these grounds—is not enough. As Marks's otherwise puzzling remarks remind us, it is all very well for Strether to be high-minded about not getting anything for himself, but he must also remember that he is not the only one affected by his decision. And we must expect Maria to be hurt to some degree by Strether's refusal: no matter how he puts it, he is still rejecting her. Yet if we are to interpret Strether's refusal as a final victory, James must plausibly represent Maria herself acknowledging it as a victory. It is for this reason, I believe, that James represents the scene in dialogue rather than in his characteristic narrative technique of showing Strether reflecting upon the action. At this point we would suspect any reflections Strether might make about how Maria feels because we know he has a vested interest in her feeling a certain way. It is only in dialogue, only in Maria's own words, that James can properly show that she herself believes that in rejecting her Strether has made the right choice. By itself, of course, James's choice of the proper narrative technique will not make the ending satisfactory; in the dialogue he must choose his language carefully if we are to believe that Maria remains true to her character and does not get reduced to a mere mechanical device for ending the book neatly. To see whether James chooses carefully enough we need to look at the final dialogue in some detail.

"I know. I know. But all the same I must go." He had got it at last. "To be right."

"To be right?"

She had echoed it in vague deprecation, but he felt it already clear for her. "That, you see, is my only logic. Not, out of the whole affair, to have got anything for myself."

She thought. "But with your wonderful impressions you'll have got a great deal."

"A great deal"—he agreed. "But nothing like *you*. It's you who would make me wrong!"

Honest and fine, she couldn't greatly pretend she didn't see it. Still she could pretend just a little. "But why should you be so dreadfully right?"

"That's the way that—if I must go—you yourself would be the first to want me. And I can't do anything else."

So then she had to take it, though still with her last defeated protest. "It isn't so much your *being* 'right'—it's your horrible sharp eye for what makes you so."

"Oh but you're just as bad yourself. You can't resist me when I point that out."

She sighed it at last all comically, all tragically, away. "I can't indeed resist you."

"Then there we are!" said Strether.[47]

Even before James presents this interchange, he is careful to represent Strether's concern for Maria's feelings. After showing that Strether finds Maria's offer extremely attractive but impossible to accept, James shows us Strether thinking of how Maria will take his refusal, "She'd moreover understand—she always understood." The general statement in the second half of the sentence, with its repetition of Maria's own valuable ability to "understand," assures us that Strether's thought is not an expression of his complacency, but a genuine compliment. With an alternate phrasing such as "She'd understand as she always did," the compliment would not be so evident. This compliment becomes greater when we realize that at this point Strether himself doesn't know why he must refuse her offer: he holds her power of understanding in such high esteem that he can feel she will understand his refusal even before he understands it himself.

In the first line of dialogue I have quoted, Strether is replying to Maria's reminder that there is nothing in the world she wouldn't do for him. Because Strether's reply, "I know. I know," is two sentences separated by a period rather than one separated by a comma, we understand that he is not merely dismissing Maria's statement, but rather acknowledging her generosity. But because he has already made his decision, because she has had to repeat her pledge, and because he does not respond more directly to it, it is clear that he is thinking of other things as well. When we read "He had got it at last," we see that those other things are the reasons why he cannot accept the offer. The way Strether formulates his refusal—"But all the same I must go"—shows his care for Maria's feelings. He does not make the refusal directly and personally, e.g., "I must refuse" or "I can't accept" but rather he acknowledges the compliment she pays him—" 'I know [you would do anything in the world for me] but all the same' "—and uses the language of necessity to say what he will do instead—"I must go."

This formulation of the refusal becomes more important when we learn his reason—"To be right." Had he phrased his refusal more personally or more directly, his "to be right" would have implied that there was something less than "right" about Maria, and his high-mindedness would have turned him into a prig. But as it is, his refusal is clear without being cruel, and his reason is one that he knows Maria will understand.

Yet Maria is human enough not to give him up without a struggle. James's representation of that struggle throughout this passage is especially fine. Her first reaction is to seek a better explanation, and she keeps the focus directly on Strether's reason by turning his phrase into a question, "To be right?," pronouncing it with "vague deprecation." It's almost as if by trying it out herself, she may overcome some of her skepticism and see what the phrase means for Strether. And she succeeds. By the time she has finished, Strether "felt it already clear for her." By seeing it so quickly, Maria is proving herself worthy of Strether's compliment to her understanding, but at the same time her "vague deprecation" indicates that she is not yet emotionally ready to accept this reason.

Strether elaborates, trying to win her acceptance: "That, you see, is my only logic. Not, out of the whole affair, to have got anything for myself." Again Strether's language displays his care for Maria's feelings: the phrase "my only logic" is general enough to apply not only to his refusal of her offer, but also his pattern of action in "the whole affair" so that again the refusal is not seen as a personal rejection but rather as part of a sacrifice he must make in order to comply with his sense of right. Furthermore, his formulation of that sense with its contrast of "the whole affair" and "not . . . anything for myself" makes us, who know how much he has invested and lost in the "whole affair," see just how strict his sense of right is, and just how much he has grown since the beginning of the affair when he judged things largely according to Mrs. Newsome's sense of right.

Meanwhile Maria's struggle continues. Strether's reply has given her pause—"She thought." What she thinks of is an objection, which she expresses rather convincingly, praising his "im-

pressions" and saving their important consequence for the end:
"But with your wonderful impressions, you'll have got a great
deal."

Strether's reply, after he admits the justice of the objection,
shows a new side to his refusal. It has, after all, had a great deal to
do with Maria personally—"But nothing like you. It's you who
would make me wrong." Maria, quite simply, is too good.
Strether uses Maria's objection as part of his praise, and then
uses that praise as part of his refusal: he agrees that his impressions have given him "A great deal," but adds that they are
still "nothing like" Maria, thereby acknowledging how much she
would give him. His conclusion, then, "It's you who would make
me wrong," is at once high praise and a clear refusal. His language is both honest and full of care for Maria.

Maria's own moral sense begins to make her accept Strether's
refusal. And since this acceptance comes at her own expense, the
narrator explicitly praises Maria, explaining how she is able to
understand: "Honest and fine, she couldn't greatly pretend she
didn't see it." Yet although she knows she has lost, she is not
quite ready to surrender: "Still she could pretend just a little. 'But
why should you be so dreadfully right?'" Her question makes us
see that the pretending really is "just a little." In the phrase
"dreadfully right," she is letting Strether know that although she
finds the consequences unpleasant, she is ready to accept the fact
that he is right. The attitude of the conversation has shifted
somewhat here; they both can relax now that the conclusion of
the dialogue is no longer in doubt. Maria here in a sense is asking
Strether, now that he has generally convinced her that he is right,
to win her completely over.

His reply is yet another compliment to her. In effect, when he
says, "That's the way that—if I must go—you yourself would be
the first to want me," he is saying that he must refuse Maria in
order to be right with Maria. By using the conditional, Strether
makes his praise more general and his point more convincing;
because his going is conditional, his assertion is about Maria's
general sense of right; and at the same time, his language is emphatic ("you yourself") about her high standards. It's as if he is
saying, "Considered in the abstract, this is the way you would
want me to be." Then, given the particular case, in which he has
no choice—"I can't do anything else"—he must live up to those

high standards of hers. She would want him to be "dreadfully right" even if it meant refusing to marry her—and it does.

"So," as the narrator tells us, "then she had to take it, though still with her last defeated protest." James's representation of Maria's struggle against what she soon knows is both right and inevitable not only makes the scene plausible but it also clarifies a little more at each step just how fine Strether's moral vision now is. Her final, defeated protest is actually the ultimate compliment to that vision—"It isn't so much your *being* right—it's your horrible sharp eye for what makes you so." His eye is both "horrible" and "sharp," because it now sees everything as it is, and refuses to be compromised in accepting the consequences of that vision. Maria's mock-complaint is somewhat wistful—oh, for blissful ignorance!—but it also acknowledges that she looks upon Strether's refusal as a victory for that horrible, sharp eye: it has seen with piercing clarity what is right.

Strether, for his part, returns Maria's compliment, but like her he puts it in the form of a complaint: "Oh but you're just as bad yourself." He is insisting on the equality of their moral vision, and therefore, is also saying that her own horrible sharp eye is as responsible for his refusal as his own; if *he* didn't see that he couldn't have her and still be right, *she* would soon see it. Moreover, he knows that she likes him to think of her as an equal: "You can't resist me when I point that out." This sentence with its strong negative language ("you can't resist"—no matter how hard you try) points to the vicious circle of attraction Strether and Maria are now in. It is their equally sharp sense of right that makes him refuse the offer, and makes her see that he is right to refuse it; that, in turn, only increases their attraction, and hence increases Maria's desire to make her offer.

It is this circle of attraction, a cause for both laughter and tears, that Maria at last sighs "all comically, all tragically, away." This sighing and her final words, "I can't indeed resist you," signify that she knows what her situation is, that she does not freely and happily choose this situation (again James uses the strong negative language), but that she is willing to accept it. Her struggle is over; and because she still finds Strether irresistible, we see that rather than being hurt by Strether's refusal, she is in agreement with it. In finding him irresistible, she has, in a sense, ended where she had begun, but now she understands more fully *why* he is irresistible and why she cannot, indeed, should not marry him.

Strether recognizes that Maria's struggle is over, that she is willing to accept her situation and his, that they have, in fact, reached an end. He sums up all these things and his own acceptance of them in their favorite phrase, "Then there we are!" There is also a note of triumph in this phrase, reflecting Strether's knowledge that he has, after all, been "right" with himself—and in this internal action, that's all that matters.

On this account, then, James's ending seems more than satisfactory. He has found a way to bring Strether's relationship with Maria to a close while also illuminating and reconfirming the moral vision Strether has attained in the course of his experience in Paris. Although we did not know at the outset that this mature moral vision was the desired end toward which Strether was moving, we recognize, once we see it, that it is the most desirable fate he could achieve. He has, in effect, achieved a complete independence and a full mautrity. We need not fear how he will cope with his external circumstances, however impoverished, when he returns to Woollett.

Furthermore, on this account, the success of the ending is to a large degree a result of the success of James's language. I have tried to show that only the subtlety and precision of the dialogue as James writes it could enable us to accept as plausible Maria's acknowledgment that Strether is right to refuse her. My analysis here, then, has corroborated my earlier conclusions about the decisive role language plays in *The Ambassadors*. Without James's complexity of style, the complexity of response—and in this case, the value of his book—would disappear.

Notice, however, that the analysis of the language of the final dialogue strongly supported but did not prove by itself the general statements about the success of the ending. We could not have a notion of what constitutes a successful ending without an idea of the book's form that is based not on its language but on those things represented by that language: James's characters in a particular sequence of actions. In spite of the importance of James's language in *The Ambassadors,* it remains a means to an end; it is the wonderful instrument, both delicate and sharp, that James needs to portray the subtle but sure process of Strether's growth—but it is finally an instrument, not an end in itself.

We may tentatively conclude, then, that language may become

decisive for the success of a work, but that it never becomes the organizing principle of a work; that it may be the most important single element in the construction of a work, but that it is never equivalent to that construction. We shall consider a serious challenge to this conclusion in the next chapter where we examine the approach to language in fiction taken by David Lodge.

3

Literary Discourse, "Ordinary Discourse," and Intentions: David Lodge and the Language of *Sister Carrie*

I

David Lodge, a critic whose statements seem to carry added weight because he is also a successful novelist, has advanced what is perhaps the most comprehensive formulation of the position that the medium is all-important in the art of fiction. Lodge puts the case in a variety of ways—"the 'synthesizing principle' of all literary structures is language: all plots are plots of language";[1] "the writer's choice is, strictly speaking, unlimited" (p. 63); "all good criticism is . . . necessarily a response to language" (p. 78)—and seemingly refutes some of the main arguments against it—what he calls "the argument from translation" and "the argument from bad writing."

Lodge's approach raises especially provocative questions about the relation between language and fiction when we consider it in connection with a novel of "bad writing" such as *Sister Carrie*. Dreiser's novel has pleased readers for nearly three-quarters of a century, yet Dreiser himself has been described in such phrases as "the Caliban of American fiction," and "the worst writer of his eminence in the entire history of literature."[2] Although a few critics finally defend Dreiser's use of language, no one denies that according to the usual standards by which an author's style is judged, he is a bad writer.

Applying Lodge's terms, we might express our questions this way: if all plots are plots of language, and Dreiser has used language poorly, then what pleasure can readers take in his novel? Or more generally, if we deny that form and content are separable, even for analytic purposes, then when we say that Dreiser's style is deficient, are we not also saying the same about the whole novel? On the other hand, if all plots are plots of language and generations of readers have in fact found Dreiser's novel moving, then can it be correct to say that he has used language poorly? Or again if form and content are inseparable, and we find that the novel as a whole has a powerful effect on us, then can we justifiably criticize Dreiser's use of language?

I shall begin trying to solve the paradox suggested by these questions by examining the theoretical basis of Lodge's position. Unlike Fish, Lodge does have a consistent, coherent theory; but he does not conform to that theory in his practical criticism. Since I am much less interested in Lodge himself than I am in the implications of the language-is-all position, I shall consider only his theory.[3]

Lodge believes that criticism of the novel has suffered because critics have accepted a false dichotomy between literary and nonliterary language, and hence have not paid sufficient attention to the language of the novel. According to this dichotomy, literary language, as exemplified by lyric poetry, is, in I. A. Richards' terms, primarily "emotive" and nonliterary language primarily "referential"; since language in fiction is deemed more like language in ordinary discourse than like that in lyric poetry, it is considered "referential" and consequently unworthy of critical attention.

Lodge attempts to show that this dichotomy is false by pointing out on the one hand that a great deal of literature—"traditional poetry, not to mention drama and fiction" (p. 17)—seems to be more referential than emotive, and on the other, that even the most avant-garde lyric poetry must have a significant referential aspect (p. 25). Therefore, Lodge proposes a view of language "as a continuum in which the proportion of 'emotive' to 'referential' varies, but in which neither element is ever entirely absent" (p. 17); furthermore, the proportion of one to another in a work will not correspond to a hierarchy of literary value (p. 26).

It is important for us to see here that Lodge's view of language as a continuum is not as sharp a break with New Critical theory as he would have us believe; instead it is only a slight shift that allows him to extend the claims that New Critics make for the importance of language in poetry to language in fiction. The crucial point for Lodge is that language in poetry (unlike language in ordinary discourse), is nonparaphrasable; its important corollary is that form and content are inseparable. Lodge's discussions of the "argument from translation" and of the "argument from bad writing'' illustrate how making these two assumptions would powerfully affect the way we understand literary experience.

Lodge uses two strategies to refute the argument from translation: personal testimony, and a comparison of a passage from Proust with its translation. He says first that although he has read many novels in translation with pleasure, he feels that he has never "possessed" them in the same way he possesses many English novels. He can only attribute this feeling to the insecurity of the reading process, "the accumulative effect of innumerable minute uncertainties, awkwardnesses, anomalies, and ambiguities in the language" (p. 20). It is revealing that Lodge sees this phenomenon as evidence *against* the argument from translation rather than evidence *for* it. He does not argue, as he might, that in spite of these problems with the medium, he can still read a translation with pleasure, still feel he is reading say, *Crime and Punishment* rather than a different novel by the translator, and that, therefore, language cannot be all-important in the art of fiction. Instead, he views the "innumerable uncertainties" as more important than the commonality of experience he has with someone reading the original: since every aspect of the two experiences will not be the same, and since the differences can be accounted for by differences in language, then the argument from translation is finally unconvincing, and language must be all-important in fiction. Lodge solves the paradox of his position— the translation isn't a true paraphrase, yet it also isn't a new work—by saying that we make a different "contract" with a translated novel than we do with one in our own language (p. 20).

The conclusions Lodge draws from his analysis of the Proust passage are also determined by his belief in the nonparaphrasability of literary language. In a skillful and sensitive discussion, he shows what the translator, Scott Moncrieff, has and has not been able to preserve from the original (pp. 20–23). Although Lodge never doubts that Moncrieff's translation describes the same experience as the original, and with almost the same affect, the differences are more important for him than the similarities. His argument boils down to this: the translation of a novel, though it may convey most of the aspects of the meaning of the novel, cannot convey all those aspects, and therefore, it is something quite different from the original. In effect, it is this condition that we accept when we make our "contract" with a translated novel.

In his handling of the argument from bad writing, Lodge demonstrates his belief in the assumption that form and content are absolutely inseparable. He maintains that a work of art may still be good if small parts of it are badly written, but when the bad writing becomes frequent, then either the work no longer deserves our admiration or the criteria for determining good and bad writing are inadequate. Lodge sums up his case: "it seems necessary to assert that the badly-written great, or even good, novel is a contradiction in terms. A work of art cannot be successfully achieved if its medium is misused" (p. 27). Thus, for him, *Sister Carrie* is either well written or a bad novel.

Lodge's conclusions here depend, finally, on what he believes about "the philosophical heart of the matter, the relation of literary language to reality" (p. 18). Lodge presents the argument for his fundamental beliefs twice, once in philosophical terms, and once from the point of view of the working novelist. I shall consider the philosophical argument first.

Relying on the work of J. M. Cameron, Lodge argues that because literary language is not related to reality in the same way that nonliterary language is, literary statements are not paraphrasable, while nonliterary ones are. In ordinary discourse, Lodge and Cameron maintain, paraphrase is possible because "the adequacy of what is said is governed by some state of affairs prior to and independent of what is said" (p. 36), that state of affairs being the real situation in the real world. Since there is no such state of affairs in fictional descriptions, since, in other words, "fictitious descriptions are neither true nor false in the way real descriptions are," it is not possible to "give an *alternative* poetic description, for there could be no criterion (as there would be in the case of a real description) for deciding whether or not the alternative description had succeeded" (p. 36). Consequently, the poetic description "exists only as *this* description, these words in this order" (Cameron's emphasis, p. 36). If we did change the linguistic form of a fictional description, we would not merely alter that description, we would create an entirely new one.

Later on, in speaking of the working novelist, Lodge says that Cameron's argument recognizes the paradox "at the heart of literary language," i.e., "the imaginative writer creates what he describes" (p. 62). Consequently, "every imaginative utterance is an 'appropriate' symbolization of the experience it conveys, since there is no possible alternative symbolization of the same experience" (p. 62). In other words we cannot, in literary discourse, separate what is said from how it is said. Thus it is misleading to talk about an author making appropriate choices of language. Lodge puts it this way:

> Clearly the writer's practice of his art can be described as a process of choosing certain verbal formulations in preference to others. But whereas in non-literary description, choice is limited by what there is to be described, the writer's choice is, strictly speaking, unlimited. If I wish to describe an actual person Mr. Brown, I might be able to choose between calling him *tall* or *big, dark* or *swarthy,* and this would be stylistic choice in Warburg's sense. But I could never "choose" between calling him *tall* or *short, dark* or *fair.* If he is a character in a novel, however, I can choose to describe him as tall and fair, or short and dark, or short and fair, or tall and dark. I can also call him Mr. Green or Mr. Grey or by any other name. I could conceivably call him all these things for a special literary effect: *Mr. Brown, or Green as he was sometimes called, was short, but tall with it. His fair-complexioned face was swarthy. As one of his friends remarked, "Grey is a difficult man to pin down."* [pp. 63–64]

The logical conclusion of this position, of course, is that everything in a novel (or in a poem) can be explained by reference to its language. Lodge is saying that since literary statements are nonparaphrasable, terms like "character" and "plot" do not refer to separate elements of a novel's construction—elements that would remain constant in a paraphrase—but rather to "abstractions formed from accumulated messages conveyed through language" (p. 17). If the linguistic forms change, then the messages change and so do the abstractions formed from those messages. In short, because the writer's choice at any point in the construction of a novel is unlimited, the novel, for Lodge, is all and only language.

II

When we begin to examine the consequences of Lodge's position for practical criticism, we begin to see its limitations. Suppose a critic who shares Lodge's theoretical beliefs reads what he decides is a bad novel; on what grounds can he justify his judgment? He cannot say it is poorly plotted, that it sets up expectations it fails to fulfill, because he believes the writer's choice is unlimited. He cannot say that the characters are inconsistent or that they are not properly suited to the action because he believes that these elements are merely abstractions from language. And, finally, he cannot even criticize that language except on invalid grounds, or by some external criterion he chooses more or less arbitrarily. If he suggests that particular descriptions in the novel be altered, he is, in effect, suggesting that the author describe different things, or in other words, he is not granting the author his subject. The only way to justify his judgment is by reference to an a priori criterion of good and bad writing, a criterion which will be applied to all works.

The criterion Lodge himself chooses is "realization," "the art which exploits the resources of language in such a way that words 'become' what in ordinary discourse they merely represent" (p. 63). As Lodge points out, this notion of realization bears a strong resemblance to Wimsatt's concept of the "verbal icon," i.e., "the verbal image which most fully realizes itself by presenting not merely a bright picture . . . but also an interpretation of reality in its metaphoric and symbolic dimensions."[4] But Lodge goes further than Wimsatt; for him, the devices of literary language "*present* the things which language is otherwise occupied in designating" (p. 63).

This criterion of realization, though a priori in the sense that it assumes all works strive to achieve it, is consistent with Lodge's other assumptions: if language is all in fiction, then it makes sense to say that the linguistic forms themselves should not only signify their references, but should also (somehow) imitate them. Let us test the adequacy of this criterion for analyzing the successful use of language in fiction by examining a specific case.

In the last sentence of *A Farewell to Arms,* "After a while I went out and left the hospital and walked back to the hotel in the rain," Hemingway represents Frederick Henry's response to the death of his lover Catherine Barkley. As Henry speaks this final sentence, he has full knowledge of the world's destructiveness—the world kills all, and it kills the very good or the very brave first—and full knowledge of the great loss he has suffered in Catherine's death. He is doomed and knows it. Yet he speaks this final sentence and we are moved. Why?

In Lodge's terms, Hemingway must have created a successful realization, his words must have "become" what they would ordinarily represent. In this context, "become" must be taken to mean that the collocations of words and the sentence structure will, in a metaphorical sense, reflect the actions or objects represented. Thus, this simple, deliberate, and precisely detailed sentence gives us as much of a sense of Henry's action as the meaning of its words. The step-by-step account ("I went out; I left the hospital; walked back to the hotel"), which might have been concisely expressed "I returned to the hotel," "becomes" an imitation of Henry's action: although Henry does not use any adjectives or adverbs, the form of the sentence tells us that Henry's walk is slow and deliberate. The sentence is realized, and hence, successful.

But to stop there, as a measurement of realization must, will not enable us to account fully for the sentence's effectiveness. We cannot, for example, explain why this particular kind of realization at this point in the novel is more appropriate than another kind. Suppose the final sentence were "After a while I went out and left the hospital and stepped into the rain, suddenly cursing, weeping, laughing furiously, uncontrollably, simultaneously, raging against my fate." This sentence is clearly realized: just as Henry suddenly explodes into violent, irrational action, so does the sentence. Its straightforward orderly description of Henry's exit is suddenly broken by the series of participles and adverbs which consists of illogical, even contradictory collocations of words, and which is not clearly connected, in a grammatical sense, to the rest of the sentence. It would even be possible to argue that my sentence is more realized than Hemingway's and hence, according to Lodge's theory, superior.

But of course no one would agree with that conclusion. To explain why and to explain the effectiveness of Hemingway's sentence, we must move beyond a consideration of the language alone. We need to understand that the sentence is effective in part because of what it does not say, and to do that we need to include character and plot in our consideration of it. Although the action of walking back to the hotel is small and simple, we know that it is neither small nor simple for Henry. If it were, if he were able simply to walk away from what has happened, then we would feel that he was an ignorant, unfeeling, virtually subhuman creature, not someone we admire. In point of fact, however, we know that in the face of his awful knowledge of the destructive world and his enormous grief at the death of Catherine, Henry has no reason to do anything but despair. Since in his world all acts eventually lead to destruction and admirable ones lead there sooner, any act other than one that expresses his despair will be tremendously difficult. Therefore, when, in the last sentence, we see Henry exhibiting no sign of despair, but instead maintaining his dignity and taking the small, difficult, deliberate, and *positive* action, we are moved. It is an admirable response to a doom that he will never be able to escape. Furthermore, since the pattern of the plot represents Henry growing in stature as he grows in knowledge of his destructive world, it is just such an action that is called for at this point. Because of this plot pattern, we would be moved by any sentence which allowed us to see Henry taking this positive action with dignity.

Although the language of Hemingway's sentence does not by itself create our sense of the nobility of Henry's response, it significantly enhances that sense. It is hard to think of a sentence that would be more appropriate. Hemingway begins with a reminder of Henry's doom: "After a while" concisely suggests how difficult it is for Henry to leave Catherine's room, but that at last he accepts the finality of her death. Hemingway then moves to the matter-of-fact description of Henry's action: "I went out and left the hospital and walked back to the hotel." As we saw in the discussion of the sentence's realization, this description indicates that it is a slow and painful action for Henry to take; at the same time, his matter-of-fact tone and the absence of modifiers indicate Henry's enormous personal control and quiet dignity in acting this way at this time. The final phrase, "in the rain," further increases our sense of Henry's dignity. Catherine had predicted that she would die in the rain, and throughout the novel, rain has been associated with the world's destructiveness. Now when Henry is being literally hit in the face with the cruellest reminder of his doom, he reports the fact neither with bitterness nor despair but only with a matter-of-factness that signifies his calm dignity and noble suffering.

In short, Hemingway's is a brilliant sentence, but it is not brilliant only because it is successfully realized. Instead, it is brilliant because it is especially appropriate for the particular character of Frederick Henry in the particular action of *A Farewell to Arms*.

This analysis, I believe, demonstrates that if we view character and action as nonlinguistic elements of fiction we shall be better able to account for the role of language in fiction than if we assume that everything in fiction can be explained by reference to language. However, it is still possible that the analysis may be illegitimate because it runs counter to what Lodge calls "the philosophical heart of the matter," the relation of literary language to reality. Let us examine Lodge's argument about the nonparaphrasability of literary language.

According to his system, nonliterary discourse is paraphrasable because "there is some state of affairs prior to and independent of what is said," and against which we can judge the adequacy of any paraphrase, while literary language is nonparaphrasable because it does not refer to any such prior state of affairs. What distinguishes nonliterary from literary discourse is not actual knowledge of the prior state of affairs but a belief that such a state of affairs exists. In one sense, then, Lodge is saying that as long as we believe in the existence of a prior state, the differences between any two sentences describing that state are stylistic; and that once we cease believing in that state, the differences between the same two sentences are differences in meaning: each sentence creates a different state of affairs.

In order to appreciate the special nature of Lodge's position, we should distinguish it from other positions that have been taken on this question. Some theorists, e.g., Nelson Goodman, argue that paraphrase is impossible in any discourse because any change in the linguistic form of an utterance introduces a change in its meaning.[5] Other theorists, e.g., E. D. Hirsch, Jr., argue that there are occasional contexts in which paraphrase is possible; in these cases the surrounding words and the general intent of the speech make it possible for one word to be substituted for another without altering the meaning.[6] Our working hypothesis, as we have seen in the previous chapter, says that the differences between two sentences such as "The lion ate the lion-tamer" and "The lion-tamer was eaten by the lion" are different in kind from those between either one of them and "It snowed today." In this view, the differences between the first two sentences are stylistic and the differences between them and the third are differences in meaning. The first two are paraphrases of each other, the third is a nonsynonymous sentence.

There is no essential disagreement among our position, Goodman's, and Hirsch's. Ours does not argue that all paraphrases are identical in meaning; theirs do not argue that all sentences are equally nonsynonymous. Each of us is simply defining the terms "meaning," "paraphrase" and "style" in different ways, and consequently each will get different insights into the nature of language. However, each assumes that those properties of language that must be considered in taking a position on paraphrasability (e.g., how semantic meanings of different words are related, how syntax affects meaning), are an intrinsic part of the linguistic system, i.e., that they are common to language in all its manifestations. Lodge is doing something quite different: he is saying that in nonliterary discourse language works the way our position has described it (e.g., substituting words that are closely synonymous produces paraphrase), while in literary discourse it works the way Goodman has described it (e.g., substituting words that are closely synonymous produces a totally new, nonsynonymous utterance). In this view, these properties of language do not inhere in language itself, but rather are determined by its relation to reality.

Lodge's position can, I think, be refuted empirically. Consider my two sentences about the lion and the lion-tamer. Because we know the English language, we do not need to believe in the existence of a real lion and a real lion-tamer to decide whether "The lion ate the lion-tamer" and "The lion-tamer was eaten by the lion" are paraphrases. It makes no difference whether the two sentences are to occur in a newspaper or in a novel; the relation between them, the meaning that they have in common is not affected in the least by whether or not we believe there is a prior state of affairs which they describe. Whether we want to call these two sentences paraphrases or not is, in one sense, irrelevant; the important point is that we can make a decision about their relation solely on the basis of our knowledge of language. There is a criterion for determining paraphrase in literary discourse and it is the same criterion that we use in nonliterary discourse: linguistic competence.

Lodge himself implicitly acknowledges the importance of our

linguistic competence in his discussion of paraphrasability in nonliterary discourse. There are only two ways we can recognize that two statements about some preexistent state of affairs refer to that state: (1) we have direct (nonverbal) knowledge of that state of affairs (we saw the lion eat the lion-tamer); (2) our knowledge of language tells us that the sentences could refer to the same thing. And surely Lodge does not want to be in the position of saying either that in nonliterary discourse we always have knowledge of that prior state of affairs, or that paraphrase is possible only when we have that knowledge, because then he is no longer fully distinguishing between literary and nonliterary discourse: it is often the case that the listener in nonliterary discourse does not have knowledge of the prior state of affairs.

When we look more closely at Lodge's system, we see that even on its own terms it cannot fully distinguish between literary and nonliterary discourse, between paraphrasable and nonparaphrasable utterances. The principles of his system lead to conclusions that violate its spirit. Novelists often describe historical personages or events, or choose real places for the settings of their novels. According to Lodge's principles, then, it would seem that descriptions of these things could be paraphrased, while the rest of the novel could not. But this means some statements in literary discourse are paraphrasable while others are not. Or to take a somewhat different case: some works of literature, e.g., *Oedipus Rex*, are based on stories so well known that we can justifiably say that they describe a "prior state of affairs." Is Sophocles' play paraphrasable while, say, Arthur Miller's *Death of a Salesman* is not? The principles of Lodge's system lead us to believe so, but this conclusion again contradicts the spirit of his system, i.e., that literary discourse is not paraphrasable. And again this conclusion is at odds with our knowledge of language. There is nothing intrinsically different in the language of the two plays that makes one paraphrasable and the other not.

Although Lodge's answers are finally unsatisfactory, he raises questions that we must consider in order to understand the nature of style in fiction. To what extent do factors other than our linguistic competence affect our judgments of paraphrasability—or more generally, our response to language? Is there any essential difference in the language of literature and the language of so-called ordinary discourse? Even if our knowledge of language tells us that all statements can be paraphrased (in the sense I am using the term), is it possible for some statements to exist in literature that cannot exist in ordinary discourse, e.g., Lodge's statements about Mr. Brown-Green-Grey? In order to answer these questions we need to look more closely at the way our understanding of sentences is affected by their use in context.

Out of context almost all sentences are potentially ambiguous, if only because they can be interpreted metaphorically. Although it is true that we can specify a great deal of information about a sentence regardless of its context—we can analyze its semantic content, its deep structure, the transformations that account for the surface structure, the surface structure itself, and its phonetic representation—and although all these components of the sentence will have a bearing on its meaning, they will not exhaust its meaning nor will they tell us under what conditions it will take on one meaning rather than another. In order to account for these aspects of the sentence, we must examine it as part of a whole speech event.

The term "speech event" includes not only the language of the speech but all the nonlinguistic factors, i.e., factors that cannot be accounted for by a grammar, which nevertheless affect our response to the language. The most important of these factors are (1) the relation of speaker and audience—we will react in one way if we hear a Democratic president call his chief of staff "Sir" and in quite another if we hear him call his chauffeur "Sir"; (2) the relation of speaker and subject—we respond in one way if a Democratic president criticizes the Democratic Party, and in quite another if a Republican does it using the same sentences; (3) the relation between audience and subject—we react to a Democratic president's criticism in one way if we're Democrats, in quite another if we're Republicans; (4) the occasion of the utterance—we react in one way if the president makes his remarks at the Democratic national convention, in quite another if he makes them at a cabinet meeting; and (5) the intention of the speaker—we react in one way if we think the president is ironic when he says "The Democratic Party is controlled by big business," and in quite another if we believe he intends the statement to be taken literally.[7]

As we have seen briefly in chapter 2, our knowledge of these nonlinguistic aspects of the speech event will have a significant bearing on what we consider paraphrases. Even sentences with identical linguistic forms can have widely different meanings in different contexts. If a friend who has just come from the circus tells me, "The lion ate the lion-tamer," I shall understand his statement literally. If a few minutes later another friend who has just been to an athletic contest and could not have heard about what happened at the circus speaks the identical sentence I shall interpret it metaphorically and understand it to mean something like the following: in the match-up between the outstanding offensive player and the outstanding defensive player the offensive player won.[8] On the other hand, once we know the nonlinguistic aspects of speech events, we may consider sentences that in isolation would be nonsynonymous as paraphrases of each other. If someone is telling me the story of how the lion ate the lion-tamer after I have told him that I heard what happened but didn't hear how or why, he might conclude, "And so, the lion made his displeasure known to the lion-tamer." In this context, I will understand that sentence as a paraphrase of "And so, the lion ate the lion-tamer"; it is not as closely synonymous to that sentence as "And so, the lion-tamer was eaten by the lion," but nevertheless it clearly expresses something in common with both those sentences that "And so, they lived happily ever after," does not.

There is, of course, a limit to how far the meanings of two sentences can diverge before we will stop seeing them as paraphrases, regardless of the context. The sentence, "And so, the lion drank water," will not be a paraphrase of "And so, the lion ate the lion-tamer" in this or any other context. The meaning of any utterance derives both from its linguistic form and from the nonlinguistic aspects of its speech event.

In some cases, there is also another significant factor that contributes to the meaning of a sentence: our encyclopedic knowledge of the world. Suppose that we are reading a novel and we encounter the sentence, "The cat slept in the oven" in a description of a character's household. Suppose we also know that in the society represented in this novel cats sleep in the oven only in houses where there is no central heating; in other words, part of the meaning of this literal, unidiomatic sentence is that the character lives in poverty. The crucial variable in our recognizing that the sentence "He lived in poverty" is a paraphrase of "The cat slept in the oven'' is neither our linguistic competence nor our knowledge of the nonlinguistic aspects of the speech event but our encyclopedic knowledge of that society.

In summary, then, our response to language is determined by our knowledge of the linguistic system, our understanding of the nonlinguistic aspects of the speech event, and at times by our encyclopedic knowledge of the world. Sentences can take on widely different meanings in different contexts, but because the linguistic system is independent of any one speaker, we cannot use a sentence to mean whatever we like.

The related problem which Lodge's approach has raised is whether it is possible to distinguish literary from nonliterary discourse on the basis of the way language is used in each. It seems fairly clear that there is no single criterion which will distinguish all literary discourse from all nonliterary. In many, if not most, cases we cannot decide by looking at the language; sentences like "Emma Woodhouse, handsome, clever, and rich, with a comfortable home and a happy disposition, seemed to unite some of the best blessings of existence," and "Stanley Fish is a brilliant and provocative critic" could be either literary or nonliterary. There is nothing in either sentence which tells us whether its subject is real or imaginary; our knowledge of the nonlinguistic aspects of the speech event must tell us.[9] Furthermore, it seems that any sentence that can exist in nonliterary discourse could also exist in literary: for any sentence that we come across or can imagine, we can always imagine a fictional character who can utter it. It is not, however, equally clear that any statement in literary discourse could occur in nonliterary. As we have seen, Lodge himself has argued that his description of Mr. Brown-Green-Grey could not exist in nonliterary discourse.

His argument is valid as long as we understand "could not" in the proper sense. Clearly we could make the statements Lodge has made about Brown-Green-Grey about Lodge himself and we could understand it as nonfictional discourse: "Mr. Lodge, or Wimsatt as he was sometimes called, was tall but short with it. His fair-complexioned face was swarthy. As a friend of his remarked, 'Beardsley is a difficult man to pin down.'" We cannot, however, understand these statements literally, the way we can those about Brown. Our encyclopedic knowledge tells us that no real person can have these contradictory physical qualities. We can either take the statements metaphorically (Lodge, like other New Critics, is extraordinarily difficult to pin down) or decide that the speaker is unreliable. If we want to take the statements literally, then we must conclude that this is literary discourse.

In some cases, we will get linguistic clues that we are reading fictional discourse: "Once upon a time, a boy named Rocket Power propelled only by his magical boots was hurtling through space." Again our encyclopedic knowledge tells us that if we are to take the statement literally then we must be reading fictional discourse, but here both "once upon a time" and "Rocket Power" are additional clues. In a sentence like "anyone lived in a pretty how town/ (with up so floating many bells down)" the clues are almost all linguistic—the character's name, the highly unusual syntax, the rhythm, the rhyme of "town" and "down," all contribute to our sense that this is fictional discourse. But even here I hesitate to say that it is impossible for the statement to exist in nonliterary discourse—we shall understand it as a "poetic" metaphor, but given the right context we might still apply it to a real person.

We have seen that although the language of a speech event may tell us either very much or very little about the nonlinguistic aspects of that speech event, those aspects are always important. And from our point of view, the most important of them is intention. It is, in a sense, the most comprehensive feature of the speech event and it is necessary for evaluating style. Given a particular speaker with a particular subject and a particular audience on a given occasion, we can still think of numerous different intentions that speaker might try to achieve, each of which will shape his choice of language (and the response of his audience) in quite different ways. On the other hand, these other features of the speech event must be subsumed in any full description of the intention. In this sense, our questions about whether one sentence is a paraphrase of another and whether it is literary or nonliterary discourse can be subsumed under our questions about the intention of the sentence. Furthermore, once we discover the intention we can make judgments about how well the style—those aspects of the language that could be altered in a paraphrase— contributes to the success of the whole event. It will be helpful to clarify these points with an example.

Let us consider Lodge's description of Mr. Brown-Green-Grey once again: "Mr. Brown, or Green as he was sometimes called, was short, but tall with it. His fair-complexioned face was swarthy. As one of his friends remarked, 'Grey is a difficult man to pin down.'" As we have seen, Lodge offers this description as evidence for his position that the writer's choice is unlimited; it is, in fact, evidence for the opposite conclusion. Consider the last sentence. It is primarily a summary of Brown-Green-Grey's character as revealed in the previous two sentences, but it becomes more than just a straightforward one with the introduction of the new name that the omniscient narrator himself did not initially seem to know: we get a sense that this character is the ultimate chameleon, able to "change" not just from one opposing quality to another, but even to things that our omniscient narrator cannot see in advance. The sentence, in short, is an apt conclusion to the description of the character.

Now suppose the last sentence read, "As one of his friends remarked, 'Brown is an easy man to pin down.'" I think it is clear that we should respond to the sentence in one of two ways: either we would interpret it as inadequate and irrelevant because it contradicts what we know from the first two sentences, or we would interpret it ironically: given everything that we have just been told about Brown-Green, we cannot believe that a friend of his could say he is easy to pin down without speaking ironically. In either case, our response depends on the fact that by the end of the second sentence we have inferred that the intention of the passage is to describe a chameleonlike character.

This example demonstrates first that the writer's choice is not unlimited. There is no way for Lodge to convince his readers in the last sentence that Brown is an easy man to pin down. What a writer does first puts constraints on what he can do later, and what he wants to do later puts constraints on what he can do first.

This example also illustrates that character is more than just an abstraction from language. Even though we may postulate that Lodge's intention is to create a chameleonlike character, if we believe that character is merely an abstraction from language, then we have no reason to read a sentence without any internal clues to irony like "Brown is an easy man to pin down" as anything but a straightforward assertion. Since we believe that character is just an abstraction of accumulated messages of language, not an entity with any real independent existence, we shall use the new messages of this sentence to alter our understanding of the intention rather than allowing our understanding of the intention to alter the way we read the new messages. But this procedure plainly contradicts our experience in reading the sentence. In order to account for that experience, we must assume that our concept of character, though formed from language, is an element independent of it, and that once our concept is formed, it can affect the way we respond to new language.

Now suppose that the last sentence of Lodge's description were not "As one of his friends remarked, 'Grey is a difficult man to pin down'" but the clearly ironic "As one of his friends remarked, 'Grey is an easy woman to pin down.'" Our concept of the intention tells us that the original is a better summary for the following reason: the friend in the original is created largely to give some "external" confirmation to the narrator's remarks about our chameleonlike character; he is not interesting in himself, and our attention remains squarely on Brown; although the new ironic paraphrase is funnier than the original, it shifts our attention away from Brown toward his friend—we begin to wonder about him and his sense of humor—and consequently, the force of the sentence as a summary of Brown is attenuated. It is possible to impose other intentions on the passage as a whole in order to account for the ironic version of the last sentence, e.g., the author is describing not just a single character but a whole society where our normal judgments are to be reversed, but we do so at the expense of our ability to account for the first two. Our evidence for this revised specification of the intention is weak: we have only two characters, not a whole society, the second character is only introduced in the very last sentence, and there is nothing in the passage that asks us to see them as representative types. Although this passage might be the beginning of a description of such a society, it is presented to us as whole and complete. Even if we say that the author's main intention in the passage is to create a funny description, we account for the ironic last sentence at the expense of the first two. Why be funny in this way? Only if his intention is to create a particular kind of funny description— that of a chameleonlike character. All things considered, we can better account for the ironic paraphrase by seeing it as a summary that is just a little too clever.

Now suppose that the last sentence were, "As one of his friends remarked, 'Grey is a difficult woman to pin down.'" Our understanding of the intention tells us that this is a better conclusion than the original: it does everything the original does—gives external confirmation to the narrator's remarks without calling undue attention to the friend, summarizes the character's nature with a twist—but it does something more. It gives the summary a double twist, as it were; it adds another dimension to our understanding of Brown's chameleonlike nature (he can "change" sex), and it contributes to the special humor of the description (the narrator cannot quite keep up with this chameleon).

In this connection, we should also note that our concept of intention can explain our reaction to a concluding sentence such as "As a friend of his remarked, 'Brown is an intelligent man.'" In spite of the fact that the sentence gives us additional information about the character, we react to it as irrelevant because it does not tell us anything further about his *chameleonlike* nature. Nor can we think of another intention that makes sense both of this sentence and the previous ones. We react to such sentences as irrelevant because they do not contribute to the perceived intention of the description, and they do not alter our perception to the point where we can formulate a new, coherent intention about the passage.

This analysis also shows that although the concept of intention has considerable explanatory power, it is not identical with the meaning of a text. It is only because we can distinguish intention from linguistic meaning that we can decide that some sentences describing Brown are better than others; if we could not distinguish between meaning and intention, then each new last sentence, with its introduction of new meaning, would lead us to formulate a corresponding new intention.

Because our concept of intention has so much explanatory power, we need to examine more closely the paradoxical relationship between the sentences of a discourse and our understanding of its intention. Again Lodge's description of Brown-Green-Grey provides a useful sample test. My analysis of it here is not meant to describe the conscious mental processes that occur as we read it, but rather to explain what we must somehow intuit in order to understand it as we do.

After we read the first sentence, "Mr. Brown, or Green as he was sometimes called, was short, but tall with it," we do not know much about the intention of the whole passage. The passage still has many possible directions; we can think of numerous second sentences that will be related to the first, e.g., "These qualities made him a good detective," "Consequently, he was an object of curiosity in his neighborhood," "These peculiarities gave him a superiority complex," and so on. In fact, the second sentence does not even have to be about Brown-Green, e.g., "Smith was fat but thin with it." However, we do know that if the description is not to be an incoherent sequence the information we are given in sentence two must eventually be somehow related to Brown-Green and/or his peculiar physical characteristics. So, while it is true that there are more sentences relevant to the first than we would care to list, it is also true that there are countless sentences that are irrelevant, e.g., "Rembrandt was a great painter," "my love is like a red, red rose," and so on.

After we read the actual second sentence, "His fair-complexioned face was swarthy," our understanding of the intention is clearer. Our knowledge of the first sentence allows us to make sense of the second—his complexion is not as important in itself as it is a sign of his ability to possess opposing qualities simultaneously—and our knowledge lets us see that it is this aspect of the first sentence that the passage will pursue. In short, we understand intuitively that the intention of the passage is to describe a chameleonlike character. The final sentence, then, may add some information that will lead us to refine our notion of the intention, but, as we have seen, it cannot lead us to alter markedly our notion. If, however, as in our alternate ending, "As a friend of his remarked, 'Brown is an easy man to pin down,'" the language does not clearly relate to the previous sentences, we shall not know for sure how to interpret it: is our alternate sentence ironic, or is it inappropriate? If there were an internal linguistic clue, e.g., "Grey is an easy man to pin down," we would know that it should be interpreted ironically.

Now suppose the description included a sentence before the three that we now have, "Mr. Brown was a hardworking man." It seems clear that by the time we finished the third sentence, i.e., by the time we had closure on the description, we would recognize that this first statement was not in keeping with the intention of the rest of the sentences. In other words, we shall not try to force our experience of the later sentences into an interpretation based on a rigid notion of intention formed from the first, but rather shall reformulate our understanding of the intention based on the new information. Thus our notion of intention is affected by our experience of sentences, and our experience of sentences is affected by our notion of intention, but neither one completely determines the other. Sentences accumulating in a given speech event enable us to perceive the intention, but are not identical in meaning with it, and accumulating sentences are interpreted as relevant or irrelevant, efficacious or not, as taking on one meaning rather than another, in light of the perceived intention.[10]

With the idea that meaning and intention are two distinct entities, we begin to touch upon issues that make "intention" one of our most vexed critical terms. Although the preceding discussion explains the concept of intention as I use it here, the discussion does not fully justify that use. For the sake of clarity I have skipped over some difficulties that Lodge's text does not immediately raise. But since the concept of intention is crucial not only to our investigation of Dreiser's language but also to our general theory of language in fiction we need to address those difficulties directly before turning to the style of *Sister Carrie*. We primarily need to make more explicit the relation among an author's intended meaning, the meanings various readers may discover in the text, and the meaning of the text itself.

As suggested by our attention to both text and context, our hypothesis about the way we understand texts implies that although authors and texts are finally more important determiners of meaning than readers, the relation among author, reader, and text is one of mutual dependence. No one of them can properly create a meaning independently of the other two, and no one of them is completely controlled by the other two. We can express the relationship several ways depending on whether the author, the reader, or the text is the focus of the description. Authors create meanings, but succeed or fail in creating the meanings they intend according to how well they use language to embody their intention in a text, and their success or failure can be measured by how well readers understand that meaning. Texts by themselves are highly ambiguous, but they are never by themselves: they are always the product of some controlling consciousness and intended for some audience; our knowledge of that consciousness and its relation to its audience enables us to choose among the various possible meanings offered by the text. Readers bring different assumptions, beliefs, experiences, and expectations to texts, but because they share a knowledge of language with an author who has a different set of assumptions, beliefs, experiences, and expectations, they will not merely find what they bring to the text confirmed in it, but will find there an independent meaning created by the author and realized in the language of his text.

The apparent difficulties with this position and its consequences for our understanding of intention and meaning can perhaps best be seen by comparing it with Stanley Fish's recent arguments that the crucial determinant of a text's meaning is the reader's interpretive assumptions, and E. D. Hirsch's contention that the crucial determinant is the author's intention. But first it will be beneficial to illustrate how this position is based upon our experience with language.

As we have seen in chapter 2, the sentence, "John, the door is open," can have numerous meanings, but when a particular speaker uses it on a particular occasion it has a determinate meaning. Let us suppose that the speaker is John's boss to whom he has gone to ask for a raise; and suppose further that the boss has a rule that all conferences with his subordinates are to be held behind closed doors. Thus, when the boss says, "John, the door is open," he is giving John a command to close the door by subtly reminding him of the rule. As we have seen, John is able to interpret the command because of both his linguistic competence and his knowledge of the boss and the boss's rule. The more interesting question now is under what conditions the communication between John and his boss will fail.

Each party can make two kinds of mistakes, each of which is likely to produce failure. The boss may not say what he means, i.e., what he says may not accurately reflect his intention. If he wants John to close the door but says, "John, the window is open," his expressed meaning will not match his intended meaning and so the communication will probably fail. If John's knowledge of his boss and the boss's rule does enable him to deduce what the boss intended to say, he will also know that the boss's text had a different meaning from the one intended: intention and verbal meaning are distinct entities. Similarly, John may be responsible for a faulty communication by mishearing the boss. If, say, John is deliberately looking out the window to avoid his boss's eyes as he asks for the raise, he may be so intent on the window that he hears the boss say "John, the window is open" instead of "John, the door is open": audiences cannot properly understand texts if they cling to their initial preoccupations, prejudices, and expectations.

On the other hand, the boss may mean what he says, but because he does not choose his words with his audience in mind, his expression may be ineffective. If John is a new employee and the boss is not certain that John knows the rule that all conferences take place behind closed doors, his saying "John, the door is open," will most likely not be an effective way of expressing his intention. If in fact John does not know the rule and does not know the boss very well, he may justifiably understand the sentence as meaning something besides a command to close the door, as perhaps an invitation to leave. Although the boss will have meant what he said and meant it in only one way, what he said is in this case ambiguous; an author's verbal meaning conveys his intention only if that meaning makes the intention discernible to his attentive audience. But if John has been working closely with his boss for a long time, and starts to leave the room soon after the boss says, "John, the door is open," the boss would be justified in saying that John has misunderstood him. John has not paid attention to things he should know—his boss's characteristic manner, the rule about conferences—and consequently has caused a failure in the communication: audiences must seek to discern a speaker's intentions through their knowledge of that speaker and of the occasion.

In literary texts, of course, we have a communicative situation that is different from the one between John and his boss. For the most part, authors have general audiences not particular ones, and audiences very often know little or nothing about the author apart from his work. But these differences do not make our activity in understanding a text different in its essentials, although they do often make it more difficult. What is essential about John's knowledge of his boss and of the situation in which the boss speaks to him is that it allows him to infer the boss's intention. In order to achieve, in our interpretation of an author's text, a degree of probability similar to John's in his interpretation of his boss's "text," we need some way to discover our author's intention, something that can be the equivalent of John's knowledge of his boss and of the situation in which the boss speaks. That equivalent, our analysis of Lodge's description suggests, is the author's language. Just as John's boss needs to include more specific directions in his sentence if John is a new rather than a long-time employee, so too an author will adjust his language for his audience. And just as John will have less difficulty understanding his boss's intended meaning if the boss elaborates on his sentence "John, the door is open," so too we have less difficulty understanding a controlling intention in a literary text because we are dealing with numerous related sentences. As we saw in chapter 2, and in our discussion of Lodge's text, each additional sentence contributes to our understanding of the intention, and our understanding of the intention affects our response to new sentences.

Both Fish and Hirsch would challenge this position by arguing that it makes texts more autonomous than they really are, though each challenge would come from a different direction. Fish's position, which he has been developing in his more recent work, is that the meaning of sentences and texts is not the result of anything intrinsic to their language nor even the result of that language viewed in the light of an author's intention, but rather the result of the assumptions readers bring to it.[11] Fish's literary example is *Samson Agonistes* and his focus there is on the dispute over whether Milton's play should be read typologically or not. Fish maintains that the dispute cannot be solved because there is no independent evidence that can be appealed to: the text itself is not such evidence because critics on each side have already construed it as typological or not. Even the fact that Christ is never mentioned is evidence for both sides; in spite of what we might initially think, it is evidence for the typological interpretation because typology insists on the difference between type and prototype and on the type's own lack of knowledge that he is a type (NC, pp. 627–29).

Although this dispute cannot be resolved, says Fish, it can be understood; we must realize that although each side is dealing with its own stable text, that text is stable in different ways, or in other words, that each group of critics is dealing with a different *Samson Agonistes*. Fish summarizes his position this way: "there is always a text . . . but what is in it can change, and therefore at no level is it independent and prior to interpretation" (NC, p. 627); furthermore, although a text is stable, "it is always stable in more than one direction as *a succession of interpretive assumptions gives it a succession of stable shapes"* (NC, p. 629, my emphasis).

Fish's conclusion raises a further question: where do the interpretive assumptions themselves come from? Fish does not explicitly address this question, but at a later point in his argument he gives an implicit answer to it, an answer that repudiates his own conclusion.

As part of his larger case that sentences do not have intrinsic properties which determine their meaning, Fish points out that the sentence, "I have to eat popcorn tonight," can be what John Searle has said it cannot, a direct speech act rejecting a proposal. All we have to do to see that it can, says Fish, is imagine the right situation: if student *x* works nights as a popcorn taster and if his roommate student *y*, proposes that they go to the movies, student *y* will interpret the reply "I have to eat popcorn tonight" as a rejection of his proposal (NC, p. 639). Notice that the meaning here, as even Fish's commentary suggests, is created not by student *y* but by student *x* (though how he creates it is influenced by his relation with student *y*). Student *y* discovers the meaning, and he does so through his knowledge of student *x*, of the speech situation, and of language. In other words, student *y*'s interpretive assumptions come from the text, and from the occasion in which it is spoken by a particular individual. Student *y* cannot properly choose on the basis of some interpretive assumptions independent of that speech situation (and, of course, his own knowledge of language) to interpret the sentence as an acceptance of the proposal, as an insult, or as anything but a rejection of his proposal.

It is possible, of course, that student *y* may forget for a moment that his roommate works as a popcorn taster, and so he might interpret the sentence as a non sequitur intended as a wisecrack, or as a sign that his friend has not heard *him* correctly, and so may repeat his proposal. But each of these responses is based on a misinterpretation, as *we* recognize immediately, and as student *y* will recognize as soon as he remembers that eating popcorn is student *x*'s job. The fact that misinterpretation can exist is, of course, evidence that correct interpretation is possible, and that meaning is not created by readers alone.

These considerations throw light on Fish's analysis of the dispute over *Samson Agonistes*. He treats Milton's text not as something which has been placed in a context by Milton's publishing it in 1671,[12] but as something which readers may import into different contexts, and so create different valid understandings of. Fish no doubt would object here that the different critics of *Samson Agonistes* do not "import" the text anywhere, but are already in a context when they read it, a context which causes them to understand it as typological or not. But the objection must be overruled because although we are always in a context, *there is nothing inevitable about the particular context we are in*, especially when we read a literary text; we can to a great extent choose our contexts, and we can choose well or badly. Just as student *y* may not stop and remember that student *x* works as a popcorn taster and so choose the wrong context, so we may cling to an a priori context and not pay enough attention to our knowledge of Milton and the details of his text. And just as forgetful student *y* will be likely to misunderstand his roommate's remark, so a priori we will be likely to misinterpret Milton.

The way out of the predicament Fish describes is to become self-critical of our context. We become self-critical by asking questions about the particular linguistic details of a text, as well as about authors and occasions. If we are typological critics, we shall want to ask not only the obvious question of whether it makes sense that Milton would write the work typologically, but also whether those details of the text that present the most difficulty for a typological interpretation point to an error in the approach. If these difficulties are only apparent, if after careful attention to the pattern of the whole text we feel the typological approach is justified, and if the presentation of our evidence also persuades other knowledgeable readers, then we shall have established the typological interpretation with a high degree of probability.

The last points, of course, will remain only assertions unless I can show through a detailed analysis that the language of the text as created by Milton does allow us to choose between typological and nontypological interpretations. However, since what is at issue here is not the specific interpretation of *Samson Agonistes* but the principle of how textual meanings are created by authors and understood by readers, I shall demonstrate the justice of the principle by considering a different, more manageable, though perhaps more problematic text: Wordsworth's "A slumber did my spirit seal." This poem will also require us to consider Hirsch's challenge, which in some respects is the polar opposite of Fish's.

> A slumber did my spirit seal;
> I had no human fears:
> She seemed a thing that could not feel
> The touch of earthly years.
>
> No motion has she now, no force;
> She neither hears nor sees;
> Rolled round in earth's diurnal course
> With rocks and stones and trees.

Hirsch's well-known discussion of the poem begins with the problem posed by the two extremely different, yet quite persuasive interpretations offered by Cleanth Brooks and Frederick Bateson. Brooks sees the poem as suggesting the "lover's agonized shock at the loved one's present lack of motion," whereas Bateson sees it as expressing a "single mood mounting to a climax of pantheistic magnificence in the last two lines."[13] Hirsch argues that we cannot choose between the interpretations by examining the language of the text; he views each interpretation as legitimate, correspondent, and coherent, i.e., each is permitted by the language, each accounts for every component of it, and each renders the individual meanings into a coherent whole. Consequently, says Hirsch, since there cannot be a meaning without a meaner, the way to decide between the two interpretations is to establish the most probable context for the poem, to consult evidence about Wordsworth's attitudes in 1799. Since what we know about Wordsworth in 1799, writes Hirsch, indicates that for him "rocks and stones and trees" were not inanimate things, but parts of nature that shared the life animating the whole universe, Bateson's interpretation, though a bit too optimistic, is more probable. If, however, we found out that Wordsworth had a brief period of pessimism during which he wrote the poem, then we would conclude that Brooks's interpretation was the more probable one (VI, p. 240).[14]

The reasoning behind Hirsch's analysis of the dispute depends on his contention that verbal meaning is above all a willed type. Although he demonstrates that verbal meaning is both a willed and a shared type, in the final analysis he gives preeminence to the will. Hirsch uses Saussure's distinction between *langue*, "the system of linguistic possibilities shared by a community at a given point in time" (VI, p. 231), and *parole*, the actual utterances made by the members of a speech community (VI, p. 232), to argue that a bungled text has no determinate meaning because its author did not will the meaning his language might seem to have (VI, p. 234). If we say that the text represents a *parole* other than the author's intended one, he maintains, we imply that the *parole* is the speech community's. But since a *parole* must belong to an individual speaker, the *parole* of a whole community is a nonexistent thing, so we must conclude that the meaning is either the author's intended one or that it is indeterminate.

Our experience with language indicates that Hirsch's reasoning here is flawed. It insists on an either/or distinction where a third possibility exists. Let us return to the hypothetical speech situation with John and his boss in which the boss says, "John, the window is open." According to Hirsch, the boss's sentence has no determinate meaning. But suppose that John has been looking out the window and that the boss notices him looking, when the boss utters his sentence. Clearly the sentence will have a determinate meaning, and just as clearly its meaning is distinct from the boss's intention of reminding John about the conferences-behind-closed-doors rule. The sentence is still the boss's *parole*—indeed, because it is, John knows which window the boss is referring to—but because every *parole* must be understood according to the rules established by the *langue*, willed meaning cannot take precedence over shared meaning. John may soon discover that the boss's intention was to remind him of the rule about conferences—perhaps through finding the window closed or through the boss's revision of his command or through later sentences the boss utters—but that discovery will not alter his understanding of the first sentence; rather he will realize that the boss did not say what he meant.

The distinction between authorial intention and verbal meaning not only accounts more accurately for our experience with language, but also allows us—indeed, requires us—to make more rigorous discriminations among probable interpretations than Hirsch's position does. If discovering Wordsworth's attitudes in 1799 is useful but not decisive evidence for deciding between

Brooks's and Bateson's readings of "A slumber," and if we do not want simply to accept the conclusion that the poem is ambiguous, we are going to take a longer, more careful look at its language than Hirsch's position requires us to do. We shall not settle only for a probable interpretation, but shall continually test the degree of its probability against both our knowledge of the author and the language of his text.

Testing Brooks's and Bateson's readings this way, we find each at least partially deficient. If Brooks is right and Wordsworth wanted to express the speaker's shock at the beloved's "utter and horrible inertness," then Wordsworth has made some curious linguistic choices. The first is the relatively gentle description of aging and death in stanza 1 as "the touch of earthly years." The speaker is speaking with the knowledge of hindsight here: it is only after the beloved has died that the speaker recognizes he was in a "slumber" and that what he lacked were "human fears." If he is greatly shocked at the beloved's horrible inertness, why would he, with his new knowledge, refer to death or even aging as something relatively gentle? The second puzzling choice under this construction of the poem is, as Hirsch points out (VI, p. 191), the inclusion of "trees" in the catalogue of the last line, and its emphasis as the last word of the poem. Why should a poem stressing the lover's inertness end with an image of her connection to living things? A related problem is the order of the main clause and the participial phrase in the last stanza. If it is the loved one's lifelessness Wordsworth wants to emphasize, he would have done so more effectively by showing the speaker's thought moving from her connection with other natural objects to her individual situation of powerlessness, e.g.,

> Rolled round in earth's diurnal course
> With rocks and stones and trees,
> She has no motion now, no force
> She neither hears, nor sees.

Bateson's interpretation also renders several aspects of the poem puzzling. As Hirsch points out (VI, p. 239), if the mood of the poem is one of pantheistic magnificence, why are lines 5–6 so strongly negative? Furthermore, if there is a single mood why are there so many devices that emphasize a break between stanzas 1 and 2? Not only does the poem shift to the present tense, but, as

Norman Holland points out, the rhyme scheme reinforces the break—"hears" is in the interior rather than at the end of line 6, where it would have continued the "fears"-"years" sequence of the first stanza.[15] Furthermore, the lines of "pantheistic magnificence" not only lack any specific language which would give them that quality, they are syntactically tied to the expression of the negatives in lines 5–6, serving as a participal phrase modifying the "she" who has no motion, force, hearing or sight, while also completing the description of her individual powerlessness.

Finally, both Brooks and Bateson fail to account for one of the poem's most prominent features: the lack of any *explicit* emotion in the second stanza, the speaker's stance there of describing the facts about his beloved's present state. It is this feature of the poem which makes it so problematic and which leads to such widely divergent readings: we must infer the emotions behind the speaker's descriptions. But this feature itself helps us to decide what the emotions are, and provides an important piece of evidence in understanding Wordsworth's intention in the poem as a whole. By representing the speaker as directing his attention away from himself to his beloved and to a factual description of her existence after death, Wordsworth is also representing and making prominent the speaker's movement from "slumber" to knowledge of human mortality. Furthermore, this factual description in both its tone and details helps us to see that the speaker has moved beyond grief and comfort to an acceptance of the facts about human mortality; indeed, acceptance is implied in full knowledge.

Those aspects of the poem which are puzzling in Brooks's and Bateson's readings also provide evidence for this view of Wordsworth's intention; equally important, this view does not render any of Wordsworth's other choices puzzling. The language of the first stanza helps us to understand the more problematic language of the second. As the speaker describes his blissful ignorance in lines 1–4, his retrospective knowledge also allows him, as David Ferry has shown,[16] to suggest that his ignorance detracted from his bliss: it caused him to slumber, it put him beyond the state of having "human" fears, and it led him to think of the beloved not as special or unique but as a "thing," that concept that cuts across almost all categories. In this way, the description of the speaker's attitude toward his beloved before she dies indicates his genuine grief, his regret for not appreciating what he had. Yet he views death itself, the agent which took her from him and awakened him from his slumber as relatively gentle, as "the touch of earthly years." It is not death which bears the blame for the speaker's regret, but the speaker himself. In the second stanza, lines 5–6 with their shift to the present tense and their insistent negatives, express both the shock of the speaker's awakening and his realization of the enormous loss that death brings. The implied grief is very clear. But the final lines, while completing the description of the loved one's powerlessness, show her not as overpowered by the earth in its diurnal motion, but as absorbed by it. Since the beloved is not "dragged" or "whirled," but "rolled," the speaker sees her as a *part* of the earth in its natural movement. Since he sees her as part of it along with "trees" as well as "rocks and stones," Wordsworth emphasizes not lifelessness itself but the difference between human life and other forms of existence.[17] There is consolation in the speaker's seeing the beloved one move beyond time by becoming part of it, but there is also a clear sense of what has been lost; she has given up motion, force, hearing, sight—qualities which formerly distinguished her from the nature she is now part of. Because the speaker dwells on neither the consolation nor the sadness, because he forgets himself and focuses on the beloved, because he admits both the loss and the compensation, we see the last stanza as presenting the speaker's clear and honest vision of his own relation to his beloved, and her relation to both her former life and her new place in nature. Now that she is dead, he is finally awake.[18]

Thus, though it can be understood through careful, self-critical attention to its language, the literary text is not autonomous because we cannot properly construe that language without some conception, either conscious or intuitive, of its author's organizing intention, which again may be conscious or intuitive. Our notion of the author's intention, though formed from the language of the text, and hence constantly being refined as we read, is distinct from the literal meaning of the text, guides our understanding of that meaning, and, indeed, allows us to judge the relative efficacy of the meaning of the parts, when considered one by one. At the same time, because our notion of intention is formed from the language of the text not from our interpretive assumptions or external knowledge of the author, we can reconstruct the intention with a high degree of probability. Furthermore, if we make mistakes in our formulation, if, for example, my inferences about the intention of "A slumber did my spirit seal" are faulty, we are able to recognize those mistakes: the intention is not ours, but Wordsworth's and it is embodied in a language which we share (or at least *can* share) with him. We shall, in the next chapter, consider a radical challenge to this faith that language can embody a reconstructable intention, but for now we can use our concepts of intention and verbal meaning to answer our questions about the role of Dreiser's much criticized language in *Sister Carrie*.[19]

III

Considered out of context, Dreiser's style seems to deserve its reputation. His faults are many, and he displays them often. John Flanagan has offered a useful summary of those faults:

> they are of two kinds, verbal and syntactical, and it is perhaps debatable which occasions the greater annoyance. The first category includes inaccuracies, pretentiousness, archaisms, faulty idioms, triteness, inappropriate use of foreign terms, and unfortunate coinages. The second category includes faulty reference, dangling modifiers, failures in agreement and a curious substitution of participial constructions for finite verbs.[20]

To put it in even stronger words, Dreiser is liable either to write sentences virtually incomprehensible because of their ungrammaticality, as in this example from *Sister Carrie*—"He simulated interest in several scenes without which he did not feel"[21]—or to write painfully self-conscious ones because of his attempts at eloquence, as in this passage from it:

> A lovely home atmosphere is one of the flowers of the world, than which there is nothing more tender, nothing more delicate, nothing more calculated to make strong and just the natures cradled and nourished within it. Those who have never experienced such a beneficent influence will not understand wherefore the tear springs glistening to the eyelids at some strange breath in lovely music. [p. 74]

The most common defense of Dreiser's style is that these faults are actually virtues because of his subject. Vern Wagner argues that Dreiser's crude, confused style is deliberate and appropriate because finally Dreiser "offers no answers, only musings, only confused defeat for his characters." [22] Walter Blackstock maintains that Dreiser's faults are not serious because he was seeking the common touch and those faults "were the sad, lovable faults of humanity itself." [23] These defenses are, I believe, finally unsatisfactory because they are too easy: it is one thing for an author to represent a character groping unsuccessfully for answers to basic human problems, but it is quite another for him to create an omniscient narrator groping unsuccessfully for the language he needs to represent that character. As readers we require different things from limited characters than we do from omniscient narrators; it is difficult to believe that the narrator's description of "a lovely home atmosphere" reinforces our sense of Carrie's own struggle just because the narrator himself seems to be straining for his linguistic effects. Or to make the point another way: Frederick Henry certainly suffers a greater defeat than Carrie Meeber, yet no one complains that *A Farewell to Arms* is marred by Hemingway's inability to imitate that sense of defeat in his language; instead the clarity and control with which Hemingway uses language is correctly seen as one of the book's strongest virtues.

Any plausible defense of Dreiser's language in *Sister Carrie* cannot be based on a simple correspondence between that language and the action of the novel considered in the abstract, but must, as we have seen, be based on how particular uses of language do or do not contribute to the particular intention of the whole.

Perhaps the key problem in specifying that intention is to define properly the relation between the novel's elements of thought—its social criticism, its statements about the nature of work, of money, of love, and about their roles in shaping individuals' lives—and its representation of characters in action. Does Dreiser subordinate the story of Carrie's rise in society and Hurstwood's decline to a larger purpose of exemplifying the workings of that society, or does he subordinate his social commentary to a larger purpose of representing Carrie's progression from small-town girl lost in the big city to successful, yet finally unfulfilled woman of the world. The two aspects of the novel are closely related, but ultimately, I think, Dreiser's intention is to represent Carrie's progress rather than illustrate a truth. The logic of the organizing intention works as follows: since certain things about society are true, what happens to Carrie, Hurstwood, Drouet, and the other characters is especially moving, not, since certain things happen to the characters, we must draw certain conclusions about the society.

Consider the very effective scene of the last chapter in which the narrator describes Mrs. Hurstwood and Jessica's triumphant train ride to New York. Not only does Jessica now have a rich husband in tow, but she also has the added satisfaction of attracting covetous glances from other men, glances that she can turn away "with a show of indifference" under the guise of "wifely modesty" while she is secretly gratifying her vanity. Mrs. Hurstwood now has the satisfaction of both seeing her daughter married to money and of being able to participate in many of Jessica's resulting advantages, such as their present trip, the first stage on a voyage to Europe. Although the scene underlines Dreiser's criticism of people like Jessica and her mother, and of the values in the larger society which influence such people, its effectiveness derives primarily from another function: the way it increases our emotional response to both Hurstwood and Carrie. Dreiser places the scene right before the description of Hurstwood's last hours, which end with his turning on the gas in his rented room, and then follows that scene with a last view of Carrie, sitting in her rocking chair dreaming of such happiness as she will never feel. Hurstwood's suicide takes on an added poignance because of its juxtaposition with the scene of his wife and daughter's vain and supercilious behavior. And their smug self-satisfaction with their material success throws into relief Carrie's dissatisfaction with her own. Although we sympathize with her distress, we respect her superior intuition which leads her, in contrast to Jessica and Mrs. Hurstwood, to sense the inadequacies of wealth as a foundation for real happiness. If Dreiser's primary intention were to use the characters and their stories to demonstrate the truth of a certain view of society, the scene with Mrs. Hurstwood and Jessica would be quite superfluous: it neither adds anything new to our understanding of their characters or of larger society nor provides a necessary completion to that understanding. But the scene is effective because Dreiser is using his depictions of them and his view of larger society as a means of shaping and intensifying our emotional response to the main characters. His primary intention, to which even the Hurstwood plot is subordinated, is the representation of Carrie's movement toward her very qualified success at the end of the book. Let us consider a few other aspects of the book as evidence for this view of the intention.

In the course of introducing his characters, Dreiser always points out that they are types: Carrie "was a fair example of the middle American class—two generations removed from the emigrant [*sic*]"; Drouet "was a type of travelling canvasser for a manufacturing house—a class which at that time was first being dubbed by the slang of the day 'drummers'"; he was also "one whose dress or manners are calculated to elicit the admiration of susceptible young women—a 'masher'"; Hurstwood "was altogether a very acceptable individual of our great American upper class—the first grade below the luxuriously rich."

At first glance, this fact might seem to contradict the assertion that *Sister Carrie* is designed to trace Carrie's movement toward her qualified success; if the characters are types then it would make sense to postulate that Dreiser finally is not interested in them for their own sake. However, as we look more closely at the novel, we see that Dreiser is not writing a parable about the interaction of social types. Although the characters are representatives of their class, we do not feel that all members of their class will act the way they do. The characters have individual psychologies, and they meet fates that are rather uncommon for members of their respective classes. Not all members of the upper middle class will end like Hurstwood and not all members of the lower middle will end like Carrie. However, because Dreiser has emphasized the representativeness of his characters, their individual fates have a greater impact; they have implications beyond the merely personal. Because we see that Hurstwood's fall takes the form of one general pattern by which men decline, we feel a greater sense of loss in his doom. Because we see that Carrie achieves the wealth and fame that are every shop-girl's dream, we feel that her failure to achieve lasting happiness is even more poignant. In short, the fact that Dreiser emphasizes that his characters are representative types contributes to his intention of making their individual fates moving.

The Hurstwood subplot contributes significantly to our sense

of the limitations of Carrie's success. There is an emotional interaction between the two plots: because Hurstwood remains a
sympathetic character, once we see him meet his doom, we cannot feel unalloyed pleasure in Carrie's success; moreover, once
we see that doom, we can better appreciate Carrie's dissatisfaction with the wealth and fame she has attained. Having seen
Hurstwood both at the height of his powers and during his decline
toward suicide, we better understand Carrie's longings for something more: wealth and fame do not guarantee happiness, nor can
they be relied upon to last; they do not offer much of real worth,
and the little they do offer may soon vanish.

Dreiser creates Carrie's character in such a way that we find
her limited success plausible and moving. Carrie is uneducated
but possessed of a keen intuition; she cannot always specify what
it is that she wants, but she can always tell whether or not something is giving her what she wants. Furthermore, she has a strong
and constant desire to find happiness. The general pattern of action in the novel shows Carrie successively attaining wealth and
fame, those things which her society has identified as necessary
for happiness; and with each new stage in her material success,
Carrie believes she will be happy, only to find out once again that
she is wrong. At the novel's end she reaches an impasse: having
attained the things society values most, she no longer knows what
to seek—yet she remains unhappy. Carrie has got what she
wanted, and though far better than life in a shoe factory, what she
wanted is far less than what she expected.

As with *The Ambassadors,* our analysis of a passage from the
novel will help us specify the intention further. I have chosen one
fairly long passage which, because it represents quite well
Dreiser's characteristic habit of mixing errors with more service-
able prose, will enable us to reach sound conclusions about the
role of Dreiser's style in this novel. The passage is from chapter
32, "The Feast of Belshazzar: A Seer to Translate," and it is part
of the section in which Dreiser's narrator describes Carrie's first
outing with the Vances in New York. Carrie has participated for
the first time in the Broadway parade of fashion, and now she is at
the theater:

> [1]The play was one of those drawing room concoctions in
> which charmingly overdressed ladies and gentlemen suffer the
> pangs of love and jealousy amid gilded surroundings. [2]Such

bon-mots are ever enticing to those who have all their days longed for such material surroundings and have never had them gratified. [3]They have the charm of showing suffering under ideal conditions. [4]Who would not grieve upon a gilded chair? [5]Who would not suffer amid perfumed tapestries, cushioned furniture, and liveried servants? [6]Grief under such circumstances becomes an enticing thing. [7]Carrie longed to be of it. [8]She wanted to take her sufferings, whatever they were, in such a world, or failing that, at least to simulate them under such charming conditions upon the stage. [9]So affected was her mind by what she had seen, that the play seemed an extraordinarily beautiful thing. [10]She was soon lost in the world it represented and wished that she might never return. [11]Between the acts she studied the galaxy of matinee attendants in front rows and boxes, and conceived a new idea of the possibilities of New York. [12]She was sure she had not seen it all—that the city was one whirl of pleasure and delight. [p. 262]

Sentence 1: "The play was one of those drawing-room concoctions in which charmingly overdressed ladies and gentlemen suffer the pangs of love and jealousy amid gilded surroundings."

This is perhaps the most successful sentence in the passage. Without being heavy-handed Dreiser clearly communicates his attitude toward the play; the connotations of his description tell us how he feels about it. It is important for us to see the deficiencies of the play clearly so that we understand Carrie's mistake when she is taken in by it; at the same time, it is important that Dreiser does not explicitly condemn the play because we might then feel that Carrie is too obtuse to be worthy of our sympathy. Because Dreiser[24] describes the play as "one of those . . . which" rather than as an individual work, we see that he has little respect for it, and that we should not take its values and attitudes seriously. The specific descriptions reinforce and expand our understanding of his attitude. In the phrase "drawing-room concoction," "drawing-room" is not just a description of the setting, it is also a pejorative term which suggests that the play has little serious substance, that it is just something put together according to an established formula. The phrase "charmingly overdressed" contains a double criticism. The excess of the play is clearly spelled out, and perhaps even worse, this excess is made to seem "charming." At the same time, this criticism is extremely gentle, almost benevolent: to be *charmingly* overdressed seems no great failing. We understand that the whole thing is too shallow to be taken seriously. Furthermore, Dreiser describes the characters as "ladies and gentlemen" rather than "men and women" in order to remind us of the genteel, polite, and artificial society to which they belong.

Having seen these attitudes, we cannot take the characters' "pangs of love and jealousy" seriously either. These are not real emotions but part of the conventional code of behavior for "charmingly overdressed ladies and gentlemen . . . amid gilded surroundings." The syntax of the phrase suggests how shallow and undifferentiated these emotions are; love and jealousy are equivalent, both causing characters to "suffer pangs." By describing the sufferings as "pangs," Dreiser suggests the conventional language of these plays, and by concluding with "amid gilded surroundings," he reinforces our sense that the affluence of the characters in these plays is more important than their emotions. We clearly understand Dreiser's attitude: the play is shallow and sterile because it values the gilded surroundings more highly than human emotions.

Sentence 2: "Such bon-mots are ever enticing to those who have all their days longed for such material surroundings and have never had them gratified."

In this sentence, Dreiser shifts his attention from the play itself to its impact on part of its audience. He also displays some of his characteristic faults. His first two words, "Such bon-mots," imply a connection to the previous sentence, but no such connection exists: he has made no reference to the conversation of the overdressed ladies and gentlemen. In fact, we may even wonder if Dreiser knows the meaning of "bon-mots": why should he isolate this aspect of gilded society to show its attraction for the lower classes, especially since he has just been talking about the "suffering" of the gilded? On the whole this is a most curious beginning.

The end of the sentence is also curious: Dreiser, in effect, uses a pronoun to refer to a verb. When he says, "those who have all their days longed for such material surroundings and have never had them gratified," we cannot, according to the rules of English grammar, assign any antecedent to "them." The logical choice "surroundings" is ruled out because it is ungrammatical to say "they had their surroundings gratified." Moreover, the semantics of the sentence rule out this possibility. At the same time, the semantics enable us to understand that Dreiser is referring to the longings of those who have never had such material surroundings; he has, in other words, used "them" to refer to "longed."

It is difficult to imagine how we could plausibly argue that these faults are actually virtues, that they increase the power of the passage. Because they are vague and confusing, they clearly interfere with the thought that Dreiser is trying to express; in other words, they do not contribute to his intention of showing why these plays are attractive to those without wealth. But to see how serious these flaws are we need to look at the rest of the sentence.

Again Dreiser's attitude toward what he is saying is as important as what he says. Dreiser emphasizes the sympathetic elements in the plight of those without wealth; he describes their constant longing not with "always" but with the more emphatic "all their days," and he describes the results of their longing with the absolute negative—they "have *never* had" their longings gratified. Consequently, we see that Dreiser's attitude is one of sympathetic understanding. Furthermore, these linguistic choices which emphasize the longings of those without wealth also contribute to the plausibility of the general claim Dreiser is making in this sentence. Because we see their longing described this way, we are more likely to believe that the have-nots find the bon-mots—or perhaps "pangs," or even "stylish furnishings"—enticing. Perhaps what is most revealing about Dreiser's error and our subsequent confusion here is that the consequences for our understanding the intention of the sentence are relatively small. Suppose first that Dreiser means what he says. Although we may wonder about the transition to this subject, the bon-mots would still clearly represent for those without wealth the pleasant trappings of a life with it; they, too, are a part of the gilded surroundings. Although our knowledge of the previous sentence will tell us that these bon-mots are probably about as witty as the emotions of the characters are deep, we will still clearly see that for those without wealth they will nevertheless be enticing. This knowledge also enables us to specify further the implied author's attitude. Although he understands and is sympathetic toward the have-nots, he does not share or endorse their values. Consequently, we both maintain our sympathy for Carrie and recognize her mistake when she is affected by the play. If Dreiser meant to say "pangs" or "stylish furnishings," our analysis would be pretty similar, and most importantly, our conclusions about his attitudes would be virtually identical. The faulty pronoun reference, while perhaps momentarily confusing, also does not significantly interfere with either our understanding of the information Dreiser wants to convey or his attitudes towards it. Because these attitudes are the most important parts of what Dreiser intends to convey in the sentence, our confusion over the grammatical mistake and about the specific information he wants to express in the beginning of the sentence does not seriously mar its effectiveness. But these are only two faults in one sentence. Let us look at others.

Sentence 3: "They have the charm of showing suffering under ideal conditions."

Again Dreiser begins with an unclear reference: what is the antecedent of "they"? There are three possibilities from sentence 2, all unsatisfactory. Any one of these possibilities—the final "them" (which we understand as "longings"), or "surroundings," or "bon-mots"—would make sentence 3 ungrammatical. We must go back to sentence 1, to "concoctions," in order to find a satisfactory antecedent. Again the vague reference is a genuine fault, but again it is not a destructive one. We soon conclude from the sense of the previous two sentences as well as from this one that "they" must refer to the plays Dreiser is describing.

The rest of the sentence is more effective. Dreiser's attitude here is more matter-of-fact; his language describes the attraction of these plays in a straightforward manner, and we accept his assertion: these plays "have the charm of showing suffering under ideal conditions." Our response to this sentence is largely controlled by our response to the previous two as well as by its particular language. Because we have clearly seen in the first sentence the deficiencies of the play, we can admit with Dreiser that it has a genuine charm while still knowing that such a charm is not enough to redeem it. Because we have seen in sentence 2 Dreiser's sympathetic attitude toward those in Carrie's situation, and because he admits here that the play has real attraction in itself, we never feel that he disdains Carrie for falling under its charm. Clearly both responses are desirable: Carrie must remain sympathetic yet we must see that her understanding of what constitutes happiness is deficient if we are to feel that she has achieved a limited victory in the end.

The particular language of the sentence helps us see that the play's attraction, while real, is not of superior quality. "Charm" recalls "charmingly overdressed" of sentence 1 and suggests a lack of substance to the attraction—"charm" is not enough to save these plays. The paradoxical quality of "suffering under ideal conditions" again suggests a lack of insight in these plays—as if any conditions could be "ideal" for real suffering.

Sentences 4 and 5: "Who would not grieve upon a gilded chair? Who would not suffer amid perfumed tapestries, cushioned furniture, and liveried servants?"

The rhetorical questions of these two sentences have effects that are similar to those of sentence 3. The assumption underlying the questions, i.e., that *everyone* (not just the have-nots) would prefer to take this sorrow amid gilded surroundings, itself points to the attractiveness of these plays, and exonerates Carrie for falling under their charm. Furthermore, Dreiser uses his language to emphasize the play's attractiveness. He could have used either sentence alone to convey their new information, or he might have combined them into one sentence, e.g., "Who would not suffer upon a gilded chair or amid perfumed tapestries, cushioned furniture, and liveried servants?" in order to expand upon his basic point. By posing the questions in two distinct sentences and by building from the shorter first to the more inclusive second with its final series of three items, Dreiser gives considerable force to his assertion of the play's attractiveness. And he needs to emphasize its attractiveness because Carrie is to fall wholly under its spell.

Sentence 6: "Grief under such circumstances becomes an enticing thing."

This is the last sentence devoted to the attractiveness of these plays, and on the whole it is a good one. It not only follows as a logical conclusion from the rhetorical questions, but it also effectively summarizes the charm of the plays. Dreiser focuses on "grief," the least welcome of all emotions, and shows what happens to it in the circumstances of the plays. The important word is "becomes" with its connotations of change. The charm of these plays is that they can transform even grief into something not just attractive, but "enticing." This charm, while it may be deficient, is also hard to resist. But again Dreiser is a little sloppy; he uses "under" when he means "in." Yet this fault is a minor one; it does not substantially impede the thought he is trying to communicate.

Sentence 7: "Carrie longed to be of it."

Here Dreiser begins to apply his general statements to Carrie's particular state of mind. He shifts the focus to Carrie, and quite properly describes her with her fertile imagination not as passively "enticed" but as actively longing. When Dreiser describes what she longs for, he again gets careless, indeed, extremely so. Not only is there no antecedent for "it" in this or the previous sentence, but there is also no single noun we can substitute for "it" here. We need a whole phrase: properly revised, the sentence would read "Carrie longed to live in such a world." Yet we recognize rather easily that this is Dreiser's intended meaning so that again though Dreiser commits an error, that error does not seriously mar the effectiveness of his sentence. We need to inquire more deeply into the reasons for this consequence after we examine the rest of the passage.

Sentence 8: "She wanted to take her sufferings, whatever they were, in such a world, or failing that, at least to simulate them under such charming conditions upon the stage."

In this sentence Dreiser specifies the nature of Carrie's longing and uses his language to reveal how her longing is misguided. In the first part of the sentence, Dreiser emphasizes that living in the gilded world is more important to Carrie than her sufferings: he ends the clause with "in such a world," thereby giving it the greatest emphasis; moreover, that phrase specifies the kind of world she wants to suffer in, while the description of that suffering—"her sufferings, whatever they were"—is so vague that it implies a dismissal. Dreiser's representation of Carrie's desire—"she wanted to take her sufferings"—suggests a further misunderstanding on her part. While "to take one's sufferings" does not clearly imply that its subject is the agent of the action, the phrase does suggest more control for its subject than "to suffer." Consequently, we get the impression that Carrie, to some degree, has the illusion that she can control the sources of her suffering.

The second half of the sentence further emphasizes Carrie's misunderstanding. Again the "charming conditions upon the stage" receive the emphasis, and her sufferings, referred to simply as "them," receive little attention. Furthermore, the successive phrases, "failing that, at least," imply that Carrie views simulating her sufferings upon the stage as only different in degree from experiencing them in real life. We see that Carrie not only does not discriminate between real and false emotions or between the relation of one's suffering and one's surroundings, but also that she does not properly discriminate between life on the stage and real life.

Sentence 9: "So affected was her mind by what she had seen, that the play now seemed an extraordinarily beautiful thing."

In this sentence Dreiser summarizes the play's effect on Carrie. The first clause is less than successful because Dreiser is too vague. It makes sense for him to distinguish Carrie's mind from her sight, rather than simply saying "she was so affected," because he quite properly wants to emphasize that her judgment of the play is distorted. However, his all-inclusive reference, "by what she had seen" causes problems: in the first place, given her situation as a spectator at a play the phrase seems tautological, and hence not worth mentioning (what else would affect her mind in that situation?); second, "what she had seen" presumably refers to the whole play and therefore, Dreiser appears to be making the fatuous remark, "her mind was so affected by the whole play, that the whole play seemed beautiful." But our experience of the rest of the passage tells us that this is not Dreiser's intention; he has been speaking not about the whole play, but one aspect of it—the gilded surroundings. Therefore, we must correct him here and understand that he means to say her mind was so affected by those surroundings that the play seemed beautiful. So again while Dreiser's language is imprecise, the imprecision does not do irreparable harm to what he is trying to accomplish in the passage.

Dreiser's language in the second half of the sentence is more successful. His syntax makes us shift our focus from Carrie to the play and consequently, we see more clearly how much this "drawing-room concoction" is transformed. It is true that Dreiser could have created much the same effect by saying that her mind was so affected that "she now regarded the play as an

extraordinarily beautiful thing." The difference is one of emphasis. In Dreiser's version, the emphasis is less on Carrie and more
on the transformation of the play as a thing in itself. Consequently, we see even more sharply the power of the gilded
surroundings on Carrie: they can alter this shallow play into
something "extraordinarily beautiful."

Sentence 10: "She was soon lost in the world it represented and
wished that she might never return."

Here Dreiser concludes his description of the play's effect on
Carrie. In general, it is a good conclusion because it describes the
most powerful effect. Furthermore, it is a reminder of Carrie's
own potential as an actress; her sympathetic nature is such that
she can become totally absorbed in the action of the play—for her
the play is real and everything else is forgotten. However,
Dreiser's semantic logic is faulty here: the second half of the
sentence partly contradicts the first. Carrie's wish that she might
never return implies a consciousness that she knows where she is
and knows where she came from; it implies, in other words, that
she is not lost. We can see why Dreiser constructed the sentence
this way: he emphasizes the fact that for Carrie the play represents another "world" that is so attractive she becomes "lost" in
it, that the end of the play will mean not simply that she must
leave the theater, but that she must "return" to her own world.
However, in this case, the contradiction of one-half of the sentence by the other seems to override these effects: the effects
don't work because we are not sure what to believe about Carrie's state of mind.

Sentence 11: "Between the acts she studied the galaxy of
matinee attendants in front rows and boxes, and conceived a new
idea of the possibilities of New York."

Here Dreiser expands the concerns of the passage to include
Carrie's reaction to the gilded society attending the play. Unfortunately, Dreiser does not provide an adequate transition to
these concerns. Although his description of the Broadway parade
has prepared us for this discussion of the audience, he moves to it
from sentence 10 too abruptly: he has just finished saying that
Carrie wished she might never return, and now he launches directly into a description of what she does when she returns.

A second weakness of the sentence is Dreiser's description of the audience: "galaxy of matinee attendants" is overdone. We can see that Dreiser uses this language to indicate that the audience is socially and financially superior to Carrie and that Carrie feels the difference, but we also see that this diction is wrong in this context. Calling the audience "matinee attendants" gives the description a stiff, formal, mannered quality that is absent from the rest of the passage, and that calls unnecessary attention to itself. The metaphor of the "galaxy" does not seem apt either: it is not vivid enough to convey how dazzling Carrie finds the rest of the audience. It does convey the sense that there are a great number of these finely dressed people but then the next phrase "in front rows and boxes" puts a limit on that number, a limit that we do not associate with stars in the galaxy. On the whole, the metaphor is a failure.

The second half of the sentence—"conceived a new idea of the possibilities of New York"—is more successful. Dreiser is presenting the fruits of Carrie's study, and his language emphasizes the significance of her conclusions. The language is general—"the possibilities of New York"—so we see that her "new idea" will apply to more than just her experience in this theater. Furthermore, the phrase, "the possibilities of New York," is quite suggestive: it implies that there is a power in the city itself as well as in what its inhabitants do, i.e., the possibilities are inherent in the environment as well as in the activities. And since Carrie has been living in New York for two years, we better understand the impact this "new idea" has on her.

Sentence 12: "She was sure she had not seen it all—that the city was one whirl of pleasure and delight."

Here Dreiser spells out what Carrie's new idea was. He carefully builds to the final clause and consequently, it receives a heavy emphasis. He starts with a positive assertion—"she was sure"—then moves to a negative expression of what she was sure about—that "she had not seen it all"—then moves finally to the positive expression—"that the city was one whirl of pleasure and delight." The language here further emphasizes the significance of this thought for Carrie: the "whirl of pleasure and delight," besides being suggestive in itself, directly contrasts with the phrase Dreiser normally uses to describe a routine life like Carrie's—"a dull round." At the same time, the absolute quality

of the characterization—*one* whirl of pleasure and delight—marks
it off as the product of Carrie's naïveté, and reminds us of her
misunderstanding of real value.

There is, however, a minor problem with the sentence, and
again it is a lack of precision in the description: although Carrie
has not seen all of New York, she has seen some of it—and that
part is not a whirl of pleasure and delight. And although Carrie is
naïve, she is not stupid; she should not be represented making
such a mistake. As I have said, this is a small point, and again
though the linguistic failure cannot be denied, we do understand
Dreiser's intention.

IV

Perhaps the most common feature of Dreiser's style that our
analysis uncovered was the "not quite destructive" flaw: we recognized that Dreiser was being vague, sloppy, or awkward yet
we also recognized—in most cases—what he was trying to do. In
other words, although the language was deficient, the intention
was clear. The first conclusion that we can draw is the obvious
one: if Dreiser's language were improved, the book would be
improved to some degree; the book does not benefit from the
vagueness, sloppiness, and ungrammaticality of the language, but
if it succeeds at all, it does so in spite of them.

The crucial question now is how serious these linguistic faults
become over the course of the whole work: is it the case that
although they generally do not seriously mar individual sentences, they have a cumulative effect that is destructive to the
whole? We can begin to answer this question by considering the
relative success of the entire passage, and then determining how
well these intentions contribute to Dreiser's larger intentions in
the book. We can then return to the question of how well he
achieves his intention in the passage, and try to reach some conclusions about the cumulative effect of his linguistic faults.

The passage is designed to show Carrie's growing awareness of
and attraction toward the gilded society of New York; because it
concentrates on the effects of wealth—the effect of the play on
the audience, the effect of both on Carrie—we also see it is designed to show that in the eyes of society, wealth equals happiness. At the same time, it is designed to show both that Carrie is

naturally and blamelessly attracted to this view of happiness and that this view is deficient. Finally, the passage is intended in part to be a reminder of Carrie's attraction to the stage.

These intentions of the passage also contribute to the intention of the whole novel, i.e., the representation of Carrie's movement toward and achievement of her qualified victory. Our judgment of Carrie in this passage, i.e., that she is blamelessly adopting the wrong values, influences the way we respond to her later actions, most notably her decision to leave Hurstwood. Because we see how strongly she feels the pull toward material success and especially to success on the stage (and of course, because of Hurstwood's own lack of initiative), we do not condemn her for leaving him, but accept Carrie's action as inevitable.

The more general point here is that we must remain sympathetic toward Carrie in order to feel some pleasure in her final victory. This passage plays an important role in properly shaping our response. In order to understand why Carrie feels unfulfilled at the end of the book, we must, as we do here, see that society's values are deficient; otherwise we will feel that Carrie is unjustified for being unhappy amid her wealth. Furthermore, in order to remain sympathetic toward her, we must understand that it is not she who is to blame for adopting those false values, but rather society. And once we understand this, her final plight becomes even more poignant: she has obtained everything that society taught her to seek yet she remains unsatisfied. We feel that she has, to some degree, been duped.

Finally, this passage serves as a standard by which we can qualitatively measure how much Carrie has grown in understanding. The strong attraction she feels for wealth here provides a sharp contrast to her dissatisfaction with it at the novel's end. And as we have seen before, this growth in her understanding is an important part of her victory.

On this account, then, the intentions of the passage positively contribute to the success of the whole. Assuming that this passage is a representative one, we can now answer our question about the cumulative effects of Dreiser's lapses—and about the role of language in general—by considering how well and by what means the intentions of the passage are communicated. Perhaps the best way to judge the cumulative effect of the faults is to determine how much difference it would make if they were corrected. Consider the following paraphrase:

¹The play was one of those drawing room concoctions in which charmingly overdressed ladies and gentlemen suffer the pangs of love and jealousy amid gilded surroundings. ²The bon-mots that these suffering characters speak are ever enticing to those who have all their days longed for such material surroundings and have never had their longings gratified. ³These plays have the charm of showing suffering under ideal conditions. ⁴Who would not grieve upon a gilded chair? ⁵Who would not suffer amid perfumed tapestries, cushioned furniture, and liveried servants? ⁶Grief in such circumstances becomes an enticing thing. ⁷Carrie longed to live in such circumstances. ⁸She wanted to take her sufferings, whatever they were, in such a world, or failing that, at least to simulate them upon such a stage. ⁹So affected was her mind by these gilded surroundings that the play seemed an extraordinarily beautiful thing. ¹⁰She was soon lost in the world it represented, and wished that she might never return. ¹¹When she did, she studied the dazzlingly well-dressed matinee audience in the front rows and boxes, and conceived a new idea of the possibilities of New York. ¹²She was sure she had not seen it all—that part of it was one uninterrupted whirl of pleasure and delight.

How superior is this passage to the original? How much more clearly do we understand its intentions? How much does it alter our response to Carrie both here and later in the novel? The answer, I think, is not much. Knowing the antecedents of the pronouns, improving the transitions, and correcting some of the diction does not change the overall effect of these sentences because they do not change our understanding of the implied author's attitude toward the things he represents, and the nature of those things is such that these stylistic alterations do not seriously affect our understanding of them. What is important in this passage is its thought, and that thought is not especially precise or carefully modified in the course of the passage; instead, one main thought is introduced at the outset—the values of the plays and of the society represented in them are deficient—a new one is brought forth—these plays are naturally attractive to people without wealth—and then both are reiterated and slightly expanded in the rest of the passage. Because the thought is of this general nature, it will remain fairly constant from one paraphrase to the next, and all that is required of the language is to communicate this thought; in fact, we could, up to a certain point, introduce further awkwardness or vagueness similar to the one we have with "such bon-mots" in sentence 2 into the passage without seriously weakening it. In short, because the language of Dreiser's passage does convey that general thought, its faults are relatively unimportant. Dreiser can write "bad sentences" and still write an effective passage.

In any given passage, of course, it will not always be the elements of thought that are important; sometimes it will be the characters or the actions represented. In general, however, it is true that because Dreiser takes characters who are representative types and because he represents them acting in readily discernible patterns, our conceptions of the response to them will not change substantially in any paraphrase of Dreiser's language. To the extent that Dreiser successfully works out the patterns he has established early in the novel, and to the extent that we can admire his "thought," i.e., his values as expressed in the book, we shall, in spite of the particular language, admire his book. It is for this reason that we can say that Dreiser is both a bad writer and a good novelist.

Perhaps putting it another way will clarify this explanation. Suppose that Dreiser had written *Sister Carrie* in James's style, one that we have judged as positively felicitous. Rather than writing a better novel he might have written a worse one. No style is felicitous for every intention, and James's style would interfere with Dreiser's intention to about the same—or perhaps an even greater—extent than his own style does. James's style would not prevent us from understanding what is represented or the implied author's attitude toward those representations, but it would make us feel that the omniscient narrator was endlessly belaboring the obvious. I suppose it is a moot point whether in this novel that would be a greater fault than the grammatical and rhetorical errors Dreiser makes. But imagine reading *Sister Carrie* written in sentences like these: "The play was one of those so common to the period, a concoction set in a drawing room, in which ladies and gentlemen, overdressed but charmingly so, suffer amid surroundings gaily gilded the pangs of love and jealousy. The bon-mots spoken by the ladies and gentlemen who are the characters in those plays always become enticingly beautiful for those members of the audience who have all their days longed after surroundings even approaching the beauty of those they see before them without ever having the gratification of seeing those longings fulfilled.'' The style does not alter the nature of the thought represented, but this narrator seems like an incurable windbag.

No one paraphrase will be especially superior to all the others. We can improve Dreiser's style by eliminating his faults, but those aspects of writing that we abstractly associate with good style—precision of description, nuance of meaning and so on—are really beside the point. The important thing to be communicated is that X quality which the paraphrases share in common; it is that X quality which contributes to the refinement of our understanding of the intention, and so long as it is communicated the passage will be successful.

In our passages from *The Ambassadors,* however, almost the opposite is the case. Almost any paraphrase will radically alter the way we understand the intention of those passages. The X quality of the paraphrases is less important than what the sentences do not have in common—the style. Precision of description and subtlety of meaning are crucial for the success of the book as a whole: they constitute the difference between seeing the novel as a melodrama with cardboard characters and seeing it as an intrinsically significant work of art.

Generalizing from these cases, then, we can see that language can play widely different roles in the successful accomplishment of intentions. Different intentions require different things from the language in which they are expressed. That is why we intuitively sense so much diversity in the language of fiction.

By this point, our hypothesis about the way we understand texts is virtually complete, and its consequences for our understanding of language in fiction have been sufficiently demonstrated for us to formulate a tentative theory of language in fiction. Though created *out of* language, the worlds we experience in novels are more than worlds of words; they are, more accurately, worlds *from* words, worlds that contain the elements of character and action, which are essentially nonlinguistic and which are more central to our experience of those worlds than the words which create them. Thus, language remains a medium, a means by which authors accomplish their intentions of representing characters in action either for the sake of the representation itself or for some rhetorical purpose. But at the same time, the role of the medium is not fixed: for successfully accomplishing some intentions, the particular language (the style) an author chooses is absolutely crucial, while for successfully accomplishing others, the particular language has little or no consequence.

This theory rests on the belief, not fully examined so far, that language is a reliable medium, one that an author can use to embody his intended meanings and that self-critical readers can examine to recover those intentions. In the next chapter, we shall subject this belief to a rigorous test by considering the deconstructionist position that all literary meaning is indeterminate because language is ultimately unreliable, a system ultimately out of our control. At the same time, we shall continue our investigation into the roles of the medium in successful fictions by examining Jane Austen's *Persuasion*.

4 Determinate and Indeterminate Value in the Linguistic System: J. Hillis Miller and the Language of *Persuasion*

I

Virtually every conclusion we have reached so far is called into question by the reasoning about language that underlies the work of the group of critics known as deconstructionists. This group, whose members include Jacques Derrida, Paul de Man, Geoffrey Hartman, and J. Hillis Miller, among others, believes that the study of literature depends upon the prior study of language as a sign system. And because they view language as a system without a center, without any independent standard to guarantee the meaning of individual signs, they view literary texts as similarly decentered, and hence, as containing so many meanings that they are indeterminate.[1] The critic's job, in their view, is to open up the endless free-play of meaning that exists in any text; one of their favorite strategies is to show how an apparently univocal meaning is actually so equivocal as to be indeterminate.[2]

The deconstructionist challenge to our theory is so radical because it casts doubt not only on our conclusions, but also on the legitimacy of our questions. A deconstructionist would say, for example, that we cannot legitimately ask whether Stanley Fish's reader-response theory is consistent with what we must know in order to read, because what we think we know is only an illusion based on a faulty conception of language and meaning. More generally, from a deconstructionist's point of view, it is wrongheaded to ask whether language plays different roles in different works because such a question assumes it is possible to understand the determinate meaning of a given work and to specify the determinate role language plays in that meaning.

Because the deconstructionist challenge is so complete, it will lead us to some fundamental questions about language as a system, about, that is, the relationships among the signs which constitute a language and the relationship between a language and the community that uses it. In one sense, their challenge will lead us to face the most basic issues upon which our theory rests. Again, because the challenge is thoroughgoing, its consequences for the practical criticism of style in the novel can be demonstrated with any text—all styles in all texts lead to indeterminacy. Nevertheless, two considerations lead us to *Persuasion* as our example text. Working with Austen's novel will dramatically illustrate the radical nature of the deconstructionist position, since, from a more traditional point of view such as ours, the value of the novel derives from Austen's successfully accomplishing an extraordinarily difficult task of determinate communication. Austen chooses to show her heroine, Anne Elliot, suffering throughout much of the action at the hands of the man who is to be her eventual husband, Frederick Wentworth; yet Austen's skill is so great that we do not merely refrain from judging Wentworth negatively, but we also interpret Anne's sufferings as signals that she and Wentworth will be happily reunited. Working with Austen's novel also will allow us to examine another possible role of language in fiction. Even our brief description of Austen's accomplishment suggests that her particular linguistic choices must be quite important for her success, yet specific actions in the novel, most notably the engagement itself, have a great effect on our response and seem as if they would have a similar effect regardless of the language in which they are represented.

Since Derrida is the theorist who has most fully formulated the view of language underlying the deconstructionist position, it makes sense to begin with his work. However, since that work is extremely broad in scope, touching on questions in metaphysics, epistemology, and psychology as well as linguistics and grammatology, I shall not pretend to treat Derrida comprehensively here, but shall focus on his work to the extent that it provides a basis and impetus for the literary theory and criticism of J. Hillis Miller. Miller is my ultimate concern because his brand of deconstruction, which insists that every text contains a path to perpetual doubt about its meaning, is most antithetical to the theory we have developed so far.

II

In linguistic terms, Derrida's work is an attempt to redefine the relation between what Saussure called the signifier (the "sound-image" we associate with a word), and the signified (the

"concept" we associate with that sound-image). The consequences of Derrida's redefinition, however, affect not only linguistics and literary criticism, but all disciplines concerned with
meaning; they signal a revolution in metaphysics itself. In Derrida's view, traditional Western metaphysics, what he calls "the
metaphysics of presence" or the "logocentric tradition," has assumed that the signified exists prior to its designation by a
signifier, and that it is this prior existence, this presence, that is
the origin of meaning. In this view, a word has a meaning because
it designates a preexistent thing. Moreover, Derrida points out,
this tradition has believed that behind all the relations between
signifier and signified is a transcendental signified—a Platonic
ideal, a Christian God, a Heideggerian Being—which is the ultimate and final guarantor of those relations. Derrida illustrates the
intrinsic hierarchy of this system by pointing out how it glorifies
speech at the expense of writing. Speech is closer to the preexistent signified; there is less of a gap between speech and the
presence which calls it into existence than between writing and
that presence. Writing is not equivalent to speech but is the sign
of the sign which is speech. In the logocentric tradition, then, the
chain of priorities is arranged this way: transcendental signified,
signified of any signifier, signifier as expressed in speech, signifier
as expressed in writing.[3]

Derrida sets out to deconstruct this tradition, to upset this
chain of priorities by applying in a most rigorous way Saussure's
principle of value in difference, the notion that the value of any
sign in the linguistic system derives not from any positive attribute it possesses but rather from its differences with regard to the
other signs in the system. Saussure demonstrates its validity on
both the phonic and the conceptual level. In reference to the
latter, he says that although it is true that social convention in-
separably links signifier and signified to each other (wherever
we have the sound-image "snow" we also have the concept
"snow"), it is misleading to take this description of *signification*
as a description of the source of *value*. The value of anything, he
points out, is always determined by a dissimilar thing that it can
be exchanged for (a word for its concept; a dollar for what it can
buy) and by similar things that it can be compared to (other
words, other units of currency). The value of "snow," for example, depends not only on the concept "snow," but also on the
value of "rain," "hail," "sleet," "drizzle," and so on. If these

latter words (or other words that would be linked to these concepts) did not exist, then "snow" would widen in meaning to include the concepts they signify; similarly, if in addition to these words, words for different kinds of snow also existed, then "snow" would take on a more specialized meaning. The point is that the positive relation between a sound-image and a concept, signified by a word, will exist as that particular relationship only because of its differences from all the other words in the system. Once the other words change, the particular relationship also changes.[4]

Similarly, phonemes have particular values because they are distinct from each other. There can be variation in the pronunciation of any phoneme as long as that variation does not result in the confusion of phonemes. The same holds true for the pronunciation of words; Saussure puts it this way: "Since one vocal image is no better suited than the next for what it is commissioned to express, it is evident, even a priori, that a segment of language can never in the final analysis be based on anything but its noncoincidence with the rest. *Arbitrary* and *differential* are two correlative qualities."[5]

Derrida uses the principle of value in difference together with Hjelmslev's distinction between form and matter—i.e., the idea that the formal essence of a sign is distinct from the particular material substance in which it may be embodied—to build a model of the "origin" of language.[6] If difference is the source of value, and if the linguistic system has a form apart from its phonic substance, what is it, he asks, that allows difference to function, and the form of the system to establish itself? Derrida's answer is "the trace," and he reasons this way:

> On the one hand, the phonic element, the term, the plenitude that is called sensible, would not appear as such without the difference or opposition which gives them *form*. . . . Here the appearing and functioning of difference presupposes an originary synthesis not preceded by any absolute simplicity. Such would be the originary trace. Without a retention of the other as other in the same, no difference would do its work and no meaning would appear. It is not the question of a constituted difference here, but rather, before all determination of the content, of the *pure* movement which produces difference.[7]

To paraphrase: before meaning, there exists only a pure movement of undifferentiated sound and undifferentiated thought; in the course of this pure movement there occurs a moment when a segment of sound and a segment of thought are retained in the memory as new segments are reached (this is the point of the originary synthesis); at this point, difference is introduced into the system (there is a trace of the previous moment in the present one), and consequently, meaning can be produced. Perhaps the most important point to understand about this description of the trace is that the trace itself is not a positive preexisting thing. It is not the first word; it is not a specific sound or thought. It does not have a discernible form, it is not itself a presence; it is the shadow of a presence, a presence-absence, a being-nonbeing. It is "merely" the condition that allows difference to function, and as such is responsible for the "formation of the form"[8] of language.

At the same time, Derrida also describes the trace as that which constitutes the difference between form and substance, so that in another sense it is the "being imprinted of the imprint,"[9] i.e., the formalization of the substance. Derrida explains this sense of the trace by focusing on Saussure's distinction between the "sound-image" and the objective sound, the appearing of the sound and the sound appearing. "The sound-image is what is *heard;* not the *sound* heard but the being-heard of the sound."[10] The sound-image constitutes the form of the signifier, while the objective sound constitutes its substance. The space between, the unheard difference between the appearing and the appearance, is the trace.

Taken together, the two descriptions of the trace show that "it is the absolute origin of sense in general. Which amounts to saying once again that there is no absolute origin of sense in general."[11] One of Derrida's other names for the trace is *differance,* a word coined from *difference* and *deferance,* and designed to indicate both the eternal play of difference and the endless deferral, the putting off of a final resting place or a ground for meaning.[12]

With this view of the trace as the origin/nonorigin of sense, Derrida proceeds to deconstruct the chain of priorities of Western metaphysics. He shows that the signified is no more privileged than the signifier. The transcendental signified has disappeared; there is no prior presence that guarantees meaning, no center to the system of meaning; there is only difference. Furthermore, there is no gap between signifier and signified; each is the function of the other. Derrida puts it this way: "the signified is originarily and essentially . . . trace . . . it is always already in the position of the signifier.''[13]

Derrida makes his deconstruction more dramatic by demonstrating that the traditional order of priorities between speech and writing should be reversed. Writing is not derived from speech, but rather both forms of expression are made possible by the system which the play of difference initiated by the trace produces. Speech will be intelligible only after this system exists, and this system can be seen as a kind of writing, because it lacks the presence of an originating mind. Derrida distinguishes between this arche-writing and writing in the narrow or usual sense. Writing in the narrow sense does not really replace speech in its privileged position—it, too, depends on the arche-writing—but with its absence of an originating consciousness and its difference created by marks on a blank page, it is more closely connected than speech to the arche-writing, the model of all language.

III

The recent work of J. Hillis Miller dramatically demonstrates the consequences this view of language has for literary theory and criticism. As we might expect, Miller takes as his first principle the heterogeneity of any text. Because the linguistic system has no center, a text which consists only of language also has no center; therefore, it can only open out, can only offer a reader its own unceasing play of differences, its own countless meanings. Miller often begins his criticism with the apparent referential meaning of a text, the one which the logocentric tradition sees as the only one, and then shows how this reading unwittingly contains its own deconstruction. He pays special attention to the referential, univocal, logocentric reading not because it has a privileged or a priori status, but because showing how this reading is based on an illusion, how it actually deconstructs itself is the best way of demonstrating the indeterminacy of all meaning.

Perhaps the most brilliant example of this use of apparent meaning is Miller's reply to Wayne Booth's charge that the deconstructionist reading of a work is ''plainly and simply parasitical'' on ''the obvious or univocal one.''[14] It will be useful to consider this example in some detail because it demonstrates the other main features of his criticism.

Miller begins discussing various images suggested by the obvi-

ous or univocal meaning of Booth's accusation—one plant feeding off another until it chokes its food-source to death, an alien
guest within the house, feeding off and perhaps about to kill the
host. Then he moves to a separate consideration of each major
element of these figures, of parasite and of host. He analyzes the
parts of the word "parasite" (*para* plus *sitos*), its etymology, and
its relation to other words beginning with "para." He also
analyzes the etymology of "host," and considers at some length
the various social relations that can exist between host and guest.
He establishes that parasite and host are double antithetical
words, i.e., they are not only opposites but they contain their
opposites within themselves. He shows that a parasite is a guest
and a guest is a host and a host is a parasite, or in other words,
that Booth's statement might mean "the univocal reading is
plainly and simply parasitical on the deconstructionist one." But
that statement, of course, can be deconstructed in its turn. We are
left with the indeterminacy of the statement. Neither the univocal
meaning nor the deconstructionist one (if there could be a single
deconstructionist reading, which there can't) is right. We are at
an impasse, a moment of aporia; we can go on examining the
meaning of the statement forever without being able to say that
any one meaning is more accurate than another. The statement
contains all those meanings; its meaning is indeterminate.

Summarizing his activity, Miller also justifies it: "It is an argument for the value of recognizing the great complexity and
equivocal richness of apparently obvious or univocal language,
even the language of criticism."[15] This complexity and equivocal
richness, Miller explains, "reside in part in the fact that there is
no conceptual expression without figure, and no intertwining of
concept and figure without an implied story, narrative or myth.
Deconstruction is an investigation of what is implied by the in-
herence of figure, concept, and narrative in one another." In this
sense, then, "deconstruction is a rhetorical discipline."[16] Deconstructionist activity is also meant to demonstrate the hyperbolic exuberance experienced in "letting language go as far as it
will take one"; and it can take one through "all the family of the
Indo-European languages," and "all the literature and conceptual
thought within those languages."[17]

Miller's own language is worth noting here: language takes the
critic as far as it will go, not vice versa. The critic is not an

ingenious importer of meanings into a text, but rather a faithful servant who uncovers the countless meanings that are already there. The text, Miller insists, always already contains its own deconstruction.

Furthermore, there is more than one path that will lead to the discovery of the indeterminacy of meaning. Since all language is heterogeneous and indeterminate, almost any word, certainly any word that recurs frequently, will provide a path to aporia.[18] Aporia itself is an end of the path only in a deconstructionist sense: just as there is no absolute origin and no absolute center, there can be no absolute end. We reach aporia the moment we realize how a particular text creates its endless play of different meanings; we can participate in that play endlessly, but once we open ourselves to it we cannot resolve any of the conflicting meanings it offers us. Nor is aporia one and the same for all texts; all texts are indeterminate, but the indeterminacy itself is not the same for all texts, e.g., the indeterminacies of "host" and "parasite" are different from the indeterminacies contained in the figure of the line.[19]

We can further understand Miller's deconstructionist criticism by analyzing *Persuasion* according to his principles. As with the Fishean analysis of *The Ambassadors,* I do not claim our theorist would analyze the novel exactly as I do, but that the analysis is faithful to his system. The important point is not whether I take the same path Miller would, but whether I can show how the path I choose leads to aporia. I take the path offered by the title word.

"Persuasion" is a key word in the univocal reading of the novel. Anne Elliot, at the age of nineteen, yielded to the persuasion of her good friend Lady Russell, refused the hand of Frederick Wentworth, and deeply regretted it ever since. Eight years later—the time at which the novel opens—when Wentworth returns to her neighborhood, Anne must try to persuade him that she still loves him and is still worthy of his love, even though she is in a position in which "her word had no weight." She can persuade him only by being herself. In the meantime, she must endure his initial coldness, his occasional polite kindness, and his apparent infatuation with Louisa Musgrove. She must wait for him to learn the difference between foolishly resolute minds like Louisa's and reasonable ones like her own—minds which may on occasion be persuaded by reasonable arguments. She must suffer in her awareness of his genuine superiority and of her own loss.

But because of that superiority, she must succeed in the end. By being herself she persuades him of her own incalculable merit. By speaking from her heart to Captain Harville about the constancy of women, she persuades Wentworth that she will welcome a renewal of his proposal. Having learned the lessons of "persuasion," Wentworth can also learn that in marrying Anne he is happier than he deserves.[20]

But in this determinate reading we never question the meaning of "persuasion," never open ourselves up to the play of differences it contains. Let us look more closely at it. It appears, at first, not indeterminate but ambiguous. In a phrase such as "Anne's persuasion" two opposing meanings are united: the persuasion of someone by Anne, or the persuasion of Anne by someone. In the first case, Anne is the agent, the performer, the person with the power of persuasion; in the second, she is the persuadable one, the patient upon whom the power of persuasion is worked. These meanings seem mutually exclusive, and we might think that they are merely the result of a coincidence in surface form created by the nominalization and deletion transformations on the two deep structures of "Anne persuades x" and "x persuades Anne." If this is the case, then we cannot make much of this ambiguity; as with other ambiguous phrases such as "flying planes can be dangerous" the context will tell us which meaning is intended. However, the explanation offered by generative grammar is not the only one.[21] We can begin to see some real significance in this union of two apparently exclusive meanings in the single word when we begin to examine a figure suggested by "persuasion."

To persuade someone is to win him over to a certain way of thinking. When you persuade someone, you move him from a position he occupied before he heard your argument to the position you want him to hold. If you are skillful in the art of persuasion, you are powerful; you can get other people to vote for your candidate, buy your product, think as you want them to think. You convince another of something, you convert him. Bolstered by your persuasion, he will have new conviction, he will maintain your position with the zeal of a convert. To wield the power of persuasion is to wield great power indeed. We see this view of persuasion in Austen's novel in Henrietta Musgrove's words about Lady Russell: "I wish Lady Russell lived at Uppercross

and were intimate with Dr. Shirley [who might promote her fi-
ancé]...I always look upon her as able to persuade a person to
anything."[22]

But let us look more closely at the other person in our
figure, the one who is persuaded. The persuadable man is, in
the words of our figure, movable, mobile. He readily gives up
one position for another that seems more attractive. To be persuaded is to be subject to the influence of others. It is, to some
degree, to lack resolution, to be weak-willed, to fail to have the
courage of one's convictions. The persuadable man is one who
does not know where to stop. It is foolish to believe that you can
persuade him to a position from which he will not be moved, for
your own argument, to the extent that it has been successful, has
shown him the advantage of mobility. The power of persuasion,
on closer examination, seems to be an illusion: your audience is
either unpersuadable or equally subject to the arguments of your
opponent. As Wentworth says, the worst evil of the persuadable
character is "that no influence over it can be depended on" (p.
88).

Moreover, the persuader, in his desire to succeed, becomes the
victim of the persuadable. The apparently weak, mobile man actually wields the power: I will move, he says either implicitly or explicitly, but only if you do x or y or z. Suddenly the positions are
reversed. Who is persuading whom? The persuadable man persuades the persuader to persuade him in a certain way. And the
persuader, in order to succeed, will be persuaded to use different
techniques for different persuadable audiences. He moves this
way, now that; he must be as mobile as the person he would
persuade. In *Persuasion,* Mr. Shepherd must move from one position to the next to the next in order to win Sir Walter over to the
idea that Admiral Croft will be an acceptable tenant for Kellynch
Hall.

The verb "persuade" contains this shifting power relationship
within itself. Its meaning encompasses a range of verbs from
wheedle to coerce, each implying a different power relationship
between agent and patient: cajole, plead, coax, urge, beseech,
beg, recommend, reason, induce, influence, prevail upon, appeal,
inculcate, dissuade, set straight, overcome, convince, convert.
"Persuader" and "persuadable," like host and parasite, are double antithetical words; they are not only opposites, but each contains the other within itself.

Perhaps if we cannot clearly distinguish between the qualities of the persuader and the persuadable, we can distinguish between the persuadable and the unpersuadable. The unpersuadable man will not move while the persuadable one will move anywhere. But this apparent difference only conceals a deeper similarity. Recall Wentworth's words: the worst evil of the persuadable character is that "no influence over it can be depended on." In our terms, the persuadable man is one who does not know where to stop. Both Wentworth's accusation and our definition also apply to the unpersuadable man. Because he refuses to heed any other arguments than those that support his position, the unpersuadable man does not really know where anyone else stands, which is another way of saying that he does not know where he is, does not know where he has stopped. Nothing has any influence over him because his only concern is to be fixed in his position.

The best illustration of this in the novel is Wentworth's experience with Louisa at Lyme. Wentworth himself is the most important person, the one who would logically wield the most influence over Louisa, and he advises her not to jump from the Cobb a second time. But even his influence cannot be depended on, and unpersuadable Louisa, not knowing where she is (in a double sense), jumps and injures herself.

So persuader/persuadable/unpersuadable all blend together in this shifting interchange of meaning. The more we try to pin down the relations among them, the more indeterminate their meanings become. This indeterminacy is built into the structure of the words, into the relation between the prefix *per* and the root word *suadere*. The root is fairly stable, meaning to "urge," "advise," or "recommend" (OED), but the prefix contains contradictory meanings within itself. It can mean "over," "through," "by means of," as in "perlocutionary," so that we can understand a "persuasion" as the moving of someone over to a new position. It can mean "thoroughly" or "very" as in "perfervid," so we can understand a persuasion as a conviction or a conversion. "Per" can also mean "through and through, to completion," as in "persevere" so we can understand how a persuasion to a new position implies the complete abandonment of the old. And "per" can mean "away, entirely to destruction" as in "perish" or "pervert" so we can understand someone's persuasion as a sign of his weakness or impotence. A look at some of the other words in "per" that are also related to "persuasion" as devices, methods, or consequences of it opens up the play of difference even more: persevere, permeate, perturb, pertain, perorate, perceive, persist, perspective, perforate, perfect, perform, perchance, perjure.

By this point, we can recognize that any determinate statement about "persuasion" in Austen's novel is a naïve misreading. In fact, all reading is misreading, all paraphrase is parody because it prematurely stops the play of different meanings contained in any text. Our path into *Persuasion* leads not to any enlightenment but to an impasse; "persuasion" has taken us only to aporia, perpetual doubt about its own meaning. "Persuasion" has deconstructed itself, and in so doing, has also deconstructed *Persuasion*.

IV

Perhaps the most notable feature of this deconstructionist criticism is its ability to stand up to objections. If we say that it is too ingenious (and our example does not come near Miller's own work for sheer ingenuity), that it compares literal and metaphorical uses of "persuasion" without acknowledging that it does so, the deconstructionist will reply that that is just the point. Because in his view there is no presence which governs meaning, there is no difference between literal and metaphorical uses of language; all language is metaphorical, and it is his task to open up the play of metaphor contained in every work. If we argue that although by itself "persuasion" might contain all the meanings he points to, in any particular case we will know its meaning because we can understand the intention of the utterance, he will rightly point out that we are not really objecting to his analysis, we are just complaining that he does not share our philosophical premises. As M. H. Abrams has pointed out, the impasse which deconstructionist criticism always leads to is the logical conclusion from its philosophical premises; once we grant a deconstructionist those premises, we must accept his method and his conclusion.[23]

Yet as Abrams also points out, the deconstructionist seems to work by a double standard. He appears to assume that the language of the text he is deconstructing works in one way while the language of the text he is writing works in quite another, i.e., that the language of the literary text is indeterminate, undecidable, purely differential, while his own language is determinate and referential. Only by assuming that language can have determinate meaning can the deconstructionist communicate his message that the language of any text is indeterminate. What we have, then, is a system whose very presentation of itself violates or contradicts itself. Abrams summarizes his objection this way: the deconstructionist critic cannot be taken seriously, in Hegel's sense of serious; that is, he does not "entirely and consistently commit himself to the consequences of his premises." Deconstructionist criticism then becomes merely an elaborate game whose only real value is its occasional byproducts—its insights into the diversity of language and the surprising likenesses and differences it can uncover in our literary and philosophical heritage.[24]

Although Abrams's objections may initially seem convincing, they finally do not undermine Miller's position. Abrams fails to do justice to Miller's contention that every text contains its own deconstruction, that the text *not the critic* is the real agent of deconstruction. In speaking about Miller's text, Abrams says that "there is no law which can prevent a deconstructive critic from bringing his graphocentric premises to bear on [it]," but that those who "stubbornly refuse to substitute the rules of the deconstructive enterprise for our ordinary skill and tact at language" will have no difficulty understanding Miller's text.[25] For Miller, however, it is not a question of choosing between logocentric and deconstructive rules of interpretation; it is a question of seeing or not seeing the deconstruction that is always already in the text—in any text including his own. He believes that his own words also have unstable, indeterminate meanings, and yet this belief does not undermine his enterprise. The language of his text, like the language of a literary text, will appear to mean something—that the literary text deconstructs itself—but then that apparent meaning will vanish once we open ourselves to the play of difference his language offers us. This process ultimately supports rather than undermines his criticism because it too ends in the impasse he is trying to demonstrate. It, too, proves that all language is indeterminate. Miller expresses this point more compactly:

> The deconstruction of the referential reading of a text . . . is necessarily formulated in such a way that it can be taken as referential in its turn, or else it would not be able to perform its

act of deconstruction. But the deconstruction has been under-taken to deny the referentiality of the language in question. Aporia, impasse, *malconfort,* in which we can neither sit nor stand.[26]

If Abrams's main objection against the deconstructionists does not hold, and if other objections are really only complaints that the deconstructionists do not share our philosophical premises, then it seems we are faced with a single choice: either de-construction or traditional Western metaphysics. The two philo-sophical positions share no common ground, and so we must choose on the basis of the consequences of each. It is a question of viewing *Persuasion, The Ambassadors, Sister Carrie, King Lear, Being and Time, Of Grammatology*—all texts—as paths to different moments of aporia, to various abysses of indeterminate meaning, or of viewing them as different determinate human communications, each with its own unique meaning. In this deci-sion, each of us must create his own value; anything we might ordinarily appeal to (experience of texts, knowledge of language) is itself being called into question. For my own part, I have no trouble choosing Western metaphysics; I infinitely prefer a *Per-suasion* with a determinate meaning over one which leads to aporia.

Nevertheless this is not a very satisfactory solution. The de-constructionists still have the last word, for they believe they have shown that traditional metaphysics is based on an illusion. Those of us who choose determinate meaning can be made to appear as naïve and sentimental fools clinging to a hopelessly romantic view of the world: "it would be nice if things were that way," the deconstructionists gently but firmly tell us, "we all wish they could be, but the simple fact of the matter is that they're not." From the deconstructionists' viewpoint, it is not a question of choosing between two *equal* alternatives, since their alternative contains within itself the deconstruction of the other. And although we could reply that they cannot "prove" in any final, mathematical sense that their account of the "origin" of meaning is superior to the one offered by traditional metaphysics, this will not positively help us either. We only get back where we started, having made a choice which is susceptible to their decon-struction.

There is, however, a way to a more satisfactory resolution of the problem posed by the deconstructionists: following Abrams's lead, we can reexamine their premises, and the rigor of the reasoning that leads to their conclusions. But first it will be helpful to look once again at their view of language.

The deconstructionists believe that language is treacherous by nature; on inspection its apparent meaning always gives way to indeterminacy. Like skywriting, the longer we look at it the more its apparent substance becomes diffuse, the more it melts from one shape into the next. Language, for Derrida and Miller, is not a system that man controls but a system out of his control. Man does not use it to express determinate meanings, but rather it teaches him that all meaning is indeterminate. Miller puts it this way: "Language is not an instrument or tool in man's hands, a submissive means of thinking. Language rather thinks man and his 'world' . . . if he will allow it to do so."[27]

Miller's statement is the logical conclusion of the deconstructionists' emphasis on difference as the source of meaning. Miller's statement also points to the most fundamental disagreement between his position and the theory we have developed so far, a disagreement over man's relation to language. Our theory rests quite heavily on the assumption that language, though not merely man's submissive tool, is nevertheless a human creation that can often be used to serve man's ends. This disagreement over man's relation to language can be resolved, and resolved in favor of our theory, because Miller's work, finally, does not deconstruct our basic assumption but also in part depends upon it. Before showing how it does, we need to explore more fully the differences between the two views of man's relation to language.

Derrida's model of the origin/nonorigin of meaning, though very astute in showing how the linguistic system does not depend upon preexistent signifieds (transcendental or otherwise), is from our point of view incomplete. According to the model, the trace initiates the play of difference, and this play produces an independent, autonomous system of language, with its own laws and regularities, a system that develops and functions on its own. The model is incomplete because it leaves out—or tries to leave out—the uses of the system. Although it is unfair and too easy to argue that our view is implicit in Derrida's model—Derrida describes the trace as "the retention of the other as other" and so seems to imply some consciousness that does the retaining and gives the trace significance—it is not unfair or too easy to argue that the play of difference cannot introduce meaning without the consent of the linguistic community.

This view does not imply that the community *creates* the trace or that the play of difference is completely controlled by man. It does not bring preexistent signifieds back into the system, but is willing to agree that the content of signs can only be explained by other signs in an endless regress. The relation between man and the system implied in this view is one of mutual dependence. The system of meaning created by the play of difference which the trace produces has significance—its potential as a meaning system becomes actual—only because man consents to it. Man relies on the independent functioning of the system to make meaning, and he cannot fully express everything he thinks or feels because he is limited by that system: he can only express those meanings that the play of difference has introduced into it. Man does not totally control language, nor language man.[28]

In a sense, this view of language brings back into focus the other half of Saussure's case about value in the linguistic system. Value derives not only from the differences among signs, but also from the arbitrary agreements about what signs can be exchanged for.[29] We must know those agreements in order to know what signs are similar to each other and how they are similar—even if we can only express those similarities in terms of other signs. Furthermore, even after difference does its work in a particular case, the proposed relation between sound-image and concept must be implicitly "ratified" or "accepted" by the linguistic community. The sound-image "snow" may signify its particular concept because of its differences from "rain," "hail," "sleet," etc., but at the same time, it can signify that concept only because speakers of English implicitly agree that it can.

Language, in short, cannot "think" man and his world, because it does not exist apart from man. It cannot exist as itself, as a system that unites sound and meaning, without a community of speakers who agree about what sounds will be united to what meanings.

Miller might still feel that this view of language does not undermine his position. He might grant this view of the relation between language and its community of speakers, but argue that the problem of indeterminate meaning remains: the community has at one point or another "ratified" so many possible meanings for any given sound-image that we cannot determine what any given use of the sound-image means. His work, in part, is a demonstration of this problem. The problem, though, is a false one because its existence depends on a contradiction in its description. This contradiction, furthermore, runs through Miller's work—indeed it makes that work possible—but finally it also makes his work unpersuasive. To be able to show, as Miller can so deftly, that a word such as "host" or "parasite" has numerous apparent meanings one must assume that the linguistic community has agreed that the same sign can have different meanings in different uses. Miller's description of the meanings of "host" implies the assumption:

> There is no parasite without a host. The host and the somewhat sinister or subversive parasite are fellow guests beside the food sharing it. On the other hand, the host is himself the food, his substance consumed without recompense, as when one says, "He is eating me out of house and home." The host may then become the host in another sense. . . . The word "Host" is the name for the consecrated bread or wafer of the Eucharist, from Middle English *oste,* from Old French *oiste,* from Latin *hostia,* sacrifice, victim.[30]

Miller is able to distinguish among and to point out these various meanings of "host," only because its meaning is *not always* indeterminate, only because in some uses it has one meaning (the sacramental host), while in others it has another (the host who is the fellow guest with the parasite). At this point in his demonstration of the indeterminacy of meaning, Miller tacitly works with the view of the relation between language and man implicit in our theory.

To go on and argue, as Miller does, that the diversity of a word's meanings reveals its ultimate indeterminacy in any one use is to switch assumptions, to assume that the value of a sign in the linguistic system is independent of the agreements made by the linguistic community. The reason Miller must try to have it both ways is that having it only one will undermine his project. If he works only with the assumption that the community assents to different meanings in different contexts, obviously he cannot show that individual texts lead to aporia. If he assumes from the outset that any use of a word is indeterminate, then he cannot isolate its different meanings: the use of "host" in "consecrated host" must have the same indeterminate meaning as its use in "your host for the night" and in "host of a parasite." And the truth of such a proposition cannot be deduced or demonstrated; to attempt to do so inevitably involves Miller's method of show-ing the different meanings the word has at different times, and that method, as we have seen, depends upon a quite different assumption about meaning. Since its truth cannot be demon-strated, the proposition about the indeterminacy of "host" is either something we take as given like a postulate in geometry, or it is intuitively obvious, something we recognize as part of our linguistic competence, or it is simply untrue, something akin to the proposition, "the sound-image 'snow' in English corresponds to the concept 'home run.'" If the proposition were either a given or an obvious fact, Miller would not have to try to demonstrate its truth; his very effort, then, indicates that the third alternative is the accurate one: propositions about the indeterminacy of lan-guage in use are simply untrue.

Thus, although our specific reasons are different, we must finally share Abrams's judgment of Miller's position; it is not serious, in Hegel's sense, because it is not fully committed to its own logic.

What emerges from our examination of the deconstructionist challenge is not only a specific understanding of the relation be-tween the linguistic system and the community that uses it but also an increased appreciation of the interdependence, the flexi-bility, and the richness of the system itself. If Miller's strategies of deconstruction do not convince us of the indeterminacy of language, they still are very powerful arguments for the *potential* ambiguity of all language, ambiguity so radical that the same ex-pressions may contain their opposites within themselves. Con-sequently, what also emerges is a greater sense of the role nonlin-guistic factors play in our understanding of language in use. Our knowledge of speaker, audience, occasion, and intention stands as a bulwark between us and the abyss of indeterminate meaning. Some of this knowledge, e.g., knowledge about occasions, seems to be a part of the linguistic system itself; a full theory of seman-tics will indicate not only the possible meanings a given sound-image may have, but also *some* of the conditions under which it will have one meaning rather than the next.[31] But other parts of this knowledge, though as reliable as grammatical knowledge, though operating in a similar tacit, intuitive way, seem to be impossible to represent in an accurate systematic manner; think, for example, of the knowledge shared in the speech-events of two friends of long years and deep intimacy. Yet in a sense even this knowledge between two such friends is of the same kind as that which allows us to distinguish between the different uses of a word like "host" on different occasions: it, too, constitutes an agreement about the linguistic system made by the linguistic community—in this case, though, the community numbers two rather than two hundred million. Finally, then, although the way we understand specific speech events depends on our knowing more than the linguistic system, that understanding also reflects an essential feature of the system: its intelligibility and its functioning depend upon our shared knowledge, our agreements.

V

Having examined these fundamental theoretical issues, and having rejected the deconstructionist analysis of *Persuasion*, let us turn now to the more practical questions posed by the language of Austen's novel. As we have seen, *Persuasion* is an intriguing case because on the one hand particular actions such as the engagement seem to be crucial for the book's success, but on the other some actions seem to be significant largely because of the way they are represented, e.g., Wentworth's lifting an unruly child from Anne's neck, his handing her into a carriage. How reliable a guide is our intuition here? Just what is the role of Austen's style in the success of *Persuasion?*

Generally stated, Austen's intention is to represent Anne Elliot's movement from an initially unhappy state to a final one of supreme happiness. As the action begins, Anne, in spite of her considerable virtues, is unloved and unappreciated by her family, and more importantly, by Frederick Wentworth, the man whom she loves and who is most suitable for her. In her final state, Anne is reunited with Wentworth in a love that is deeper and more mature than the one they had eight years before. Wentworth has the moral and intellectual powers to do Anne justice, to make him see that he is luckier than he deserves, and to assure us that with him Anne can be as happy as we have always wanted her to be.

More specifically, Austen also wants us to feel that neither Fortune nor Wentworth is as responsible for Anne's final happiness as Anne herself, because in this way we shall feel the greatest degree of satisfaction in that final happiness. However, this aspect of the intention is the most difficult to achieve because Anne is always in a position in which she cannot *directly* act to improve her situation. Austen solves the problem brilliantly: she makes us see that by being herself—by sacrificing her own pleasure for that of just about everyone else, by keeping her head after Louisa's fall from the Cobb, when all about her, including Wentworth, are losing theirs, by speaking honestly and ardently in her discussion with Captain Harville on the relative constancy of men and women, by not expecting to get any reward for her virtue—that Anne wins Wentworth. A man of his sense and discernment cannot remain unaffected by Anne.

Yet one consequence of Austen's solution is that for a time Anne will suffer at Wentworth's hands; since she remains constant in her love as well as her virtue, and he must change, she will be the "victim" of both his gentlemanly politeness and his warm-hearted kindness until she knows that his feelings have changed. As a result, Austen has another artistic problem: if we feel Anne's sufferings as intensely as she does, we shall not feel fully satisfied with her eventual marriage, since the memory of her suffering will be too strong.

One method Austen uses to solve this problem is to make us see from the outset that Anne most likely will attain a state she deserves. The first three chapters introduce us to the moral world of the novel. And because we immediately see Sir Walter and Elizabeth Elliot so appropriately punished for their self-indulgent and extravagant way of living—they must give up the seat of their power and importance, Kellynch Hall—we feel confident that Anne too will eventually achieve a fate appropriate for a woman of her merits. The other method Austen uses to guide our expectations about Anne will become clear as we analyze a passage form the novel.[32] The passage is from the Uppercross section of the novel.

Wentworth has just helped Anne, who is fatigued from walking all day, into the Crofts' carriage (volume 1, chapter 10, p. 91). This particular walk has given Anne considerable distress. Henrietta Musgrove has become reconciled with Charles Hayter and "everything now marked out Louisa for Captain Wentworth" (p. 90). Furthermore, Anne has involuntarily overheard Wentworth tell Louisa of his belief that firmness of character is the foundation of happiness, and she cannot fail to make the natural inferences about what he must think of her character. In this passage, Anne reflects on Wentworth's unexpected kindness:

[1]Yes—he had done it. [2]She was in the carriage and felt that he had placed her there, that his will and his hands had done it, that she owed it to his perception of her fatigue, and his resolution to give her rest. [3]She was very much affected by the view of his disposition towards her which all these things made apparent. [4] This little circumstance seemed the completion of all that had gone before. [5]She understood him. [6]He could not forgive her—but he could not be unfeeling. [7]Though condemning her for the past, and considering it with high and unjust resentment, though perfectly careless of her, and though becoming attached to another, still he could not see her suffer, without the desire of giving her relief. [8]It was a remainder of former sentiment; it was an impulse of pure, though unacknowledged friendship; it was a proof of his own warm and amiable heart which she could not contemplate without emotions so compounded of pleasure and pain that she knew not which prevailed. [p. 91]

Again, we shall be better able to judge the importance of the language by comparing it to a paraphrase.

[1]She had been handed into the carriage by Wentworth. [2]He had done it, she felt, because he saw that she was tired, and he wanted to let her rest. [3]Anne was very affected by what these things showed about how he felt towards her. [4]What he did here seemed to complete everything he had done before. [5]He was understood by her. [6]She was an object of some feeling for him—but she was not to be forgiven. [7]He condemned her for the past and resented it highly and unjustly, he was perfectly careless of her and was becoming attached to another, but if he saw her suffer he would try to relieve that suffering. [8]It showed that he still had some of his former feeling; it was motivated by his feeling, though he had not previously acknowledged it, that they were friends; it proved that he was warm and amiable, and she could reflect on that only with such a combination of pleasurable and painful emotions that it was impossible for her to tell which were greater.

Sentence 1: "Yes—he had done it."

Paraphrase: She had been placed in the carriage by Wentworth.

This sentence repeats the information we have received at the end of the previous paragraph: "Captain Wentworth, without saying a word, turned to her [Anne], and quietly obliged her to be assisted into the carriage." The very fact of the repetition—the paraphrase has the same effect—tells us how important his small act is for Anne. The form of the repetition tells us even more. "Yes" creates the sense that Anne is reassuring herself of what Wentworth had done; it is as if she has been so agitated by his actions that she can only now look around her and get her bearings. "Yes" also implies an affirmation on Anne's part, a positive pleasure in her realization of Wentworth's kindness— compare the effect of "Oh no—he had done it." Both these effects, which are absent from the paraphrase, are desirable because they make us begin to appreciate how keenly Anne is affected by Wentworth's action.

Finally, "yes" indicates that we are beginning to see Anne's thoughts; it seems more likely that she is the speaker of "yes" than that the narrator is. This technique, of course, does not depend on the particular choice of "yes," but it is worth noting that this form of repeating the information of the previous sentence creates this inside view of Anne while the straightforward paraphrase does not. This inside view is important because it gives us the best sense of the emotional and intellectual struggle that Anne suffers in coming to terms with the meaning of Wentworth's action.

The narrative technique in this passage is one which simulates Anne's process of thought while presenting her thoughts in the narrator's words. Consequently, Austen is able to give us an inside view of Anne's struggle to regain her composure and come to terms with Wentworth's action without making her seem like a self-centered egotist.

In the main clause of the original, we see that Anne's first thoughts are directed outwards; unlike the paraphrase, its focus is on Wentworth, not on Anne herself. It is a sign of her characteristic unselfishness; she is not immediately concerned with herself, but rather with the fact that Wentworth has acted in a certain way. Furthermore, all the responsibility for the action is given to him: "he had done it." The shift to the past perfect in combination with "yes" reinforces our sense that Anne is "coming to," and is only now getting her bearings. The action is complete, and now she can interpret it. Finally the monosyllables, the brevity, and the simple structure of the clause give us the sense that what Anne faces as she comes to is an important but basic fact—"he had done it." Having reminded herself of this, she can reflect on what it entails.

Sentence 2: "She was in the carriage, and felt that he had placed her there, that his will and his hands had done it, that she owed it to his perception of her fatigue, and his resolution to give her rest."

Paraphrase: He had done it, she felt, because he saw that she was tired, and wanted to let her rest.

In this sentence, we begin to see Anne interpret Wentworth's action. Because we understand from the first sentence that we are seeing Anne's processes of thought (though those thoughts are presented in the narrator's language), we respond to the first clause, "She was in the carriage," not only as a description of Anne's physical location but also as her discovery of that location. It is another small step in her coming to. At the same time, the way Austen structures the rest of the sentence makes us see that Anne is still agitated; the parallel structure of the three "that" clauses and the fact that they are separated only by commas, not by a connective like "and," create the sense that she is feeling all those things at once. The first "that" clause, "that he had placed her there," not only reemphasizes Wentworth's responsibility for the action, but indicates how much he had done. He did not merely "lead" Anne to the carriage or as in sentence 1 of the paraphrase "hand" her into it, but moved her from one place to another; it is almost as if Anne did not move under her own power at all. This theme of Wentworth's total responsibility for the action is continued in the next clause, "that his will and his hands had done it." In a sense, this clause is Anne's correction, her improvement of sentence 1. Getting her bearings, she can more accurately specify how he had done it. She understands—and makes clear for us—that Wentworth's kindness is neither a mechanical gesture of politeness nor simply a good intention that never got carried out. Instead she sees that he has made a special effort: though he has not been walking with her, and though Admiral Croft is about to drive away, Wentworth not only would like to see Anne accept the ride, he joins action to intention and personally makes sure that she does.

The final clause elaborates on Wentworth's kindness, and assigns him a motive: "she owed it to his perception of her fatigue and his resolution to give her rest." Because this clause is placed last it receives the most emphasis; consequently, we see that Wentworth's motivation is more important forAnne than the action itself. The particular language of the clause emphasizes the dual aspect of his kindness, the sense in which it shows his special effort. Unlike his previous overt act of kindness to Anne— removing the youngest Musgrove child from her neck—this one is not in response to a situation where she is *obviously* in need of some relief. In this case, he notices on his own ("she owed it to his perception"), and is prompted to do something ("his resolution to give her rest"). The language of the final phrase gives Wentworth even more credit. "Resolution" suggests his firm and decisive action; secure in the accuracy of his perception, he does not allow Admiral Croft to drive off without a third passenger, and he does not allow Anne to deny her fatigue. Finally, his kindness is to "give her rest"—not merely to let her rest, or make relief available to her, but positively to relieve her fatigue with the gift of rest.

For the most part, what is lost in the paraphrase are subtle effects, nuances in Anne's interpretation of Wentworth's action. The only absolute differences between the two versions are ones of degree: in the paraphrase, we see that Wentworth is responsible for the action ("*he* had done it . . . because *he* saw . . . *he* wanted"), and that he both notices Anne's fatigue and does something about it. But with the plain diction and more simple syntax of the paraphrase we do not fully appreciate the special qualities of Wentworth's action or how well Anne herself understands them. These differences are not insignificant.

It is important for us to have all the subtle effects that emphasize Wentworth's genuine kindness here because now that he is "marked out" for Louisa Musgrove, we need an assurance that he is far better than we have seen him to be; we need to be reassured that he is worthy of Anne's high estimation of him. Furthermore, once we are reassured that he deserves that estimation, we are also assured that he and Anne will be reunited. Any man who possesses the acute perception and genuinely unselfish nature that we have seen here can neither be satisfied with a Louisa Musgrove nor long blind to the virtues of an Anne Elliot. It is also desirable for us to see that Anne appreciates his kindness as she does because such a realization reconfirms our sense of her own unselfish perception. Although in doing justice to Wentworth, Anne must also increase her own sense of loss, Austen's representation of this scene positively contributes to the success of the book. The more Anne appreciates Wentworth's action, the more *she* will suffer, but the more *we* shall see that their two minds are meant for each other. Furthermore, our understanding of and participation in Anne's noble suffering during this scene will increase our satisfaction in her deserved final happiness.[33] In this connection, we can see why it is desirable for us to sense Anne's agitation and her gradual mastery of it; we more fully understand what Wentworth means to her, and can more fully appreciate her present struggle to come to terms with his action.

Sentence 3: "She was very much affected by the view of his disposition towards her which all these things made apparent."

Paraphrase: Anne was very affected by what these things showed about how he felt towards her.

Sentence 3 marks a transition in the passage; Austen (and Anne) move from reflections on Wentworth's particular action to its broader meaning. The sentence also serves as a kind of topic sentence for the rest of the passage. It is a general statement ("she was very much affected") that will be elaborated on in each of the remaining sentences. Perhaps the most obvious feature of the sentence is its formality—an effect created by the abstract diction and complicated syntax especially in the double nominalization "view of his disposition." The first effect of this formality is that we lose the sense of Anne's agitation and feel instead that she has now mastered her emotions and is trying to understand the implications of Wentworth's kindness. The effect of *"view* of his disposition," rather than just "his disposition," is to mark off everything that follows in the passage as *Anne's* rather than the narrator's view. This small effect, which is absent from the more direct paraphrase ("she was affected by what these things showed"), has two important consequences: first, the narrator is not committed to any of Anne's conclusions—we do not feel that because we read "He could not forgive her," and then see that he does indeed do just that, we have been lied to, but rather that we have seen a movement from a point where Anne felt convinced that she could not be forgiven to one where she (quite rightly) feels that she could not be happier. Second, seeing everything in the passage as Anne's view makes us appreciate her honesty with herself and the admirable nature of her struggle to understand properly what Wentworth's action means about "his disposition towards her." We shall be returning to this point in the analysis of the remaining sentences, but even here we can see it. Austen's language suggests that Anne's view of Wentworth's disposition is based not on her own feelings or desires, but purely on the evidence at hand: on what "all these things [the various aspects of Wentworth's action] made apparent." The implication of this phrase is that Anne has no choice but to adopt the view she does.

Sentence 4: "This little circumstance seemed the completion of all that had gone before."

Paraphrase: What he did here seemed to complete everything he had done before.

In this sentence, we see Anne start to formulate her view of Wentworth's disposition by placing this action in the context of his previous actions. We see that although Anne has fully appreciated what he has done for her, she nevertheless does not overestimate its importance; Wentworth's kindness ("all these things" of sentence 3) is now "this little circumstance." Anne is intelligent and honest enough to realize that in spite of how deeply she is affected by what Wentworth has done, his handing her into the carriage must for him be "a little circumstance."

Because Anne thinks that "the completion of all that had gone before" is only "this little circumstance," we see that she does not regard that completion as especially joyful or major, but rather as a small though not insignificant step in their relationship. Because there are no agents for any of the actions, neither for the "completion" nor for "all that had gone before," we see that Anne is neither placing blame nor bestowing praise on herself or Wentworth. This is a desirable effect here for two reasons: first, to ascribe, as the paraphrase does, the responsibility to Wentworth suggests that there might be a conscious design on his part; he set about to do something and now he seemed to complete it—and such a suggestion detracts from our understanding of his act as one of spontaneous kindness. Second, Anne's thought "all that had gone before" is more encompassing than our paraphrase, "everything he had done before." It can refer not only to his actions, but to the whole history of their relationship, including her most important action—the refusal of his marriage proposal. Once we realize this we can see that the phrase has an understated quality; Anne does not become effusive thinking about "all that had gone before," but that general description suggests what she means. At one and the same time, then, she admits the importance of the "little circumstance" without letting herself be overcome by that importance.

Sentences 5 and 6: "She understood him. He could not forgive her—but he could not be unfeeling."

Paraphrase: He was understood by her, she was an object of some feeling for him—but she was not to be forgiven.

Sentence 4 states the consequence of Anne's viewing Wentworth's action as the completion of what had gone before. Having seen the whole, she can now understand his part in it. This particular expression of her conclusion has considerable rhetorical force because in this context of abstract diction and somewhat complicated syntax, it is remarkably simple and direct. We cannot fail to see the importance of Anne's conclusion. At the same time, the simplicity and directness of the statement indicate that Anne does not let herself be overcome by her emotions at reaching this understanding; instead, we get the sense that she accepts it. Finally, it is important that she and not Wentworth is the focus of the sentence. The paraphrase, "He was understood by her," directs our attention to the wrong person, makes Wentworth prominent in a place where all our interest is rightly centered on Anne: we need to see *her* thinking here, need to see her coming to terms with Wentworth's action in order to appreciate both her present complex emotions and her final happiness.

Sentence 5 tells us what Anne understood about Wentworth. Again, Austen's language is simple and direct; especially in the first clause where Anne tells herself the most unpleasant "truth" —"He could not forgive her." Because we see her face this conclusion so squarely, we can both admire her and understand the pain it must cause.

The second clause, the more positive side of her understanding, is somewhat less specific. "Could not be unfeeling" does not identify a definite emotion, but only indicates that Wentworth is more than indifferent toward her. It is like Anne to be blunt in expressing the unpleasant, and more cautious in expressing the pleasant. Yet Austen's representation of Anne's thought emphasizes the pleasant aspect of it. The order of the clauses is reversed in the paraphrase and the effect is quite different. To close the sentence with the unpleasant indicates that the pleasant can never be returned to; to close it with the pleasant indicates that there is hope for the future. In this sense, then, the narration tells us more than the specifics of Anne's thought; on balance those thoughts are more negative than positive but we interpret them as more positive than negative—we see them as another sign that Anne and Wentworth will be reunited.

The language of the first clause ("could not forgive") takes any explicit blame from Wentworth; it is not that he would not forgive her; he was unable to. In the second clause, the "could not" construction works in a different way; Wentworth's inability to be unfeeling seems to be all to his credit. His noble nature will not allow him to be unconcerned about Anne.

Finally, the particular grammar of this sentence presents us with an interesting example of the relation between an individual sentence and the whole passage. The grammatical focus of the sentence is "he," Wentworth, but the real focus, the one which the whole passage, reinforced in this case by sentence 5, makes us see is "Anne." We read "He could not forgive her—but he could not be unfeeling" and understand "Anne felt that he could not forgive her—but could not be unfeeling." The particular grammar is important because it makes us see that Anne's thoughts are directed outward toward Wentworth and his actions. In the paraphrase we see these thoughts centered on herself, and feel that she is adopting an uncharacteristically egotistical way of looking at the situation. By keeping her thoughts directed outward toward Wentworth Austen emphasizes the sense of Anne's remarkable honesty.

Sentence 7: "Though condemning her for the past, and considering it with high and unjust resentment, though perfectly careless of her, and though becoming attached to another, still he could not see her suffer, without the desire of giving her relief."

Paraphrase: He condemned her for the past and resented it highly and unjustly, he was perfectly careless of her and was becoming attached to another, but still she could not be seen suffering by him without his wanting to relieve that suffering.

Sentence 7 expands upon the direct statements of sentence 6 as it applies them to the present situation. We again see Anne's ability to be brutally honest with herself as she catalogues all the evidence against her. It is a kind of systematic catalogue in which she treats things in chronological order (initial condemnation for the past, ensuing resentment, present indifference, recent attachment to another), and the language of these "though" clauses is very strong—"condemning," "high...resentment," "perfectly careless." It is because of the strong language that the original is superior to the paraphrase. By beginning with "though," Austen immediately qualifies all this language; we know that in spite of all this, there will be something positive stated. In the paraphrase, on the other hand, the strong, negative language is completely unqualified, and each of the independent clauses builds on the case against Anne so that the positive final clause seems a very small compensation for all the unpleasantness. Wentworth's action seems rather insignificant in the face of all the negative things he feels about Anne.

In the original, however, the effect is somewhat different. Because we see that the strong language is qualified from the start, we are able to respond to the positive information of the main clause as a genuine consolation for Anne. We do not, of course, ignore the strong language; in fact because we see that Anne herself realizes all these reasons for the distance between herself and Wentworth, we understand just how noble and unselfish she perceives his action to be.

The description in the main clause emphasizes the generosity of Wentworth's nature. The absolute language—"he *could not* see her suffer *without*"—makes it emphatically clear that this spontaneous kindness is part of his nature; the implication is that if he could see her suffer and not desire to give her relief, he would not be Frederick Wentworth. Furthermore, the description of the original appropriately emphasizes Wentworth's feelings rather than his actions. It is "his disposition towards her" that we and Anne care about; the particular actions Wentworth would take when seeing her suffer are important only because of what they reveal about his feelings. The description of his feelings, "the desire of giving her relief" indicates how strong they are: he does not want merely to "help" or "assist" her, he wants to bestow upon her what she needs most.

Sentence 8: "It was a remainder of former sentiment; it was an impulse of pure, though unacknowledged friendship; it was a proof of his own warm and amiable heart, which she could not contemplate without emotions so compounded of pleasure and pain that she knew not which prevailed."

Paraphrase: It showed that he still had some of his former feeling; it was motivated by his present feeling, though he had not previously acknowledged it, that they were friends; it proved that he was warm and amiable, a proof on which she could reflect only with such a combination of pleasurable and painful emotions that it was impossible for her to tell which were greater.

This sentence presents Anne's final conclusion about Wentworth's action. Continuing her consoling thought of the previous sentence, Anne thinks of the action in positive terms: "a remainder of former sentiment"; "an impulse of pure, though unacknowledged friendship." The abstract language of the original represents Wentworth's action as arising completely out of his feelings; it is not so much that *he* put Anne in the carriage but that "sentiment" and "friendship" did. In the concrete expression of the paraphrase, we clearly see how Wentworth felt, but these feelings are not given the same prominence. Again the difference between the original and the paraphrase is a subtle one; the original is preferable because we are most concerned with what Wentworth's act reveals about his feelings toward Anne.

Here, too, Anne remains scrupulously honest with herself. She does not fail to note the negative aspects of her situation: Wentworth's sentiment is "former" and his friendship "unacknowledged." Although we can see hope for Anne in these conclusions, she does not try to fool herself.

The final "it was" clause is the most unequivocally positive of the three because it focuses solely on Wentworth's character—"it was proof of his own warm and amiable heart." We have seen that Anne has already thought of Wentworth's kindness as a physical and a mental action ("his hands and his will had done it"); it is appropriate that now when she is most concerned with feelings, she thinks of his heart. The language of praise is strong, especially when we think of how much it must mean for Wentworth to be "warm and amiable" after having seen in sentence 7 the catalogue of reasons why he should be "cold and inimical."

Although the language of the last "it was" clause is unequivocal, the consequences it has for Anne are not: "she could not contemplate [this proof of his warm and amiable heart] without emotions so compounded of pleasure and pain that she knew not which prevailed." Anne, of course, is both pleased that Wentworth has given her this proof of his admirable heart, and saddened by the realization of what she has lost. Austen's language emphasizes the complexity of Anne's emotion. Again she employs the "could not . . . without" construction to indicate the inescapability of the condition she describes. She uses "pleasure and pain" in their nominal rather than adjectival forms, and in combination with "emotions so compounded" we see them as separate and distinct elements that constitute her emotions. Finally, Austen emphasizes both this bittersweet quality and the intensity of Anne's emotion by ending her sentence with "she knew not which prevailed." Because Anne "knows not," we see how strong and confused these emotions are: they are controlling her rather than vice versa; furthermore, unlike the paraphrase's "were greater," the final phrase of the original, "which prevailed," suggests that pleasure and pain are warring within her, fighting for dominance. Because Austen's language enables us to understand and participate in Anne's struggle here, we are better able to understand and participate in her final happiness.

Our analysis of this passage, then, suggests that the style of *Persuasion* is a significant but not all-important element of its success. By paraphrasing the passage, we lose some important aspects of our understanding of Wentworth's character and Anne's struggle, but we do not lose everything. What we lose, for the most part, are subtle effects, nuances of meaning that are not totally responsible for the success of the novel but that cumulatively increase our pleasure in it. For example, from reading the paraphrase our estimation of Wentworth's character is not nearly as high as it is from reading the original because the nuances of Anne's appreciation of his act—as mental, as physical, as emotional, as done in spite of very serious objections to her—are gone. Yet from reading the paraphrase we do estimate his character more highly than we did before; the X quality of the sentences representing Anne's thoughts and feelings about Wentworth's act is itself an important determinant of our response.

If this passage is a representative one, then *Persuasion* exemplifies a third possible role for style in fiction. Unlike *The Ambassadors* where the style of James's representation of Strether's thoughts about and responses to the events is absolutely crucial for the novel's success, and unlike *Sister Carrie* where the style of Dreiser's representation of Carrie's progress in society matters little, *Persuasion* is a novel in which both the linguistic and non-linguistic elements are extremely important. And without doing another detailed analysis, we can see at least partial proof that the passage we have analyzed is representative. The immediate incident that leads to the reunion of Anne and Wentworth is Anne's speech to Captain Harville on the superior constancy of women. It is absolutely necessary for Anne to be given this chance to convince Wentworth (although she does not know he is listening), so that she will seem to be the master of her own fate rather than a helpless woman who is rescued by the noble Wentworth. (It is, of course, for this reason that Austen changed the original ending.) Regardless of the language in which Anne makes her speech, she must be given this chance. The action itself is crucial. Then, in order for us to be moved by the speech and in order for us to find it plausible that Wentworth is moved to propose, the language of the speech itself must be carefully crafted. Austen, of course, is equal to the task; without denying the virtues of her fellow creatures, and without claiming any special privilege, Anne convinces us and Wentworth of how deeply she believes in the constancy of women, and how fully she knows what it is like to love constantly even when "hope is gone."

Similar requirements hold for the reunion scene. The book builds to that scene, and it will have a great emotional effect almost regardless of the language Austen uses to represent it. At the same time, however, if the book is to be a complete success, she must use language to make us feel that Anne and Wentworth are more happy now than they could have been eight years before. Austen does so by stressing at every point the maturity and richness of their love; her style approaches what Lodge calls "realization," as the balance and rhythm of her sentences seem to correspond to the deep satisfaction they describe, e.g., Anne and Wentworth are now "more tender, more tried, more fixed in a knowledge of each other's character, truth, and attachment; more equal to act, more justified in acting" (pp. 240–41).

VI

In the last three chapters, we have developed a hypothesis about the way we understand literary texts, have used the hypothesis to gain insight into one element—style—of our understanding in novels, and in so doing have seen substantial evidence for our initial hypothesis that language is a subordinate element in the construction of successful fiction. We have seen three distinct roles for the particular language of a novel, yet the three roles are alike in being subordinate ones. The two main parts of our investigation in these chapters—the inquiry into the way we understand texts, the inquiry into the effects of language in specific novels—unite in our theory of fiction: though fictional worlds emerge from words, and though sometimes the particular words an author chooses are extremely important for creating a fictional world effectively, those worlds finally are not worlds of words, but worlds of characters, actions, emotions, and thoughts. The investigation to this point, though concerned with questions raised by both inquiries, has progressed more from the questions about and challenges to our hypothesis about the way we understand texts. In the next two chapters, we shall switch the emphasis and concentrate more on testing our hypothesis about the subordinate role of language in fiction. But before initiating that challenge, we ought to explore the explanatory power of our hypothesis a bit further; specifically, we need to consider—and at least clarify—what our conclusions about language in *The Ambassadors, Sister Carrie,* and *Persuasion* imply about our judgment of artistic success in the novel and about our understanding of language in other novels.

Although we have taken it for granted that the novels we have analyzed are successful, our findings may perhaps be construed as implying a connection between the role of style and the *degree* of success. If, for example, we modified our description of Dreiser's achievement in *Sister Carrie* only slightly and said that its success results from his skills as novelist rather than as stylist, we might seem to suggest that Dreiser is an inferior artist to James and Austen (and hence creates inferior works): he lacks skills that they possess. That conclusion we may ultimately want to accept, but it is not supported by our analysis of the three novels. It is not supported because our analysis proceeds from assumptions about success which are quite different from those that lead to the judgment of Dreiser as inferior. Someone who makes that judgment on the basis of style implicitly or explicitly divides artistic skill into various component skills and determines artistic success according to degrees of excellence with each component. We, on the contrary, assume that artistic success can more accurately be judged by considering the specific work in itself than by applying such an a priori standard to it. As a result, we try to discover artistic intentions in specific works and then determine the extent to which specific skills are required for achieving those intentions. Obviously, if the features we normally associate with a good style are not required to achieve a particular intention, their lack is actually no lack at all, and thus is no basis for judging the author of that work as inferior to other novelists.

We could make the connection between "mediocre" style and impaired success only if the kinds of intentions an author can achieve without superior stylistic talents are themselves inferior to those that can be achieved with those talents. I doubt anyone would agree with this proposition as it stands, and even amending it to say only that the two or three most worthwhile intentions are beyond the capacities of the poor or indifferent stylist will not win immediate assent from all. In order to establish that the poor stylist is ultimately the inferior artist, one would first have to establish criteria for determining the relative worth of various intentions. And there is no obvious reason why these criteria should favor intentions that depend upon some artistic skills rather than others. James, Dreiser, and Austen have quite different intentions, and each achieves his or her intention successfully, though Dreiser's sloppiness—but not his lack of grace—slightly mars *Sister Carrie*. If we want to make further evaluative discriminations, we must consider issues other than the roles of their respective styles.

Turning to the connection between our specific analyses of *The Ambassadors, Sister Carrie,* and *Persuasion* and our conclusions about language in other novels, we need first to clarify the way in which our novels are intended to stand for others. They do not exhaust the possible roles that language can play in fiction but rather represent the range of those roles: extremely important, important but not crucial, unimportant. In an investigation of, say, the role of language in *Tristram Shandy,* our hypothesis will predict not that its role will be identical to the role of language in one of our three novels, but that its role will not be substantially more important than in *The Ambassadors,* or, needless to say about Sterne's novel, substantially less important than in *Sister Carrie*. In other words, our hypothesis does not rule out but includes the possibility that language in a novel such as *Tristram*

Shandy could be more important than in *Persuasion* but less important than in *The Ambassadors,* or that, analogously, in a novel such as *Tess of the D'Urbervilles* it could be less important than in *Persuasion* but more important than in *Sister Carrie.* Thus, at this point, the appropriate schema for picturing the various roles of language in fiction is not three distinct cells but a continuum with *Sister Carrie* at one end, *The Ambassadors* at the other, and *Persuasion* somewhere in the middle.

The continuum, however, is an imperfect model at best and in some respects is even a misleading one. First, novels obviously would not fall into regularly spaced intervals along any line we might construct, but would bunch up at some points and not correspond to others. Furthermore, as we have seen as early as our discussion of *The Heart of Midlothian* in chapter 2 but can perhaps now appreciate more fully, the role of language is not always uniform within a novel. The importance of language will fluctuate with the role individual parts play in contributing to the intention of the whole. Not only can a Dreiser be clumsy throughout his work, or a Scott be sloppy for a greater part of it and enormously careful toward the end, but a Dickens or an Eliot can suffer lapses of carelessness or awkwardness without impairing the success of the whole. He or she can, that is, if the function of those awkward or careless parts can be adequately rendered by the X quality of its sentences rather than by the precise refinements that would accompany a certain paraphrase.

Finally, the continuum model is less than fully satisfactory because it might lead us to seek quantifiable results in our investigations. We have said that *Persuasion* is "somewhere in the middle" of the continuum, and that the role of its language is "important but not crucial." These descriptions, of course, lack precision, and if we become committed to the continuum model, we shall certainly want to refine them. Somewhat more precision—the kind we could obtain by testing our hypotheses about language in *Tristram Shandy* and *Tess of the D'Urbervilles*—is both possible and desirable, but a precision that would allow us confidently to place novels at more than a half-dozen or so places on our scale is neither possible nor desirable. How can we tell—and why would we want to—that in *Persuasion* language has an exactly equal importance with the other elements of construction and so belongs precisely at the midpoint of our continuum? Although we find it helpful to talk about the elements of fiction as if they were separate ingredients, although considering them separately can substantially increase our understanding of individual works, these works finally cannot be reduced to recipes consisting of so many parts style, so many parts character, so many action, and so on. The worlds created in fiction take on a life of their own, a life whose specific dependence on the individual elements of construction can no more be precisely quantified than an individual human's dependence on his organs, bones, and muscles. Just as we can understand the importance of, say, the heart in the functioning of the body, but are not able—and do not try—to say how much of the soul or spirit is in the heart, so too can we understand the importance of language in the functioning of a novel but are not able—and ought not try—to quantify precisely the role of language in creating the living world of a novel.

In the next two chapters we shall, in a sense, test the adequacy of the continuum model further by examining the idea that *The Ambassadors* roughly corresponds to one endpoint. But this challenge is more than a concern with the pictorial model, it is a challenge to one of the principles of our theory. By insisting that language never becomes all-important in fiction, are we proposing a theory that is too narrow? Does our hypothesis fail to apply to certain kinds of novels? We shall pose these questions by examining the specific examples of *Lolita* and *Willie Masters' Lonesome Wife*. And in order to understand both whatever modifications we need to make in our theory and where it stands in relation to others, we shall consider its relation first to Elder Olson's language-cannot-be-all position and then to Umberto Eco's semiotic approach to aesthetic texts, which offers a powerful alternative explanation of Gass's work.

2

Limits of the Theory

5 Verbal Artistry and Speech as Action: Elder Olson and the Language of *Lolita*

I

Our conclusion that language cannot be all-important in fiction is not incompatible with the theory about the relation between language and literature espoused by neo-Aristotelian critics such as R. S. Crane and Elder Olson. At this point in our investigation, it seems not only fair but necessary to examine their theory's connection with ours, and then to test the theory that emerges as rigorously as we have tested the language-is-all theories. Such scrutiny is necessary, first, because it will help clarify the contribution to critical theory this study is attempting to make: it will show whether our question about the role of language in fiction can be answered by extending neo-Aristotelian theory into an area where it has not often been applied before, whether our question requires a different, essentially new theory about the relation between language and literature, or whether no one theory will provide us with a full answer.

More importantly, a scrutiny of the language-cannot-be-all position is necessary because there are some authors—in addition to Nabokov and Gass, Virginia Woolf and James Joyce come immediately to mind—whose verbal artistry is so great that we must at least consider the hypothesis that the value of their novels derives almost exclusively from their language. That is, we must consider two possibilities: (1) whether the language of a novel such as *Lolita* or *Willie Masters' Lonesome Wife* is important not because it contributes to the author's achievement of a particular intention (or in neo-Aristotelian terms, a final end or power), but because it gives us pleasure in itself, a pleasure which constitutes one of the chief virtues of the novel; (2) whether in a novel such as *Lolita* or *Willie Masters' Lonesome Wife* the main intention of the work is to afford us this special kind of pleasure in language.

I choose to raise these questions in connection with *Lolita* first, because in many ways its style is more problematic than that of *Willie Masters' Lonesome Wife*. One of the problems pointed to by *Lolita*'s critical history is precisely whether Nabokov's language is subordinate to other interests in the novel or vice versa. With Gass's work, there is no doubt that he is *attempting* to create a world of words. The questions there are about his success, about whether his work is truly fiction, and about how we can properly analyze the linguistic effects he creates. We shall be better able to understand Gass's experiment after examining *Lolita*, which, though radically experimental in its own way, is from our point of view more closely related to the other novels we have analyzed so far.

What are the consequences of telling the story of the horrors inflicted by a man of thirty-seven upon a girl of twelve in a style that is playful, charming, and at times beautiful? Does the style, as some critics have suggested, "attest to a comic vision" that overrides the horror of Humbert's crimes?[1] Or does Humbert's passion for nymphets in general and Lolita in particular exist, as another critic has suggested, merely as "the vehicle that can give the greatest latitude to Nabokov's romance with language"?[2] How is the curious juxtaposition of verbal virtuosity and morally reprehensible action related to Humbert's claim that his memoir is designed to give Lolita the immortality of art? We shall return to these questions after examining the place of language in the neo-Aristotelian theory of literature.

II

At the heart of this theory are two basic assumptions: (1) that literature is not a special kind of language but rather an art form which uses language to represent characters, action, and thought, and (2) that these representations are designed to affect our emotions and intellects in certain complex but finally determinate ways. Neo-Aristotelian theorists assume that the different emotional and intellectual effects which literary works produce in us correspond to the different formal ends of those works. One of the main objects of their criticism, then, is to determine how the distinct parts of the work contribute to the single formal end or power, or in other words, how the parts combine to produce in us the single, though complex, effect. In doing this criticism, they are investigating the nature of the literary work as a made object, a concrete whole that is both ordered and complete.

Language, in their theory, is one of the elements of a work that contributes to its formal end, but it is always the least important. For them language is only a necessary condition for literature. Elder Olson, the neo-Aristotelian theorist who has most fully addressed this question, puts it this way:

> [The words of a poem] are governed by everything else in the poem. We are in fact far less moved by the words as mere words than we think; we think ourselves moved mainly by them because they are the only visible or audible part of the poem. As soon as we grasp the grammatical meaning of an expression in a mimetic poem, we begin drawing inferences which we scarcely recognize as inferences, because they are just such as we habitually make in life; inferences from the speech as to the character, his situation, his thought, his passion, suddenly set the speaker vividly before us and arouse our emotions in sympathy or antipathy; our humanity is engaged and it is engaged by humanity.[3]

Olson's remarks contain two ideas that are crucial to our understanding of the role of language in neo-Aristotelian theory: (1) that the language is governed by everything else in the work and (2) that there is an important distinction between the grammatical meaning of an expression and the inferences we can draw from it.

In order to see why Olson says that the language of a work is governed by everything else we need to see what "everything else" is. The neo-Aristotelian identifies four main elements of a work: (1) the objects imitated (characters, actions, and thoughts, including the inferences we make about them); (2) the manner of imitation (narration, dialogue, etc.), which also includes the order of imitation (the point in the work at which things are revealed to us); (3) the style, the particular diction and syntax; and (4) the final end or power of the work as a whole. The efficacy of any one of the first three elements is determined by how well it contributes to the final end.

In analyzing a given scene, let us say the final one of *The Ambassadors,* the neo-Aristotelian might reach conclusions such as these: the objects imitated include not only Strether's refusal of Maria's proposal but also the inferences we can draw from it, given everything else we have experienced in reading the book.

We can see that Strether's refusal is an act which signifies the extent of his moral and intellectual growth, the development of his sharp eye for what is right, and the strength to follow its vision regardless of the personal consequences. The refusal is, in fact, the culmination of his growth and a reassurance that his mature moral vision is turned not just on Chad and Madame de Vionnet, but on himself as well, indeed on his whole life. The scene is rendered in dialogue because that technique allows James to give us an external confirmation of Strether's growth by showing that Maria herself acknowledges that Strether is doing the right thing. The scene is placed last precisely because it is the culmination of Strether's growth, the case where his vision of what is right is most acute. At the same time, because the scene is placed last, we recognize that Strether's experience in Paris has ended in the achievement of this acute moral vision, are immeasurably pleased by this victory, and we do not worry about what will happen to him when he returns to Woollett.

The language must represent Strether's refusal (it is a necessary condition for the scene to exist), but the particular stylistic choices will not be primarily responsible for the inferences we make about that refusal (our knowledge of the rest of the book will). The particular stylistic choices may cause us to make some refinements in our understanding of Strether's situation, but these refinements should never be mistaken for the more important causes of our emotion. The language, in short, is governed by the objects imitated and the manner of representation and is relatively unimportant in itself. This account of the role of style in the final scene, you will remember, is quite different from the one offered in chapter 2.

Because our overall interpretations are the same, this discrepancy about the importance of style may appear to be simply a result of a difference in procedure. Because the neo-Aristotelian critic starts his analysis with the objects imitated and concludes with style, and because we consider them more or less at the same time, he may attribute some of the effects we claim are stylistic to the objects imitated or the manner of representation, and we may attribute effects he claims are nonlinguistic to the style. But this explanation only leads to another set of questions: How does each of us arrive at the underlying rationale for our procedures? Why does the neo-Aristotelian believe that style cannot be crucially important? In order to answer these questions, we need to examine the distinction Olson makes between the grammatical meaning of an expression and the inferences we draw from that meaning.

The distinction between the two corresponds to the distinction Olson makes between speech as meaningful and speech as action. "What the poetic character says in the mimetic poem is speech and has meaning; his saying it is action, an act of persuading, confessing, commanding, informing, torturing or what not. His diction may be accounted for in grammatical and lexicographical terms, not so his action."[4] In other words, speech as action is one of the objects imitated in the work; its essence is nonlinguistic.

Olson supports his argument that speech-as-action is always more important than speech-as-meaningful by citing some examples from Shakespeare: "[His] profoundest touches are a case in point. 'Pray you, undo this button' and 'the table's full' are profound not as meaningful verbal expressions but as actions permitting an extraordinary number of implications, in that they are revelatory of many aspects of character and situation."[5] Olson gives a partial analysis of the importance of the diction of "Pray you, undo this button," after first suggesting that from one point of view the causes of emotion at any point in a mimetic poem fall into four classes: (1) the preceding context, the action of the whole up to that point; (2) the particular speech-action, with all its implications; (3) the speech as diction; and (4) the speech as ornament. Lear's speech affects us

> (1) because the whole poem has up to this point excited certain emotions with respect to Lear and his fortunes and has left us in a certain frame of mind; (2) because the plea sets before us his utter helplessness, his anguished hope to save Cordelia, the bitter repentance implied in that plea and so on; (3) because the diction simply and starkly expresses that plea; and (4) because the ornament—in this case, the rhythm merely—affects us as well.[6]

Olson points out that of these four reasons, only the last two depend on speech as meaningful and they are obviously not nearly as important as the first two. He says that a translation "good enough to permit the operation of the first two would not be greatly inferior."[7] In other words, the particular language of the speech, its style, is important only because it is necessary to reveal the objects imitated; any other language which also revealed Lear's plea would do almost as well.

Olson's distinction between speech as meaningful and speech as action is similar to but not identical with our distinction between linguistic and nonlinguistic apsects of a speech event. Speech-as-action is one of the things we would consider as a nonlinguistic element; so is the precedent context and the present context. The nonlinguistic aspects of the speech event also include the speaker, his audience, his intention, his subject, the occasion, and so on. Speech-as-meaningful corresponds rather closely to what we would call the linguistic aspects of a speech event, i.e., those aspects of the speech that are subject to change in a paraphrase. The crucial difference between Olson's system and ours is that we are arguing that in some cases what he would call "refinements"[8] made by the speech-as-meaningful are absolutely crucial to the emotional effect of the speech. To use Olson's own example: of course the fact that Lear expresses this plea while mourning the death of Cordelia has a very significant impact on the way we respond to it; but part of our response, part of why we are so moved by the plea is what its diction and syntax allow us to understand.

If, for example, we paraphrase Lear's speech to read "I beseech you, extricate this clasp," his speech-as-action is still the same (he is still making the same plea), but clearly we will not be moved to the same degree. Once we lost the simplicity and starkness of Lear's plea, we lose much of our sense of his helplessness, his repentance, his anguished hope to save Cordelia, and so on. Any translation, any paraphrase which does not simply and starkly express Lear's plea will be markedly inferior to the original.

My argument about the last scene of *The Ambassadors* is that the particular language is even more important there. Paraphrase will alter not merely the degree of our understanding but its very nature. If we change just a few sentences—if Strether refuses Maria by saying "I cannot have you" and "you yourself don't want me to have you" instead of "I must go" and "That's the way that—if I must go—you yourself would be the first to want me. And I can't do anything else"—then he will seem to be not a man of mature moral vision but an insensitive boor who cruelly rejects his kindest friend. In one sense, what is important in this scene is not so much that Strether rejects Maria's offer but how he does it.

To summarize, we share with the neo-Aristotelians the assumption that the language of a text will be successful to the degree that it contributes to an intention, but we disagree about the ways it can be successful. We agree that the inferences we make about the characters and their situations are finally what is important, but we disagree about how we come to make those inferences. Olson says it is primarily a result of speech-as-action, one of the objects imitated; we say that only sometimes is this the case. In some situations only certain language will be capable of letting us draw the inferences that are necessary for an author to achieve his intention, for us to make the proper responses to the characters. In these cases, the language is "more important" than the objects imitated not in the sense that it is the *sine qua non* for the existence of the work, nor in the sense that it is finally what we care about, but in the sense that it is the crucial variable for the success of the work. The advantage I am claiming for our approach, then, is that it allows us a greater flexibility in dealing with the language of fiction, and to that extent it allows us potentially greater insight into the nature of successful novels.

In the neo-Aristotelian's own terms, what we have done is to argue that the elements of a work can vary in relative importance, but we have not cast any doubt upon the assumption that the individual elements are efficacious to the extent that they contribute to the final end. In fact, our discussion of the style of *The Ambassadors* depends both here and in chapter 2 completely on an (implicit or explicit) conception of its final end, i.e., that it was designed to represent Strether's internal growth. The more fundamental question of this chapter is that posed by *Lolita*: does the style of a successful novel ever become extremely important in itself, a significant source of our pleasure in the novel regardless of what it contributes to an intention or an end, or indeed, is it ever so skillfully employed that it becomes the center of our interest, and the pleasure it produces the main intention of the novel?

III

The very nature of our questions about *Lolita* indicates that specifying its intention is a difficult task. Even if we begin with the idea that it is more plausible to conceive of Nabokov's main intention as the representation of an action involving Humbert and Lolita rather than as the demonstration of his own verbal virtuosity, we are still faced with the problem of accounting for that virtuosity. Therefore, rather than beginning with a statement of the intention more specific than that the novel represents an action, I shall analyze our responses to one important scene that intuitively seems appropriate and effective, and then draw tentative conclusions from that analysis.

The final meeting between Humbert Humbert and Lolita, in which she refuses his entreaty to leave her husband and go away with him, is the high point of the book. Everything builds to what Humbert realizes during that meeting, and to our responses to those realizations. In that scene the worst that could happen to Humbert happens. He realizes more fully than ever before that he has broken Lolita's life; he realizes too that he loves her, in all her unnymphetlike commonness, more than anything else in the world; and finally, he realizes that he cannot do anything to make reparation for the awful crime he has committed against his love. The one act which he believes will relieve some of the burden he feels actually completes his doom. After killing Quilty, Humbert says, "Far from feeling any relief, a burden even weightier than the one I had hoped to get rid of was with me, upon me, over me."9

We react to Humbert's doom not with pleasure but with sympathetic pity. We know that Lolita is right to refuse to go away with him, yet we almost wish she would. We are moved when we see him drive away in tears. If this description of our response is correct, then we are led to a somewhat curious conclusion: the intention of the book is to move us to tragiclike emotions as we see the undeniably perverse Humbert move toward his doom. In order for this description to be correct, we need at least to see that Humbert is partly sympathetic and that he is proceeding toward a doom. If we can establish these minimum conditions, then we can try to show what language contributes to the intention, and *why* the book is moving.

Humbert's present tense interjections into his retrospective narration both contribute to our sense that he is moving toward a doom, and help to keep him at least partly sympathetic. Very early in the book Humbert makes remarks that suggest the regret and despair of one living in a doom, e.g., "Oh Lolita, had you

loved me thus!'' (p. 16). Humbert also often speaks of his fatal
lust and of a fate that toys with him; after one session of outdoor
lovemaking he becomes rather explicit about his later doom: ''I
was laughing happily, and the atrocious, unbelievable, unbear-
able, and I suspect eternal horror that I know now was still but a
dot of blackness in the blue of my bliss'' (p. 154). Although we are
never told the precise nature of Humbert's doom, his narration
makes it very clear that he is moving toward one.

The interjections that precede Humbert's worst crimes often
serve a dual purpose. For example, on the night that he and Lolita
become lovers, after Lolita is safely locked in room 342 of the
Enchanted Hunters hotel, Humbert says: ''Jurors! If my happiness could have talked, it would have filled that hotel with a
deafening roar. And my only regret today is that I did not quietly
deposit key '342' at the office, and leave the town, the country,
the continent, the hemisphere—indeed, the globe—that very
same night'' (p. 114). A little later, he says, ''I should have known
(by the signs made to me by something in Lolita—the real child
Lolita or some haggard angel behind her back) that nothing but
pain and horror would result from the expected rapture'' (p. 115).
Besides contributing to our awareness of Humbert's impending
doom, these interjections in which Humbert directly or indirectly
condemns himself help us to remain partially sympathetic to him
even while they emphasize the seriousness of his crimes. We
never approve of those crimes—indeed we abhor them more than
if Humbert remained silent—but his interjections do affect the
quality of our response to him. We know how much pleasure it
will give him to sleep with Lolita; consequently, when we see him
now regretting that he ever experienced that pleasure, we regard
him not as a monster but as a potentially sensitive human being.

Of course the interjections will have this effect only if Nabokov
has done other things to ensure that we can react to Humbert with
at least partial sympathy. In fact he carefully controls our response from the very beginning of the book. He shows that Humbert is, to some extent, an unwilling victim of his passion for
nymphets. He indicates that the passion itself results from a situation over which Humbert had almost no control: his abortive
love affair with Annabel Lee. Nabokov also shows that Humbert
makes numerous attempts to overcome his passion; he undergoes
psychiatric therapy, he tries to cultivate a ''normal'' life. Of
course, in the latter case, the passion itself distorts the attempt to

overcome it: Humbert marries Valeria largely because she resembles a child. This act, however, seems as much a sign of the force of his passion as it is that he is less than sincere in his attempt to conquer it. Humbert, after all, never once gives in to all his longings for nymphets until he meets Lolita.

Nabokov makes choices in his representation of the seduction scene which also help to maintain our partial sympathy for Humbert. It is crucial that Lolita seduces Humbert and not vice versa. In spite of his intense desire, Humbert resists forcing himself on the child; we are led to believe that if Lolita had not suggested that she and Humbert play the game Charlie Holmes taught her at camp, Humbert would have remained in his state of miserable longing. At the same time, however, the fact that Lolita takes the initiative does not exonerate Humbert. Her suggestion that they play Charlie's game is precisely what is needed to start Humbert on his irreversibly destructive course. After that point, Humbert can never go back to his plan of satisfying his desire without disturbing Lolita; and consequently, Lolita can never be just another American teenage girl. The chief reason why Humbert cannot be exonerated is that although Lolita takes the initiative, she is really rather naïve and innocent about sex. Humbert tells us that "she saw the stark act merely as part of a youngster's furtive world unknown to adults" (p. 123), that for her it was largely a mechanical activity, and that "she was not quite prepared for certain discrepancies between a kid's life and mine" (p. 123).[10] It is part of Humbert's crime that he turns Lolita's furtive game into a living nightmare. At the end of his account of their first cross country trip, Humbert makes another telling present tense remark:

> We had been everywhere. We had really seen nothing, and I catch myself thinking today that our long journey had only defiled with a sinuous trail of slime the lovely, trustful, dreamy enormous country that by then, in retrospect, was no more to us than a collection of dog-eared maps, ruined tour books, old tires, and her sobs in the night—every night, every night—the moment I feigned sleep. [p. 160]

While Nabokov takes care to keep Humbert partly sympathetic, he never lets us forget the seriousness of his offenses against Lolita.

Although our discussion so far indicates the description of

Nabokov's intention as the representation of Humbert's progression toward a tragiclike end is accurate, we have not yet demonstrated why Nabokov's achieving this intention would move us.
That is, it is not yet clear that Nabokov's representation of the
partly sympathetic but still perverted Humbert meeting his doom
provides us with an experience of any lasting significance. This
shortcoming is not surprising in light of the problem we are trying
to solve. The particular language Nabokov chooses may be so
important that we cannot see how the achievement of the intention moves us until we see what role the language plays in that
achievement. On the other hand, the achievement of the intention
as we have described it may only be a vehicle for Nabokov to
exhibit his marvelous style; in other words, that exhibition may
itself be the main intention of the novel. Nevertheless, by describing and providing evidence for a particular intention, we
have established a framework, however tentative, in which to
investigate the role of Nabokov's language. Let us begin with
what is often cited as one of the most beautiful passages in
Lolita.[11]

> [1]Lolita, light of my life, fire of my loins. [2]My sin, my soul.
> [3]Lo-lee-ta: the tip of the tongue taking a trip of three steps
> down the palate to tap, at three, on the teeth. [4]Lo. [5]Lee. [6]Ta.
>   [7]She was Lo, plain Lo, in the morning, standing four feet ten
> in one sock. [8]She was Lola in slacks. [9]She was Dolly in school.
> [10] She was Dolores on the dotted line. [11]But in my arms she was
> always Lolita. [p. 11]

It is worth restating here that we assume we can most fully
account for the effects of a passage by applying our knowledge of
the whole work to it, not just our knowledge up to the point where
the passage occurs. This is not to say that the effects are created
only after we have read the whole, but rather that we can better
understand why the author created those effects when he did. In
this case, for example, we can more fully understand the consequences of Humbert Humbert's making these statements at the
beginning of the book, if we draw on our knowledge of Humbert's
character as it is revealed in the book as a whole.

I doubt that anyone would argue that a paraphrase could re-
produce even most of the effects of the passage, but in order to
appreciate just how essential the particular language is, let us
briefly consider one.

Lolita, spirit of my existence, source of my passion. My error, my life. Lo-lee-ta: the tongue advancing down the roof of the mouth in three steps and finishing at the teeth. Lolita.

We called her Lo in the morning, as she stood, all four feet ten of her, in one sock. In slacks she was called Lola. At school her friends called her Dolly. Her legal name was Dolores. But she was always Lolita with me.

Besides making us grateful that Nabokov does not write like this, the paraphrase indicates that the beauty of the original derives from Nabokov's skill with all aspects of language. Our analysis must pay attention to the particular syntax of the passage, to its particular shades of semantic meaning, and to the sounds of the words, both individually and in combination.

In a sense, the whole passage grows out of the first word. Humbert reflects on "Lolita" first as a concept, then as a sound, and in both reflections he displays evidence of his complex feelings about her. It is revealing to notice that although the passage is filled with descriptions of Lolita, although her name appears in almost every sentence, the passage contributes very little to our understanding of her as a character. After reading this passage we could not predict how she would act in a given situation. What the passage does contribute to is our sense of Humbert's feelings about her and our awareness of the power of his language. The passage not only begins with the word "Lolita," but it ends with it and she is the focus throughout. At first glance, the passage seems to be a kind of celebration of the glories of her name, and by extension a celebration of her. But Humbert himself is in the passage, and the nature of his presence qualifies the way we understand the celebration.

Humbert begins with a series of metaphors describing Lolita's impact on his life. "Lolita, light of my life, fire of my loins. My sin, my soul." The power of the first sentence derives in part from its poetic quality—its alliteration and its rhythm—and in part from Humbert's development of the metaphor of "light"—"fire" of the second phrase seems to grow out of "light" of the first. Because the sentence builds to that second phrase, because it is the more original metaphor, and because "fire" itself suggests a greater intensity than "light," Humbert's expression of his physical passion receives the greater emphasis. At the same time, the very intensity of that metaphor, coupled with "my sin" of sentence 2, makes us understand that Humbert is describing not just the physical passion of any lover, but rather his lust.

The two sentences together, however, do not give greater emphasis to that lust than they do to a quite different attitude—love. Humbert's initial metaphor, "light of my life" makes us look upon Lolita as the best thing in his life, and his final description "my soul" makes us look upon her as his life itself, as that which is the essence of his existence. The style of the two sentences makes it clear that Humbert's lust is not stronger than his love, nor vice versa. In sentence 2, it is his feeling for Lolita as the moving force of his life ("my soul") that is emphasized. Furthermore, the syntax and the poetic qualities of the two sentences reinforce the equivalence relationship. All the phrases are in apposition to "Lolita" and to each other. Within each sentence, the phrases are not only parallel constructions they also have the same number of syllables, and those syllables, which share many of the same phonetic sounds, have the same stress patterns (long short short long in sentence 1, short long in 2). The result of all this careful patterning is not to obliterate the distinction between Humbert's love and Humbert's lust, but rather to make us see that they exist simultaneously in a kind of equal balance. There is no subordinate-superordinate relationship here; Lolita is not the fire of Humbert's loins because she is the light of his life, or vice versa. She is the fire of his loins in spite of the fact that she is the light of his life. Humbert expresses the basic contradiction of his relationship with Lolita in these first two sentences.

At the same time, these sentences make us see that Humbert is summing up virtually his entire being in terms of what Lolita means to him. In one sense, the series of Humbert's metaphors describes Lolita's effect on him metaphysically, physically, and spiritually. We understand that she is his all in all.

The third sentence begins Humbert's celebration of the sound of Lolita's name. The basic thought of the sentence is that pronouncing her name is a pleasure trip for the tongue; Humbert convinces us by the way he describes the act of pronunciation: "Lo-lee-ta: the tip of the tongue taking a trip of three steps down the palate to tap, at three, on the teeth." The poetic qualities of this sentence are perhaps even greater than those of the first two. The alliteration of t's, th's and p's, the internal rhyme of "tip" and "trip" with its variation in "tap," the use of "three" as an adjective and then a noun, plus the repetition of the double "e" sound in "teeth," make this sentence itself a special trip of the tongue. It is as if the act of describing one trip naturally produces the other. The sentence becomes evidence of Humbert's love for Lolita: he takes delight not only in the sound of her name, in pronouncing it himself, but also in describing how it is pronounced.

Humbert then offers us proof of what he has just said by presenting Lolita's name separated into each of its three distinct steps. "Lo. Lee. Ta." We imagine Humbert himself pronounce it, and we see him linger over it, savoring every syllable. It too is evidence of his love for Lolita.

The effects of the second paragraph, in which Humbert describes the different names Lolita had in different contexts, are equally impressive although their sources may not be quite as apparent. Everything builds to the enormously forceful last sentence, "But in my arms she was always Lolita," and its force depends in large part on how well it is prepared for. Each sentence introduces a particular variation of Lolita's name, and evokes a general image of the context in which she bore that name. The first sentence begins to establish the pattern of Humbert's description: "She was Lo, plain Lo, in the morning, standing four-feet ten in one sock." Humbert seems especially to enjoy this evocation of Lolita; he reiterates her name, and describes her most specifically here. We are reminded again of his love for her. At the same time, however, the particulars of the sentence emphasize Lolita's delicate nature, the fact that she is only a child; she has a child's name, she is less than five feet tall (it is, of course, characteristic that Humbert gives her height exactly), and she stands in only one sock. This last detail, especially in connection with Humbert's ambiguous remark that she was "plain Lo," and his next sentence which says that she was Lola "in slacks," makes her seem fragile and vulnerable. It suggests that the Lolita Humbert conjures up here is naked except for that one sock. This image of the naked child beheld by the lustful Humbert of the first two sentences reminds us of the destructive potential of his lust.

In the next three sentences, Humbert creates a kind of litany out of the recitation of Lolita's names. He develops a fairly simple, but rather strict pattern, a pattern which is a simplification of the first sentence of the paragraph. Each sentence has the same surface structure syntax: pronoun—verb to be—prepositional phrase. "She was Lola in slacks. She was Dolly at school. She was Dolores on the dotted line." The sentences are ordered by the progression of the sounds of Lolita's name—Lo, Lola, Dolly, Dolores—and by the progression of their formality. However, because of what happens in the last sentence, it is the progression of the prepositions that is most interesting.

The prepositions that Humbert uses—in, at, on—are fairly similar; they are all often used to denote a place. Despite their surface similarity, however, they are used in quite different ways. In the initial sentence of the paragraph Humbert uses "in" first to signify time ("in the morning"), then to signify not a place but a manner ("in one sock"). In the next sentence, he repeats this usage ("in slacks") as he begins to create his litany. In the third sentence, he shifts the pattern and uses "at" to signify place but that place is very generalized ("at school"). In the fourth sentence, he uses "on" ostensibly as another indication of place, but actually his use is metaphorical—Lolita herself is never "on the dotted line." Much of the force of the last sentence derives from Humbert's use of the prepositional phrase, which retains its surface similarity to the others, in a new and quite different way. Humbert returns to "in," and uses it to signify place in the most literal sense: "But in my arms she was always Lolita."

Part of the force of the sentence also derives from Humbert's inverting the order the main clause and the prepositional phrase have in the previous sentences. This inversion not only makes the sentence stand out, but it allows Humbert to emphasize the particular variation of his lover's name because it has final position in both the sentence and the paragraph. The name, of course, is "Lolita," and we are back where we began in the very first sentence.

We are back where we began not only with the utterance of Lolita's name, but also with Humbert's double attitude. His litany is beautiful, a song that expresses his love. But at the same time the very literalness of the final prepositional phrase, coupled with the earlier image of Lolita's childlike delicacy, makes us, if not shudder, at least be unsettled at the thought it expresses. Neither Humbert's love nor his lust is ever long absent from our awareness.

The style of this passage, then, is important, first because of the

inferences it allows us to make. Although Humbert never explicitly declares either his love or his lust for Lolita, we have a clear
conviction that he possesses both. It is absolutely essential that
we see Humbert's love for Lolita at the outset of the novel if he is
to remain sympathetic, because what we most clearly see in the
main body of the novel is his destructive lust. In general, it is
absolutely essential that we see both sides of Humbert's character if we are to be moved by his doom. As a minimum condition,
we need to see the potential for love in Humbert if we are to
believe his later insistence that he loves Lolita in spite of her lost
nymphethood. More importantly, we need to see that this love,
this other side of Humbert's perverted nature, is present at least in
potential form fairly early on in their relationship, if we are to feel
that anything valuable has been lost in Humbert's doom.
Although Humbert's remarks do not establish that he had this
double attitude from the very beginning they are important because they summarize his entire attitude toward her.

Humbert's statements here are not time-bound. They could
occur at any point in the novel. It is as if he were saying: "over all
the time I have known Lolita, this is what she was to me, both the
light of my life and the fire of my loins." Of course if Humbert's
double attitude is not conveyed at other points in the book, we
will not be moved by his doom; however, because we see this
double attitude right from the beginning, we have a framework
within which to respond to Humbert's other revelations about
himself.

The beauty of Nabokov's particular language does play a key
role in the establishment of Humbert's double attitude, especially
in his attitude of love. In particular, the art with which sentence 2
and the litany of Lolita's names are constructed contributes to
our understanding of the extraordinary kind of love Humbert is
capable of. In general, the lyrical force of the passage helps to
convince us of the sincerity and depth of Humbert's feeling for
Lolita. At the same time, however, I hesitate to say that the
purposes which the style serves are, in fact, sufficient to account
for its impact. Even after we see that Humbert's description of
the way Lolita's name is pronounced is a sign of his deep and
idiosyncratic love for her, we still do not account for all the pleasure of that sentence. It gives us the pleasure of watching a master craftsman display his artistry; Nabokov carefully blends the

sounds of individual words with particular meanings that suit his purpose and at the same time carefully controls the cadence of the whole. The sentence calls attention to itself and gives us pleasure as a virtuoso performance.

Let me try to put this point another way. Part of what Nabokov reveals in these first two paragraphs is frightful. However, our realization of this frightfulness does not alter our response to the beautiful style, and the style itself only slightly alters our response to that frightfulness. The lyrical beauty of Humbert's expression does, no doubt, make the frightful aspects of the passage more palatable. If Humbert expressed himself coarsely, we probably would not be able to read the book. (For an example of such an expression see my paraphrase of the next passage below.) And no doubt the beautiful style also creates some involuntary sympathy for Humbert just as the first person point of view does. But these functions of the style do not fully explain its power, do not fully account for the positive pleasure it offers; Nabokov would not have to be so magnificent if these were his only purposes.

Furthermore, these effects of the style do not obscure what is genuinely horrible about Humbert. As our analysis shows, the virtuoso style does not override our awareness of Humbert's lust and does not prevent us from judging him as morally deficient. At the same time, our perception of Humbert's lust does not make us recoil from the style; we do not feel that his sexual perversion contaminates what would otherwise be a beautiful style. Instead, we relish the manner of Humbert's self-revelation, even while we are repelled by what he reveals. In the presentation of the frightful side of Humbert's character, Nabokov, to some extent at least, separates linguistic form from linguistic function, and offers us distinct pleasures in both. In the passage as a whole, the virtuoso style remains extremely important for the success of the book and yet, in offering us so much pleasure in itself, it is not entirely subordinate to the achievement of an intention. At this point, then, *Lolita* is escaping the reach of our theory and thus may force us to modify our claims for the theory's comprehensiveness.

But based on only one passage, these conclusions must be tentative. Perhaps the best way of testing them is to examine a passage in which Humbert seems to be motivated purely by lust. In so doing, we can see both whether the style requires us to make inferences that are crucial for the achievement of the intention, and whether the pleasure of the style exists apart from our realization of the frightful aspects of Humbert's character. Let us consider an excerpt—one very long sentence—from the famous davenport scene.

> Her legs twitched a little as they lay across my live lap; I stroked them; there she lolled in the right hand corner almost asprawl, Lola the bobby-soxer, devouring her immemorial fruit, singing through its juice, losing her slipper, rubbing the heel of her slipperless foot in its sloppy anklet, against the pile of old magazines, heaped on my left on the sofa—and every movement she made, every shuffle and ripple, helped me to conceal and improve the secret system of tactile correspondence between beast and beauty—between my gagged bursting beast and the beauty of her dimpled body in its innocent cotton frock. [pp. 56–57]

In the first part of this sentence, Humbert ostensibly sets the scene—where Lolita was, where he was, what he did, what she did—but his particular descriptions reveal his attitude toward the action. He begins by describing the movement and position of Lolita's legs: "Her legs twitched a little as they lay across my live lap." What is perhaps most notable about this description is its relatively subdued quality. The alliteration, the internal rhyme of "they lay," and the suggestive phrase "live lap," all indicate that Humbert is quite delighted with this state of affairs, but given everything we have seen before, we expect more exuberance from him. This is even more true of the next clause—"I stroked them." Humbert has never taken this kind of license with a nymphet before, yet he now chooses to be matter-of-fact. Part of the reason for this surprising choice is dramatic. Humbert is building up to the description of his orgasm and he does not want to detract from its special qualities by giving too much attention to the steps along the way. We can better understand the particular reasons why he does not emphasize his delight at this point in this sentence as we look at the effects of the rest of it.

Humbert moves from this description of his action to a full description of Lolita. The description begins very generally: "there she lolled in the right hand corner." The verb "lolled" is a most appropriate pun, and it is reinforced by the name Humbert chooses for her here—"Lola." To be Lo is to loll, so to say there she lolled is to say there she was her quintessential self. Because Humbert expresses this idea in the pun, we understand that he takes considerable pleasure in the idea of Lo as Lo rather than Lo as sex object. Furthermore, because of the pun we look upon this description in a special way: he is capturing Lolita in a characteristic pose before she has lost her innocence.

Humbert brings his considerable linguistic resources to the task of capturing that image. "Almost asprawl" emphasizes the carelessness of Lolita's attitude, because of the alliteration of the *a*'s, and because its initial sound is echoed in its final one. "Lola the bobby-soxer" not only reinforces the pun on "lolled" in its sound but its generality also reinforces the idea that Humbert is describing a characteristic picture of Lolita. With these two phrases—"almost asprawl" and "Lola the bobby-soxer"— Humbert achieves Lodge's effect of "realization," i.e., he makes his sentence imitate the action it describes. He introduces a subject ("she"), then describes an action that the subject performs ("lolled"), and then returns to the subject to describe it once ("almost asprawl") and then again ("Lola the bobby-soxer"); the sentence itself lolls over its description of Lolita. This effect not only contributes to the impact of the image he is creating, but it is also a sign of the care with which he creates the whole description.

Humbert next gives us a series of participial phrases: "devouring her immemorial fruit, singing through its juice, losing her slipper, rubbing the heel of her slipperless foot in its sloppy anklet." Again the particular language emphasizes the carelessness of Lolita's action, her total ignorance and indifference about Humbert's purpose: the juxtaposition of "devouring" with its implication of ravenous hunger and "immemorial" with its connotations of tradition, antiquity, something sacred; the description of her singing as not merely "at the same time" but "through its juice," and the description of her slipper's disappearance as not a "kicking off" but a "losing," all emphasize that her actions are completely unselfconscious. Unlike Eve, who first ate the immemorial fruit, Lolita does not feel she is about to acquire great knowledge. She is simply Lola the bobby-soxer amusing herself with what's available on a Sunday morning.

Again the alliteration of the passage points towards the care with which it is constructed: here the *s* and *l* sounds of the earlier part of the sentence are not only continued with regularity (im-memorial, singing, juice, losing, heel, its, anklet) but a new pat-tern of *sl* together is started (slipper, slipperless, sloppy). This care is reflected in the precise detail with which Humbert de-scribes Lolita. His picture of Lo contains not only those me-chanical movements of hers that directly lead him to his bliss, but her whole attitude and every detail of that attitude; he tells us more than that she rubbed her foot against the magazines; he tells us that she rubbed the heel of the foot that lost the slipper, tells what she had left on the foot (a sloppy anklet), tells us what kind of magazines they were, how they were arranged, and where they were. It is a description that impresses us with the number of details that go beyond the merely sexual. Together with the other elements that indicate the care he takes in constructing this scene, all these details are evidence of the tenderness Humbert feels for Lolita even at this point when he is about to use her for his own pleasure. It is a glimpse of the other side of his nature, of the devoted love he is capable of.

These qualities of the passage become more evident when con-trasted with a paraphrase. Notice how despicable Humbert would seem if he described Lolita with a little less care:

> Her legs moved a little as they rested in my lap; I fondled them;
> there she was, stretched out in the corner eating her apple,
> singing, rubbing her foot against some magazines in the other
> corner—and every movement she made helped me to hide and
> improve the way her flesh rubbed against mine—her beautiful
> dimpled flesh against my engorged member.

It is on account of passages like the original which come at moments of Humbert's greatest lust, that we find it plausible for Humbert to fall deeply in love with Lolita. It is on account of passages like this that we see what might have been; because of them, we see how extraordinary a lover Humbert potentially was. And it is the irrevocable loss of this potential that moves us in his doom.

As the sentence continues, an important shift takes place. Humbert leaves this image of Lo in a characteristic pose and describes the physical interaction between himself and Lolita. As he does so his diction becomes more abstract: "and every movement she made, every shuffle and ripple, helped me to conceal and to improve the secret system of tactile correspondence between beast and beauty." The effect of this abstract diction is to distance us from the actual physical details of the situation. Compare the paraphrase: "every movement she made helped me to hide and improve the way her flesh rubbed against mine." Furthermore, Humbert's phrase "the secret system of tactile correspondence" and his insistence that not just every movement but "every shuffle" and "every ripple" had its effect shows that for him this is more than just mechanical push-button sex, more than flesh against flesh, or the right person's leg in the right part of his lap; it instead has a greater significance, it is a special kind of one way communication, the light of his life unwittingly kindling the fire of his loins.

At the same time, however, Humbert seems aware that his phrase is almost self-parodic, and in response pokes fun at himself by referring to himself and Lolita as "beast and beauty." Consequently, we are quite shocked when we find out in the last part of the sentence, where Humbert drops the abstract diction and becomes almost painfully specific, that he is deadly serious: "between my gagged bursting beast and the beauty of her dimpled body in its innocent cotton frock." We are clearly repelled by this image of Humbert; we get a glimpse of the potential horror of this situation that he is enjoying so much. Although we can recognize the subtle effects which indicate Humbert's tenderness, this effect is clearly the strongest one of the passage. Nabokov is very careful that we do not sympathize with Humbert to the point where we become blind to the evil of what he does.

Nabokov uses every device in his power to emphasize the potential horror. Not only is the image of "my gagged bursting beast" very vivid and very repulsive but the alliteration of b sounds connects the two metaphors only to increase our sense of their contrast ("bursting beast" and "beauty of her dimpled body"). He reverses the normal order of "beauty and beast" so that he might end with the evocation of that which is in danger of the beast: "her dimpled body in its innocent cotton frock." The metaphor of the "innocent frock" again emphasizes that Lolita is unaware of what Humbert is doing; consequently his maneuvering seems all the more perverse, all the more repulsive.

We can now see why Humbert is relatively subdued at the beginning of the sentence. Nabokov must let him evoke Lolita and his tenderness towards her first; any expression of his exuberance is likely to turn into a revelation of his perversity, and it is considerably more difficult to make his tenderness plausible after seeing his perversity than vice versa.

Even while we become distinctly aware of Humbert's repulsiveness, we admire the skill with which it is revealed to us. Unlike the first part of the sentence whose art we appreciate after some reflection, the style of the end calls immediate attention to itself; we cannot miss the skill involved in the shift from the abstract diction with its fanciful reference to beast and beauty to the vivid imagery of the final phrase where beast and beauty take on quite different meanings; furthermore, we admire both the particular word choices and the sounds of the words because they contribute so well to the revelation of the horror. Our admiration of the style is clearly distinct from our judgment of Humbert. The fact that he writes so well does not alter our condemnation of him at all. We do not feel that his ability to write like this is a compensation for his moral failings; nor do we feel that he is even more despicable because he has this talent. Instead we take pleasure in the style, while recoiling from what it reveals.

Our analysis of this passage, then, confirms our tentative conclusions. The particular language is crucial for the success of the book, but there is an aspect of it—its selfconscious power and beauty—that we cannot fully account for by looking solely at its function. I cannot find any reason why we need to know here that Humbert possesses a gift for writing extraordinary prose. But there is no doubt that his way with words contributes significantly to our pleasure in the book beyond its contribution to the intention. *Lolita,* it seems, will force us to reduce our theory's claim to comprehensiveness. But before taking this unwelcome step, let us take a broader survey of Nabokov's extraordinary stylistic skills and then consider a few other possible explanations of their function.

Lolita, I believe, is distinctive among novels because the pleasure in the style is found on almost every page. Furthermore, that pleasure is by no means always the same. Humbert is a versatile virtuoso, equally capable of producing passages of lyrical beauty and comic hilarity. Though we cannot do full justice to his skill here, it will be helpful to look at least briefly at a few more examples of it.

Humbert, of course, describes many things besides Lolita, and one of the things he describes frequently is American society—motel "culture," private schools, summer camps, and suburbia. The wit and perception Humbert displays in his parodic descriptions of these things allow us to see that the society which so severely and totally condemns a man like Humbert is in many ways inferior to Humbert himself. Yet our understanding of the function of Nabokov's style does not completely explain the pleasure we derive from it. Humbert's descriptions of his conferences with Headmistress Pratt of Beardsley School, for example, not only show how Humbert has become in part subject to her inferior, superficial mind but are also delightful in themselves, largely because he reconstructs and preserves her wonderfully self-incriminating speech: "Dr. Hummer [he has already in this speech been Humbird, Humburg, and Humberson; before it's over he'll also be Hummerson], do you realize that for the modern pre-adolescent child, medieval dates are of less vital value than weekend ones (twinkle)...?" (p. 162).

Similarly, the trail of clues left by Quilty, full of literary allusions, personal allusions, puns, and anagrams, has an important function: it further establishes the similarity between Humbert and Quilty, and it gives some wry reflections on Humbert's character and the actions he has been performing ("A. Person, Porlock, England"). But finally the pleasure that we take in it goes beyond its relevance to the book as a whole. It affords us the pleasure of recognition and the pleasure of problem solving; it engages our intellects quite apart from what it reveals about Humbert, Quilty, and their respective actions.

Perhaps most interesting in this connection is the murder scene. Nabokov has a difficult job here in controlling our response. He must avoid both making us sympathize with Humbert as the righteous avenger, and making us sympathize with Quilty as the innocent victim. His solution is daring and successful: he represents the scene farcically both in its action—Humbert has the hardest time making Quilty understand what he is about to do and then shoots bullet after bullet into him before bringing him down—and in its linguistic effects. This farcical representation is in obvious contrast to the serious desire that motivates Humbert to commit the murder—there is no doubt that he desperately wants to destroy Quilty—and consequently it makes us understand how unsatisfactory the revenge is, even to himself. This effect is necessary if we are to feel the utter helplessness of his situation, the inescapability of his doom.

But again many of the linguistic effects are so good that they contribute to our pleasure beyond what they contribute to our understanding of the scene. For example, in describing his fight against Quilty to regain control of his gun, Humbert writes: "He was naked and goatish under his robe, and I felt suffocated as he rolled over me. I rolled over him. We rolled over me. They rolled over him. We rolled over us." The style of the first sentence reveals much about Humbert's distaste for Quilty; the syntax suggests a causal link, however loose, between the two clauses; we infer that Humbert's feeling of suffocation is not just a result of the physical act of one man rolling over him, but the result of the distasteful "naked and goatish" Quilty rolling over him. Then the fun begins: Humbert continues the thought of his last clause and gives us the series of sentences describing who rolled over whom.

Many critics have commented that Humbert's playing with language here has a very serious point: he and Quilty are indistinguishable in many ways so that when he says "he rolled over me" and "I rolled over him," he is also saying "we rolled over us." Nabokov could have made the same point and he still could have made it humorously if he had written, " . . . and I felt suffocated as he rolled over me. I rolled over him. We rolled over us." The series would not be quite so humorous because we could not get the same sense of them rolling over each other again and again—and then yet again—at this most dangerous time, but we would probably still laugh at the scene.

The choices Nabokov actually makes again both make us see more about Humbert and his attitudes and make us admire the skill he has with his medium. By including "We rolled over me. They rolled over him," he not only makes the scene more farcical but makes us see just how closely aligned he and Quilty are. By saying "We rolled over me" he indicates that because he is indistinguishable from Quilty, for Quilty to roll over him is for him to roll over himself, so they both rolled over him. With "They rolled over him," he takes a distant perspective, separates one part of himself from another and looks at the situation. The effect of this distance is to make the scene more farcical. Humbert can stand aside, as it were, and let the rolling continue. It is like one of those cartoon fights where two dogs pick on a cat and the fight gets so furious that the cat can escape to the side and narrate. Only in this case the cat is still in the fight. The final sentence, "We rolled over us," sums up the situation; "naked and goatish" Quilty, black-clad and handsome Humbert have become indistinguishable as they roll endlessly over the floor.

Even while we can appreciate all these functional aspects of the sentences we marvel at the economy and simplicity with which Nabokov creates them. Our account of the purposes of the style simply does not exhaust our pleasure in it. The series is another example of what Lodge calls "realization"; the sentences describe Humbert and Quilty rolling over each other and at the same time, through the repetition of the staccato rhythm (long long long short long) for five consecutive clauses, the repetition of the verb phrase, and the variations of the first and third person pronouns, they "roll over" each other, or to put it another way, they imitate the action of rolling over in their own movement. It is a simple but still rather dazzling performance.

IV

To this point, then, we have found that the language of *Lolita* neither becomes the synthesizing principle of the novel nor remains totally subordinate to an intention. Like the language of *The Ambassadors,* it is a crucial element for the successful achievement of the intention, but unlike the language of James's novel, it is a significant and continual source of our pleasure beyond the way it functions. Explaining its function does not sufficiently explain its role in the novel. There are, however, a few other explanations of language's role which are worth considering because they help us understand both the nature of Nabokov's work and its consequences for our theory.

One approach we might take is to look at the self-conscious artistry as produced not by Humbert as a participant-narrator, but only by Nabokov. Although we would recognize that Humbert tells the story, we would not attribute the beauties of the language to him but to Nabokov in a way roughly analogous to that by which we attribute the rhymes of "My Last Duchess" to

Browning rather than the duke.[12] The consequence of this approach is that Humbert dramatically shrinks in importance while Nabokov grows. Humbert becomes responsible only for his actions, not for his confession of those actions. The power of the book then comes less from the representation of Humbert's movement toward a fate than from experiencing a special communication from Nabokov: look, I can take the most sordid situations and describe them in such a way that they will be transformed into something beautiful.

There are both theoretical and practical objections against this solution, which, in effect, says that language-is-all in this novel: the characters, action, and thought are all subordinate to Nabokov's demonstration of his verbal artistry. First, the analysis we have done so far—we have been able to explain much of the book, even much of the style, by conceiving of it as the representation of an action—argues against this solution. Perhaps even more to the point, Nabokov shows us right from the start that Humbert is a very self-conscious stylist. It is in chapter 1 that he makes his famous claim, "You can always count on a murderer for a fancy prose style" (p. 11). It is in chapter 8, only some thirty pages into the book, that he exclaims, "Oh my Lolita. I have only words to play with!" (p. 32). Toward the end he says that he has tried to make his confession become "articulate art," because he sees that as the only treatment for his misery. And he closes the book with an address to Lolita that indicates his artistry is conscious: "one wanted H. H. to exist at least a couple of months longer so as to have him make you live in the minds of later generations. I am thinking of aurochs and angels, the secret of durable pigments, prophetic sonnets, the refuge of art. And this is the only immortality you and I may share, my Lolita" (p. 281).

Humbert's remarks suggest another way in which the beauty of the language might be subordinate to the whole. It might, in fact, be a compensation for his doom, his way of atoning for what he has done to Lolita. Because Humbert is himself a created character we must consider this solution, which seems quite attractive, very carefully; we need to look first at how it works within the fiction, i.e., how it applies to us in our role as the ladies and gentlemen of the jury whom Humbert often addresses; and then we must look at how it applies to us as readers of the book *Lolita*.

Even if we take the view that within the fiction the power of the language is a kind of compensation for Humbert's crime, we run into problems. We must first recognize that Humbert's confession is only a very partial compensation. To say it is more is to get our values mixed up. To say it is more is to say that Lolita's life was worth sacrificing because it produced this confession; it is to say that the confession itself is more valuable than the life it commemorates. Humbert himself never makes this claim. The first time that he speaks of his attempt to create "articulate art," he sees it as only a "very melancholy and local palliative" for his misery. His second expression of his wish to make his confession a work of art is given in the context of a lament for his crime. When he says, "this is the only immortality you and I may share, my Lolita," he is not rejoicing about the possible immortality of his art, but grieving that he cannot spend, that he does not deserve to spend, eternity with Lolita. Given this qualification about its importance as a compensation, we can see within the fiction that the power of Humbert's language is an attempt to make his confession as memorable as possible at every point so that Lolita might live on for later generations. But what does this mean for us as readers of the book *Lolita?*

Clearly it cannot mean the same thing as it does for us as ladies and gentlemen of the jury. Both Humbert and Lolita are created characters and the immortality that is possible for them is not the kind of immortality Humbert wants. It is not the immortality given to the various lovers addressed in the sonnet sequences of the Renaissance, but the immortality of fictional characters. Whether they achieve that immortality is obviously out of Humbert's control; it is in the hands of his creator, Vladimir Nabokov.

Humbert's remarks are important to us as readers of the book because of what they indicate about his feelings. They are a clear and powerful sign of his remorse. Whether Humbert himself can actually give Lolita the immortality of art is, in one sense, irrelevant; the important thing is that he wants to: that desire shows he acknowledges what he has done, repents of it, and wants to make amends. Furthermore, we believe that he feels this way because we have experienced the art of his confession. In this way, we can see a general reason for the style and can see that it is subordinate to the intention. However, this is a weak reason. It cannot tell us why the style is especially beautiful at some points and not at others; and it simply does not seem sufficient to account for all the puns, parodies, allusions, and virtuoso performances that we discover in the book. In the final analysis we are not fully accounting for the pleasures of the style if we say that they are there only so that we shall react to Humbert's claim that he is trying to create articulate art as a sign of his repentance.

This consideration of the relation between Humbert and Nabokov further explains how our pleasure in the style is evoked. Although Humbert is himself a self-conscious artist and though we see the function of his artistry in the work, what we marvel at finally is his creator's skill. A passage such as the opening invocation to Lolita almost compels our wonder at the great gift of expression, the remarkable talent, the consummate craft that enables Nabokov to write like that. He is so much the master of his medium that even well into the book we continue to be impressed anew and to take delight in this aspect of his work.

Nevertheless, because our pleasure in the style is, in a sense, a surplus—something we experience in addition to its crucial function is accomplishing the intention—it is not sufficient in itself to make *Lolita* a successful novel. If, for example, Nabokov employed his gifts in a passage in which he undercut Humbert's remorse for what he has done to Lolita, we would no doubt still admire Nabokov's skill with his medium, but we would also feel that he was misusing his talent: if Humbert's remorse is not real, then he is not a potentially valuable human, but a monster for whom we can only feel contempt and repulsion. In general, whenever Nabokov's virtuoso effects are not also contributing to the intention, they cease being extraordinarily impressive parts of a moving work of art and become at best impressive linguistic exercises. It is one measure of Nabokov's achievement in *Lolita* that he so often gives us the pleasure of his masterful style while rarely, if ever, making us feel that he is doing linguistic exercises.

It is, of course, possible that we have been unable to account fully for the beautiful style in terms of its contribution to an intention, because we have inadequately specified that intention.[13] If that were the case, however, then we most likely would have been unable to account for other aspects of the book as well. In fact, the number of kinds of elements that we have been able to account for—the seduction scene, the representation of Humbert early in the book, as well as the many linguistic effects we have examined—give very strong support for our description of the intention. I cannot conceive of another one which will be able to account for more elements of the book; and as we have seen, any description which tries to give a full account of the beautiful style does so at the expense of its ability to account for the specifics of the action. In this case, it makes better sense to see our inability to account for the style solely in terms of the intention as evidence of a limitation of our theory. Although the theory does give us considerable insight into the language of *Lolita,* it does not enable us fully to explain its role. We must admit, then, that though our theory has substantial explanatory power, it is not truly comprehensive: it cannot give us complete insight into the role of the medium in every novel. This realization has important consequences for the conclusions we can draw from the study as a whole, but we can best understand those consequences after we examine the further challenge to our theory posed by *Willie Masters' Lonesome Wife.*

Design and Value in
a World of Words:
Umberto Eco and the Language of
Willie Masters' Lonesome Wife

I

Our analysis of *Lolita* has indicated one limitation of the theory
we developed in part one: that the role of language in a novel
cannot always be satisfactorily explained by its contribution to an
intention. In order to complete our inductive inquiry, we need to
challenge the other basic finding of part one: that language in
fiction can never be an end in itself. Gass's *Willie Masters' Lonesome Wife*, which has been called "a virtual casebook of literary
experimentalism" in which "every strategy is related to the idea
that in literature words should not merely point somewhere else
but should be admired for themselves,"[1] presents the challenge
quite dramatically.

Gass deliberately destroys such traditional fictional staples as
unity of action and consistency of characterization, and replaces
them with a cornucopia of stylistic produce. His book is filled
with striking metaphors, ingenious puns, eloquent meditations,
low humor, philosophical reflections, nonsense poetry, and epi-
grammatic prose. Gass calls further attention to his manipulation
of the medium by continually varying the typography and by
juxtaposing many passages with photographs. To give a few
specific examples: he makes his first-person narrator speak not
only in distinct voices but also as different people—Babs Masters
becomes Joe Slatters becomes a woman named Leonora; ranges
so freely in the actions he describes that he includes a one-act
farce as part of his work; reproduces one page of an imaginary
work called "The Passions of a Stableboy" and inserts it in the
middle of his own text; and prints the asterisks indicating a foot-
note in such large type that they occupy almost a whole page by
themselves.

If, after careful examination, we conclude that Gass's work is
not only a true example of fiction about its medium, but also a

successful and valuable work, we must ask some troubling questions about our theory. How can we modify it to account for both works such as *Willie Masters' Lonesome Wife* and those such as we examined in part one? How does our principle about evaluating language in light of an intention apply here? We may find that we cannot modify our theory to account for Gass's work without impairing its ability to account for novels such as *Persuasion, Sister Carrie,* and *The Ambassadors*. What must we then conclude, especially in the additional light of our analysis of *Lolita,* about our whole enterprise of constructing a comprehensive theory?

At the same time, however, our theory leads us to ask some hard questions about Gass's work. Since language in fiction, even such self-consciously employed language as Nabokov's, seems by its nature always to point away from itself toward some content, how is it possible to write a work of fiction in which language does not point away, or perhaps more accurately, points away only to point back at itself? Once the medium of fiction becomes its content as well, do we still have fiction or metafiction—or do we have an essay on language? Put another way, the question is whether it is possible to write a *successful* work of fiction in which language is an end rather than a means. We have argued that if Nabokov's self-conscious manipulation of the medium in *Lolita* did not also contribute to the representation of Humbert's progression toward his tragiclike end, that manipulation would become linguistic exercise. Has Gass given us valuable art, or a grabbag of verbal prizes, tricks, and surprises?

Let us initially put our theory rather than Gass's work on the defensive. What we turn to first, then, is an alternative approach that will enable us to put the best possible construction on *Willie Masters' Lonesome Wife*. After seeing the conclusions about Gass's work that approach leads us to, we can return to our questions about our theory and about the novel; and as part of those inquiries, we shall also examine the relation between this alternative theory and our own.

II

An approach well suited to explain the virtues of Gass's work is outlined by Umberto Eco in *A Theory of Semiotics*. Since Eco's approach to what he calls "aesthetic texts" follows directly from the full theory of sign systems he is developing, we can best understand his approach in light of the larger theory. Eco's project is the extremely ambitious one of explaining how all sign systems operate. The category "sign" for him includes "everything that, on the grounds of a previously established social convention, can be taken as *something standing for something else,*" [2] or expressed another way, everything that can be used in order to lie (p. 17). For Eco, the whole of culture can be studied "as a communicative phenomenon based on signification systems"; furthermore, he believes it should be studied this way in order to clarify some of its fundamental mechanisms (p. 22).

Eco divides his inquiry into two parts: the development of a theory of codes, or signification, and the development of a theory of sign-production, or communication. Signification is a necessary condition for communication; it defines the abstract rules (it establishes the codes) which allow communication to take place. Communication, by Eco's definition, is the passage of a signal from a source through a channel to a destination (p. 8).

The key problem in developing the theory of codes is to account for both the extreme flexibility (signs individually and in common stand for many distinct things) and the absolutely conventional nature of sign systems (signs signify according to widely agreed upon rules). Eco begins to solve this problem by replacing the traditional concept of "sign" with that of "sign-function." A semiotic entity, whether we call it sign or sign-function, consists of two functives, an expression (a sound, for example) and a content (a concept, for example) *mutually* correlated according to the rules of a given code. But neither an expression item nor a content item is bound by a single code, and in fact, many expression items are correlated with more than one content item, and vice versa. When an item with one correlation enters into a second correlation, it then becomes a new functive, thus giving rise to a new sign-function. For example, says Eco, the expression item "plane" in English is correlated with many different content items, e.g., "carpentry tool," "aircraft," "geometric concept." This is not a single sign standing for many different things, but rather many different sign-functions each participating in a different code (pp. 48–49).

The next important distinction Eco makes is that between connotative and denotative meaning. He bases this distinction on the nature of the sign-functions that produce those meanings. Denotative meaning, which Eco labels unmediated content, is a content directly correlated with an expression. Connotative meaning, on the other hand, is mediated content; it is a content correlated with *both* an expression and its denotative content. To put it another way, a denotation is the content of an expression, while a connotation is the content of a sign-function (p. 56). For example, when the needle of a gasoline gauge in a car points to "E," it denotes that there is little or no fuel left. Both that expression (the needle pointing to "E") and that denotation (little or no gasoline in the tank) combine to form the connotative content "add fuel to the tank."

Having laid his groundwork, Eco turns to the main task of the theory of codes: describing the relationships among the numerous codes, or in other words, describing the organization of the content plane of all sign systems. Eco considers both horizontal relationships and vertical ones on this plane. But he emphasizes first that the content of a sign system is independent of the objects it may be used to refer to; content is fixed not by relationships between signs and things, but by convention. Take, for example, a sign-function such as a pointing finger where we might initially think that the expression takes its content from what it points to. The case in which there is no object for the finger to point at shows that its meaning depends on convention rather than on reference: the meaning "look where I am pointing" is completely unaffected by the presence or absence of a referent. As Eco puts it, the semiotic object of a semantics is not referents but cultural units (p. 62).

Expressed another way, Eco's point is that the rules or conditions of signification (the object of a theory of codes) are independent of the rules or conditions of truth (the object of a theory of mentions). Thus, the various codes which relate expression to content "set up a 'cultural' world which is neither actual nor possible in the ontological sense; its existence is linked to a cultural order which is the way a society thinks, speaks, and while speaking explains the 'purport' of its thought through other thoughts. Since it is through thinking and speaking that a society develops, expands, or collapses . . . a theory of codes is very much concerned with the format of such 'cultural' worlds" (pp. 61–62).

Since contents are not referents but cultural units, we cannot properly explain their meaning in terms of their possible referents. We are faced, in Eco's words, with the "basic problem of how to *touch* contents" (p. 62, his emphasis). The solution to this problem takes us to the heart of the theory of codes. Eco argues that the only way we can explain the meaning of one cultural unit is in terms of other cultural units, in terms of what C. S. Peirce called the chain of interpretants of the sign-function. Since the cultural units we use as an explanation can themselves only be explained by other cultural units, this chain is actually an endless series of representations in which each successive representation represents the one behind it (pp. 68–69). The chain of interpretants may include different types of "sign-vehicles," i.e., sign functions with different material forms on the expression plane; a word, for example, may be represented not only by its synonyms but also by translations, emotive associations, drawings, typical behavior associated with it, or typical responses to it. In short, semiosis explains itself only by itself (p. 71), and since each code can only be explained by other codes, all the codes are mutually dependent.

By pointing to the chain of interpretants, we provide the first half (the horizontal dimension) of the answer to the question, "What is the content of a sign-function?" We can provide the second-half by placing that content item in a vertical dimension, in a "system of other cultural units which are opposed to it and circumscribe it" (p. 73). Ideally, says Eco, we would like to construct a diagram of the Universal Semantic Field which would relate every content unit to every other one in a fixed, clear, and permanent way. But such a diagram is not possible for two reasons: (1) the same content units often have different relationships to one another (e.g., "bachelor" and "spinster" are contraries when opposed only to each other, but are complements when opposed to "married person"), and as a result the boundaries of the content form are virtually impossible to fix; (2) many semantic fields are transitory and constantly shifting; no sooner would we construct a model of the Universal Field than we would have to reconstruct it (p. 80). Nevertheless, we need not completely abandon the idea of specifying the meaning of a content through its position in a semantic system, but we need to do it in such a way that we indicate the different fields it participates in.

Eco develops a compositional analysis designed to do just that.
Given an expression item which may participate in many sign-
functions, he will break it down into its syntactic markers
(features such as noun, + count, + singular, + animate and so
on), its sememe, by which he means its unanalyzed content, its
denotations independent of context or circumstances, its connotations independent of context or circumstance, and finally its
different denotations and connotations within different contexts
and circumstances. The schematic diagram (in which *"sm"*
equals semantic marker, *"d"* equals denotation, *"c"* equals
connotation, *"cont,"* context and *"circ,"* circumstance) looks
like this:

$$
\begin{array}{l}
\text{[sign-vehicle]—}\\
sm = \langle\langle\text{sememe}\rangle\rangle\text{—}d_1, d_2
\end{array}
\left\{
\begin{array}{l}
c_1, c_2, \text{ etc.}\\[4pt]
(cont_a)\text{—}d_3\ d_4 \left< \begin{array}{l}[circa_A]\text{—}c_3 \\ [circ_B]\text{—}c_4 \end{array}\right.\\[8pt]
(cont_b)\text{—}d_5, d_6\text{—}c_5, c_6, \text{ etc.}\\[8pt]
[circ_C] \left< \begin{array}{l} (cont_c)\text{—}d_7, d_8\text{—}c_7, c_8, \text{ etc.} \\ (cont_d)\text{—}d_9, d_{10}\text{—}c_9, c_{10}, \text{ etc.} \end{array}\right.\\[8pt]
[circ_D]\text{—}d_{11}, d_{12}\text{—}c_{11}, c_{12} \text{ etc.}
\end{array}
\right.
$$

A context is created by the presence of other sememes, other
content units (context, in other words, refers to signals within a
message itself, e.g., in a sentence it refers to the other words
surrounding the one under focus); a circumstance is created by
the presence of other sign-vehicles belonging to different semiotic
systems, or of an action or object functioning as a sign-vehicle
(circumstance, in other words, refers to signals external to a
given message). By including context and circumstance in the
compositional analysis, Eco can include the many different fields
the content unit participates in. But consistent with his whole
approach, Eco emphasizes that the contexts and circumstances
which would be included are themselves conventionally recognized semantic units, "pieces of coded information" (p. 105).
The combination of all the compositional analyses of all the
sign-vehicles would yield a diagram of semantic space. But since
every sign-vehicle is a component in the analysis of some other
vehicle we have a space that is so crisscrossed by paths from one

sign-vehicle to another that such a diagram is impossible to construct. Nevertheless, we can see that every content unit is connected with every other one; we have a system of "infinite semantic recursivity" in which it would be possible to trace a path from any given content unit (say, "literary criticism") to any other one (say, "indigestion"). The sum of our knowledge of all these relations among expressions and contents is a code; more accurately, we might describe this code as a hypercode, a "complex network of subcodes . . . some of which are strong and stable, others weak and transient," such as some relations between an expression and its connotative content (p. 125). Furthermore, because the hypercode is based on social convention rather than on inherent properties of its components, it is not a fixed, stable structure but one that changes with its use. This point leads us into the nature and importance of aesthetic texts, which Eco considers as part of his theory of sign-production or communication.

Eco defines the aesthetic text as one that is both ambiguous and self-focusing; more precisely, he defines it as a text that is self-focusing because it is ambiguous. A text is ambiguous, in Eco's sense, when it violates the rules of a code. Ambiguity may be syntactic ("John has a when"), semantic ("colorless green ideas sleep furiously"), stylistic ("I pray the Lord my soul to take"), and even total ("waf frsft onlk") (pp. 262–63). What distinguishes the ambiguity of an aesthetic text from just any violation of a code is that in the aesthetic text an ambiguity on the expression plane will correspond to an ambiguity on the content plane. Because the norms of a code are violated, we are forced to reconsider the way the code is working in this case; thus, the text focuses attention on itself (p. 264).

What further distinguishes the aesthetic text from other kinds of communication is that it focuses attention on the *lower levels* of the expression plane. Any functive in an expression plane is composed of a more basic material (e.g., the phonemes of a word, or the sand and gravel of a stone that serves as a unit in an architectural code), and in the aesthetic text the potential of this material to have a semiotic function, to participate in communication, is realized. In Eco's words, "the matter of the sign-vehicle becomes an aspect of the expression form" (p. 266, his emphasis). He cites the campaign slogan "I like Ike" as analyzed by Roman Jakobson as a prime example of this process. In that slogan, our attention is not only focused on the phonic matter of the message but that phonic matter plays a key role in creating the effectiveness of the message. As Jakobson puts it,

> both cola of the trisyllabic formula "I like/Ike" rhyme with each other and the second of the two rhyming words is fully included in the first one (echo rhyme), . . . a paranomastic image of a feeling which totally envelops its object. Both cola alliterate with each other, and the first of the two alliterating words is included in the second, . . . a paranomastic image of the loving subject enveloped by the beloved object. [Quoted by Eco, p. 308.]

Because our attention is drawn to the expression plane, we reach a better understanding of it. What had been semiotically undifferentiated matter (the sound of individual or groups of phonemes) now becomes part of the system of expression (it suggests new content). Thus, we become more aware of the expressive possibilities of the expression plane. The analysis of "I like Ike" demonstrates how the increase of functioning at the level of the expression plane gives rise to increased functioning at the level of content. "I like Ike" is a semiotically richer message than say, "I back Ike," because the matter of the expression form functions as part of the sign-vehicle to a much greater extent and adds additional significations to the content plane. In Eco's terms the "surplus" of expression gives rise to a "surplus" of content (p. 270).

Of course, in an aesthetic text like a novel, we shall be concerned not with a single message such as "I like Ike," but with a series of messages, or perhaps with a hypermessage constructed from a series of individual ones. Since a work of art has "contextual solidarity," i.e., if one element of the context is altered the others will lose their previous functions, we can conclude that it was organized by a systematic rule, a rule which governs how the norms of the code are to be violated and how these violations are to impinge on each other.

When we discover this systematic rule, we learn an "aesthetic idiolect," the author's private code which has been developed by rearranging the existing codes. As we examine the aesthetic text and discover this idiolect, we are compelled to reconsider the usual codes. Every aesthetic text, says Eco, "threatens the codes but at the same time strengthens them; it reveals unsuspected possibilities in them, and thus changes the attitude of the user toward them" (p. 274). As the user (or addressee) reflects on the code, he "becomes aware of new semiosic possibilities and is thereby compelled to rethink the whole language, the entire inheritance of what has been said, can be said, and could or should be said" (p. 274). Thus, the aesthetic text makes its addressee more skilled in the processes of signification and communication. At the same time, "it challenges the accepted organization of the content [of the existing codes] and suggests that the system could be differently ordered" (p. 274). If the impact of the aesthetic text is pervasive enough, it can in fact change semantic systems and consequently, "change the way in which culture 'sees' the world" (p. 274). Thus, concludes Eco,

> a text of the aesthetic type which was so frequently supposed to be absolutely extraneous to any truth conditions (and to exist at a level on which disbelief is totally 'suspended') arouses the suspicion that the correspondence between the present organization of the content and 'actual' states of the world is neither the best nor the ultimate. The world could be defined and organized (and therefore, perceived and known) through other semantic (that is 'conceptual') models. [p. 274]

Eco's semiotic approach can perhaps be further clarified by comparing it with Miller's deconstructive one. Eco, like Miller, sees the value and interest of aesthetic texts in their capacity to generate multiple meanings and to make us aware of the arbitrary and interconnected codes that govern all uses of language. But, unlike Miller, Eco does not see language (or any sign system) as beyond the control of those who use it; he does not, for example, argue that every text is unstable and hence likely to lead us to reflect upon the sign system out of which it is created. Furthermore, because Eco maintains his distinction between aesthetic and nonaesthetic messages, he implicitly argues for something which has no place in Miller's approach, the importance of the author—especially in aesthetic texts: that which leads to the exploration of cultural codes, and ultimately perhaps to the reorganization of a culture's world-view is the author's insight into the semiotic system.

III

The passage from *Willie Masters' Lonesome Wife* I shall analyze according to Eco's principles occurs at the very beginning of the work. Gass's narrator, Babs Masters, the lonesome wife of the title, is speaking about her early physical maturity and her father's reaction to it; on the facing page, there is a photograph of a naked woman standing with her back to the camera and her hips swayed slightly to the right. I choose this passage both because it illustrates the linguistic virtuosity Gass is capable of and because it provides an excellent place from which to compare Gass's work with the other novels we have examined. This first section of the novel is most like more conventional fiction: Gass is now presenting us with a narrator who reveals herself and her relationship with another character through her speech. Just what significance these revelations of character have for the novel as a whole is a question I shall leave until after the semiotic analysis.

[1]There was never any doubt about my bosom, buddy; breasts as big as your butt there, nipples red and rubbery. [2]A regular dairy, my daddy always said. [3]Babs' Sweet Buttery. [4]The smart ass. [5]The hairy smart ass. [6]Well, a smirk to his memory. [7]This plump little lady, he used to say, shot up like a weed when she was eight. [8]What a smart ass. [9]May the tines in his skull ache. [10]A milk-weed, he'd shout, and then he'd tickle my tummy and shatter with laughter. [11]You're going to amount to something, baby, he'd say, shaping his hands, the smart ass; you're going to be as big this sway as you are the other. [12]This *sway*, see? he'd say, and fold in delight. [13]Now he's giving his worms gas, the beery s.o.b.[3]

The playfulness of this passage will be in an obvious—and somewhat comic—contrast to the rather solemn analysis that now follows. That solemnity, of course, is appropriate to and dictated by our interest in how Eco's approach can shed light on the role of language in this passage; however, though my face will be straight as I analyze, I trust that the analysis will help the reader smile more widely at Gass's ingenuity.

Sentence 1: "There was never any doubt about my bosom, buddy; breasts as big as your butt there, nipples red and rubbery."

This sentence sets up many of the relationships among semantic fields that will be developed in the rest of the passage. First and most obvious is the relationship between "bosom" and "butt"; the content plane contains the explicit assertion that Babs's breasts are as big as a butt. The expression plane significantly adds to our understanding of this content. In making the comparison, Gass chooses the word that repeats the *b* sounds of "bosom" and "breasts" ("butt" rather than "ass" or "posterior"), and that is itself smaller in size than those two words ("butt" rather than "buttocks" or "bottom"). Furthermore, the arrangement of the description in the second clause, and the amount of space given to the description of Babs's breasts reinforce the content plane's assertion of their size. The word which on the content plane is normally associated with the largest size ("butt") is not only smaller but is surrounded on both sides by descriptions of Babs's breasts. In this context, even the description of the nipples ("red and rubbery") which has no denotations about size receives the connotation "large." The logic of the sentence works like this: a general statement about Babs's bosom is made (there was never any doubt about it), and is then supported by specific statements about its parts, i.e., breasts and nipples. Since the claim made about breasts is one about their size, and since the description of the nipples is in apposition to and has the same number of syllables (7) as that claim, the description of the nipples receives the connotation "large." This connotation nicely supplements the conventional connotation of the description, i.e., "mature."

In addition to these devices, the movement of sounds on the expression plane reflects the movement of signification on the content plane. While the equivalence of size between bosom and butt is being stressed, the *b* sounds predominate (about, bosom, buddy, breasts, big, butt) with a pattern of *r* sounds in the background (breasts, your butt there); in the description of the nipples where color and texture come into the foreground and size recedes to the background, the relationship between the sounds is also reversed: the *r*'s predominate with the *b*'s in the background ("red and rubbery").

Perhaps the most inventive aspect of the sentence is the word play of "bosom buddy." Gass divides the two words which are themselves usually "bosom buddies," and as a result, is able to emphasize Babs's aggressive tone. There is an obvious contrast between her use of the two words, and their customary use of describing warm friendship. Gass then brings the two words back together again but with still another meaning. Because the sound of "buddy" is echoed in "butt" and because "butt" is made comparable to "breasts" the sentence also suggests that Babs has a "bosom butty" (or "butty bosom"). The pun is particularly appropriate since Babs is a lonesome wife whose own body is her best buddy. Thus, not only is the semantic field of "bosom" now crossed by "butt," the field of "butt" is now crossed by "buddy."

"Buddy" also participates in other relationships that are developed later in the passage. Babs's hostile attitude toward this unidentified "buddy" is similar to her attitude toward her "daddy," who would also conventionally be thought to be her friend. This relationship between "buddy" and "daddy" is reinforced by the chain of words that leads from "buddy" in sentence 1 to "daddy" in sentence 2: we go from "buddy" to "your [the buddy's] butt" to "daddy" who is a "smart ass." I shall discuss this relationship further when I consider sentences 4 and 5.

Sentences 2 and 3. "A regular dairy, my daddy always said. Babs' Sweet Buttery."

In sentence 2, the relationship between the semantic fields of "bosom" and "bottom" becomes further complicated by the introduction of a third field, that surrounding "dairy." The content plane of the sentence seems to be moving away from the link between "bosom" and "butt" and developing the more conventional connection between breasts and milk. The exact development of the connection, though, is far from conventional. Gass creates Babs's father to be almost as inventive as he is crude. He skips over conventional associations like "breasts" and "jugs" and creates the hyperbolic metaphor of "a regular dairy." While the content plane ostensibly moves in this direction, the expression plane continues the comparison between "breasts" and "butt," through the similar sounds of "dairy" and "derriere." This effect of the expression plane ensures the success of the metaphor: although "dairy" denotes the prodigious potential of Babs's breasts, by itself it does not denote anything about their shape. With the pun suggesting "derriere," Gass includes a denotation of the shape as well as the size of Babs's "dairy."

Sentence 3 further complicates these relationships by means of another pun. "Buttery," of course, picks up on "dairy" in both the expression and content planes. Although the description of Babs's breasts is progressing on the content plane in the direction given by "dairy," the expression plane continues to state the equivalence between Babs's breasts and a bottom; they are "butt-ery." "Buttery" is used ambiguously in other ways as well: because of the context we read "buttery" as an adjective, and because of the syntax we read it as a noun. Reading it as an adjective, we supply "breasts" as the understood noun and so return to the content unit of "texture." This unit combines with the unit of "taste" denoted by "sweet" and together with some of the other elements of these three sentences that we have already pointed to, they create a sensual description of this woman's sweet, soft, big, buttery, breasts.

Reading "buttery" as a noun, we introduce another semantic field into a relationship with "bosom" (and consequently with the other fields as well)—that of a "liquor cabinet or storeroom." We skip once again over the conventional associations between breasts and milk, and understand "liquor" as a potential product of Babs's "dairy." Focusing on the connotations of the comparison, we can understand it this way: Babs's bosom is so large and so sweet that it is potentially intoxicating. The boldface type and the imitation of handprinting rather than the usual typewritten characters make us read sentence 3 as a sign hung over a door. It would be appropriate over a dairy barn, or over the door of a liquor storeroom. But when we think of it in its intended place, i.e., over Babs's chest, we understand why she is so offended by her father's remarks.

Sentences 4 and 5: "The smart ass. The hairy smart ass."

Babs's name-calling creates more meanings than she intends because these names now participate in so many semantic fields. "Smart ass" has first its conventional figurative meaning: "smart ass" is equivalent to "wise guy" which is opposed to "wise man" and so denotes someone with a specious and superficial wisdom or intelligence. But because "dairy" has been introduced and because "ass" gets repeated with the addition of the rhyme-word "hairy," we think of the farm animal and can read "smart" literally. Since the conventional connotation with "ass" is dumb, its semantic field exerts a pull on "smart," which makes us read the phrase as "smart for an ass," and Babs's remark takes its place in the unofficial catalogue of left-handed compliments.

Babs's name-calling also participates in the semantic field of "butt." Because this field is already present in the passage, and because of the addition of "hairy" in sentence 5, we read the insult as literal in this sense as well. Since "butt" has previously been equated with Babs's bosom, her insult is especially appropriate. Babs's father has, in effect, equated her identity with her bosom; Babs retaliates by equating his with his ass. She has, in more senses than one, been able to return him an equivalent insult. At the same time, the connection between "daddy" and "buddy" takes on new significance here. Babs's father is her "buddy" in this near equivalence of identities: she is only her bosom, he is only his bottom; but since her bosom is so like a bottom, she, in a sense, is also all bottom.

Finally, the adjectives used by father and daughter allow us to understand an antithesis between the insults: Babs's bosom is sweet and buttery, her father's behind "hairy" and "smart." At this point "smart" becomes related to another semantic field; it refers not only to "mental acuity" and "wisecracking" but also to "hard" and "sharp," i.e., to the opposites of "buttery."

Sentence 6: "Well, a smirk to his memory."

This sentence looks back to "Babs's buttery" with its meaning of storeroom for liquor. Babs and her buttery offer her father not the usual "drink" to his memory, but only a smirk. The already established relationships between semantic fields in the passage make this substitution of "smirk" for "drink" quite significant. "Smirk" both opposes the fields of "butt" and "bosom" and extends them. On the one hand, Babs is denying the validity of her father's claim that she is all bosom by calling attention to this action of her *mouth*. At the same time, both the content and expression planes demonstrate that she is the smart ass's daughter: the *sm* sound associates "smirk" with "smart ass" and a "smirk" after all is the characteristic facial expression of the smart ass. Thus, even the words Babs chooses to express her hostility to her father prevent her from escaping his insults and influence.

Sentences 7, 8, 9, 10: "This plump little lady, he used to say, shot up like a weed when she was eight. What a smart ass. May the tines in his skull ache. A milk-weed, he'd shout, and then he'd tickle my tummy and shatter with laughter."

Babs's father's joke introduces yet another semantic field into a relationship with "bosom." The first line of the joke (sentence 7) presents us with somewhat contradictory fields in "round" and "short" ("plump little") and "vertical" and "tall" ("shot up like a weed"). The punchline ("milk-weed") solves the problem because it participates in all these fields at once. On the literal level of content, of course, "milk-weed" provides only a specious solution: milkweeds have no more in common with pubescent girls than ragweeds do. The solution—and Babs's father's joke—works because of the way it manipulates the expression plane of the utterance. "Milk" is momentarily treated as an expression unit independent of "weed" and thus is associated with "dairy" and "breasts," thereby satisfying the semantic requirements of "round" and short." It is then reunited with "weed," thereby satisfying the requirements of "vertical" and "tall." One result of this joke is that our understanding of both Babs and "milk-weed" is changed: she can be seen as a milk-producing weed, and it can be seen as resembling a precocious young girl.

One effect of sentences 8 and 9 ("What a smart ass. May the tines in his skull ache") is, of course, to increase the effectiveness of the punchline by delaying its delivery. They also work together to produce a very effective and humorous curse on Babs's father. "Tines," which denotes plants with long and twisting tendrils, participates in the same semantic field as "weeds," and thus Babs is able to avenge herself by using weapons similar to the ones she was injured with. The choice of "skull" links up with "smart ass" in its conventional meaning of "wise guy." Babs's father has used his smart ass's skull to draw on two figurative uses of weed ("grow like a weed," "weed of milk") to make his joke at her expense. Babs now draws on literal uses of "tines" and "skull" to vent her anger. We see the clever, ingenious way *Gass* has manipulated his medium, and are educated about the flexibility of that medium in the process.

In sentence 10, Gass manipulates the expression plane so that Babs's description of her father's actions provides a humorous contrast to her own growth. In the narration of the joke, there is a succession of verbs beginning with *sh* and having *t* as a middle or final consonant—"shot," "shout," and "shatter." "Shot" is applied to Babs, while "shout" and "shatter" apply to her father. Because of the close association on the expression plane ("he'd" rhymes with "weed" and "shout" and "shatter" recall "shot"), we are more likely to see the actions as a contrast on the content plane: Babs's shooting up becomes an occasion for her father to shoot himself down. His reverse growth is especially marked by the extreme reaction he has to tickling her—he'd "shatter with laughter"—and the very telling omission of Babs's own reaction to his tickling. As a result, the distance between the fields of "growth" and "maturity" is emphasized here.

Sentences 11 and 12: "You're going to amount to something, baby, he'd say, shaping his hands, the smart ass; you're going to be as big this sway as you are the other. This *sway*, see, he'd say, and fold in delight."

In these two sentences, many of the previous relationships between semantic fields are altered, and some new ones are established. The first joke in sentence 11 depends on Babs's father using the phrase "to amount to something" in both its literal and idiomatic sense. The joke is both humorous and insulting because it establishes the two meanings for the phrase and then equates them: the growth of Babs's bosom is rendered first as the amassing of a great amount of something, and then as her greatest—indeed only—achievement. The semantic field of "bosom" has now moved from its association with plant growth to an association with physical growth in general, and it now has an ironic relationship with "social stature" as well.

"Baby" obviously participates in all the fields connected with growth, but its conventional meanings are also somewhat altered here. Her father uses the term at a time when any remaining resemblance between Babs and a "baby" is vanishing; as a result, the word has an ironic meaning in the field of physical growth. It is also ironic in the field of "maturity," since at this point Babs's father is far more babyish than she. On the figurative level, "baby" almost mocks its usual connotative association with "affection." Babs clearly has no affection for her father, and if he has any for her, he certainly has found an unusual way of expressing it.

The repetition of Babs's epithet for her father ("the smart ass") takes on new meaning here partly because it is a repetition; since it has been repeated so often, we look for new applications of it. First, it emphasizes another opposition between Babs and her father: she grows and changes, he remains the same—an incorrigible smart ass. The second, more interesting change in meaning depends both on the repetition and on the context. Because Babs's father is "shaping his hands" and making his tasteless jokes about Babs's big sway, and because on the facing page we see the photograph of a woman's bare back, we feel a pressure to read "smart ass" as applying to Babs's own body as well. Although the syntax does not naturally lead us to this reading, it does not absolutely rule it out. In the clause, "he'd say, shaping his hands, the smart ass," the most obvious way to read "smart ass" of course is as a description of "he"; nevertheless, it is also possible to read the phrase as the object of "shaping," as in "he'd say, shaping his hands, shaping the smart ass." This reading would be one that Babs herself is not conscious of creating, and as such it illustrates both the power of context and the existence of language's own life. Finally, of course, "smart" would now participate in yet another new field, that surrounding "goodlooking" and "stylish."

The "way/sway" pun moves the field of "growth" into a connection with the fields of "movement" and "direction." The vertical association of "growth" begun with "shot up" is now converted into the horizontal association of "swaying." The pun itself is of the simplest kind, but it also contains a sharp perception: Babs will be as big one way as she is the other, but each "way" will fully define itself by her "sway."

The repetition of Babs's father's words ("This *sway*, see? he'd say") at the beginning of sentence 12 is significant on the level of connotation because it emphasizes his reverse growth: he is the eight-year-old comedian badgering his audience, "Did you get it, huh, huh, huh, did you get it, huh?" The repetition makes the discourse itself sway on the expression plane; the identity of sounds ("this sway . . . this sway"), the rhyme which quickly follows in "say," and the alliteration of *s* sounds, give the last half of sentence 11 and the first half of 12 a singsong quality. The discourse swings over this ground once, appears to be moving on, and then swings back over it on both the content and the expression planes. This effect emphasizes the contrast between "swaying" and the "folding" that is mentioned in the last half of sentence 12—"[he'd] fold in delight." Babs sways because she has grown up, her father "folds" because he has grown infantile.

Sentence 13: "Now he's giving his worms gas, the beery s.o.b."

This sentence provides an effective conclusion because Babs finally finds the dismissive insult for her father, and in so doing, ties together or further alters our understanding of many of the semantic fields in this passage. "Beery" suggests the plausible inference that Babs's father made his insulting remarks while drunk; it also calls to mind "buttery" of sentence 3. Since "buttery" was connected there with "dairy," an opposition between the beer of a buttery and the milk of a dairy is now created. And this opposition has implications for the semantic fields surrounding "growth." The field of "milk" is associated with "babies" and that of "beer" with adults; and, of course, "milk" and "babies" are both also associated with women's breasts. In this passage, some of these relationships get turned on their heads. Babs's father's beer-drinking makes him infantile, and, in a sense, he expresses that condition very appropriately—through a fixation on a woman's breasts. Again speaking metaphorically, we can describe Babs's father's maturation this way: he has grown up on milk, then switched to beer, and that beer has brought him back to milk again.

Although Babs does not explicitly call her father a smart ass here, that epithet or some version of it is clearly implied in the activity she ascribes to him: giving his worms gas. So fixed is his character that he acts like an ass even after death. The final word neatly sums up Babs's attitude: the only "sob" Babs has for her dead father is the curse, "s.o.b."

This passage, then, not only does most things that Eco claims are characteristic of the aesthetic text—violates existing codes, trains our awareness of them, invents others—but it is a brilliant tour de force as well. The connections and interconnections it establishes within the somewhat unlikely group of semantic fields surrounding "bosom," "bottom," "buddy," "growth," "dairy," "milk," "weed," "liquor," "intelligence," "movement," and "direction" are so variously whimsical, serious, logical, preposterous, and ingenious that reading and analyzing the passage does train semiosis. It sensitizes us to the conventional nature of the linguistic system, to its extreme flexibility, its arbitrariness, and to its delightful capacity for ambiguity. The passage, in short, is a dazzling demonstration of the immensely rich inner life of language.

IV

The contrast between this semiotic analysis and the kind of analysis that we have done on the basis of our theory is striking. Where we see language as subordinate to character and action, Eco sees character and action as subordinate to language: the language does not work to reveal important information and attitudes about Babs Masters and her father which have consequences for the way we judge her now and later; instead, the characters are given their traits in order to reveal more effectively the relationships between the various semantic fields Gass wants to explore. This contrast between the semiotic approach and the one we have developed is even more striking when we consider an element of this passage that the semiotic analysis does not even consider: while Babs is speaking this passage, having this interior monologue, she is also entertaining the latest in a long series of lovers. The distance between her actions and her thoughts is of little or no consequence to the semiotic theorist while it obviously has important consequences for the kind of analysis our theory would have us do. To see which approach is more appropriate we must look more closely at the rest of Gass's work.

Although *Willie Masters' Lonesome Wife* has neither chapter divisions nor page numbers, it has four clearly marked parts. In the first section, the one from which our passage is taken, Babs is presented primarily as a psychologically real character in a setting which gives rise to plausible thoughts and potential action. As she entertains Phil Gelvin, a bald-headed salesman, we overhear her thoughts not only about her early maturity but also about such things as her attitudes toward sex, toward love, toward her husband, and toward men in general. A third person narrator also speaks occasionally, sometimes to remind us of the action that is happening as Babs speaks (she and Gelvin engaged in foreplay), sometimes to refer to Babs's memories of past desires. As a result, this narrator's discourse is a potentially valuable device in the characterization of Babs: his presence can emphasize Babs's distance from her actions.

In addition to these elements which point toward the realistic representation of his character, Gass, as we have seen in the semiotic analysis, also includes many elements which point toward language itself as the subject of the book. Gass's language is not only inventive and witty, it varies greatly in its range—Babs is sometimes crude, sometimes eloquent. Furthermore, because the typography is so varied and so unconventional (it is in this section that a page and its mirror image are printed side by side), we must focus on the medium to a considerable degree. As the book progresses, we give more and more emphasis to this aspect of our experience of the first part, and less and less importance to our experience of Babs as a realistic character.

Nevertheless, the potentially revealing distance between Babs's action and her thought is not rendered unimportant, but rather is given a different significance. As the book continues, Gass develops a rough analogy (it limps in several places) between language and its users, and Babs and her lovers.[4] Thus, in retrospect after we discover that Gelvin is an inept lover concerned only for his own pleasure, we see that the distance between Babs's thought and her actions is a way of illustrating the gap between the expressive potential of language and the often impoverished use we make of it. Babs, like language, has a rich and complex inner life that Gelvin never touches even when he is inside her. He uses her, but never truly knows her—and, suggests Gass, we may relate to language in the same way.

The second part of the work, which consists of a one-act play accompanied by Babs's extensive commentary, begins to make language an explicit subject of the text. The play, in which Babs once acted, is a farcical representation of a man's discovery that his penis has been baked in his breakfast bun, and his even more farcical attempt to communicate this discovery to his wife. The play, filled with puns and double-entendres, is a mere trifle, but serves as an occasion for the banquet of the commentary. That commentary soon becomes so dense that it virtually pushes the text of the play off the page, and it soon runs several pages ahead of the lines it is commenting on. Thus, our normal front-to-back pattern of reading is disturbed. As Babs comments, she displays several new voices: she employs at one point or another the abstract diction of a philosopher, the hortatory tone of a schoolteacher, the abusive attitude of a bully, the peremptory tone of a play director, the tongue-in-cheek pose of a punster, and the concise eloquence of a poet. The commentary consists of advice on how to stage the play, of questions about the meaning of the words in the stage directions, of commentary on previous commentary, and of many reflections—some serious, some playful—on the nature of language itself.

In this section Gass also continues to experiment with the typography. He gradually increases the size of the lines of commentary, and finally blows up the size of the asterisks which signal the footnotes—until we get the page at the end of the commentary which is almost completely taken up by them. In this section, too, Gass includes fragments from other narratives—a short scene from Hardy's *Tess of the d'Urbervilles* (printed inside the "balloon" of a cartoon character's speech), a sentence from Sterne's *Tristram Shandy* ("a cow broke in tomorrow morning to my Uncle Toby's fortifications") and the page from the imaginary "Passions of a Stableboy."

By this point, it is virtually impossible to make sense of the book as anything but an experiment with language. Not only has the original situation of Babs entertaining Gelvin faded into the background (it is not referred to at all in section two), but the nature of language is becoming more and more the explicit subject of the discourse. In part one, the explicit comments about language were tied to Babs's immediate situation (e.g., the narrator tells us, "She felt the terror of terminology" after she reflects on how inappropriately the word "screw" describes what a man does to a woman during sexual intercourse). Here quite often there is no special connection between either the traits ascribed to Babs or her particular situation with Gelvin and her commentary on language. Indeed, the philosophical reflections seem designed in part to emphasize the discrepancy between Babs as speaker and what she is speaking about. By flouting the conventions about consistency of characterization in this way, Gass is demonstrating another point: his character is in *essence* only words, only the sum of all the different things she says. If only she can be the speaker of all these different thoughts, then somehow we must accomodate our idea of her to that fact. This point gets made more explicitly in the short transition section between parts two and three. There Babs summarizes her position, saying in part: "I'm only a string of noises, after all—nothing more really—an arrangement, a column of air moving up and down, a queer growth like gall on a tree, a mimic of movement in silent readers maybe . . . and surely neither male nor female." Yet along with this nonhuman essence comes a nonhuman benefit. Although she may be sick or injured ("something has bitten a hole in my lining—some image perhaps, some out-of-work meaning, an unruly and maddened metaphor"), she will never die.

Part three continues both Gass's demonstration of and his explicit statements on the powers of language, but it also dwells on the limits of language as well. Gass presents several different discourses on the same page for several consecutive pages. As a result, we are again made aware of the conventional nature of the reading process: we cannot read all the way down the page without making hash out of each discourse. In the first discourse, Babs is transformed into a speaker with a male name, Joe Slatters, who explicitly reflects on the limits of communication. Slatters moves, by association rather than logic, from this topic to the arbitrariness of names, to the feeling of engulfing blackness which emanates from the blank page, and then once again to the difficulty of communication. Nevertheless, he reminds us that "only here in this sweet country of the word are rivers, streams, woods, gardens, houses, mountains, waterfalls, and the crowding fountains of the trees eternal as it's right they should be."

In the second discourse, Babs is the speaker, and she, too, moves by association from one topic to the next. She starts by elaborating on her previously expressed desire to be a poker table and ends by discussing masturbation. The main part of the discourse, though, is her attempt to find a culprit for her unhappy marriage. ("Maybe it was the walls or the windows, or the trees outside the windows, the wallpaper or the walls, the leaves, the layering dust..."). The discourse ends with Babs comparing making love with a man to masturbating ("No, it's simply not the same because when I'm masturbating, I—by Christ—call, witch up, conjure images and pictures, visions, fancies, wishes....")

Given the context of these remarks, we can make the best sense of them by understanding them metaphorically, by seeing the relations between Babs and her men as metaphors for the relations between language and its users. At the time Babs speaks these words, she is presumably having intercourse with Gelvin, yet he is so unsatisfactory a lover, she is hardly aware of him. Yet thinking of Willie offers her no solace; he pays virtually no attention to her, does not even notice when she is unfaithful. He is like those speakers who betray themselves without realizing it; too concerned with referents (walls, windows, etc.), they ignore the beauty of the system that allows them to refer. With such a poor master, Babs (and language) must solace herself with herself.

The third discourse, a dialogue involving four people (Leonora, Carlos, Angela, and Phillipe), is a clear-cut example of failed communication. Leonora, who, when she speaks of having a "shining sample salesman in his polished shoes astride me" appears to be Babs under yet another name, complains that because she is so used by men she has no place in her life for poetry; Carlos replies only with a sleepy "Hmm." Then Angela and Phillipe each express how much he or she wants to love the other, yet each pays no attention to the other's speech.

The fourth discourse, which begins after Babs's has ended, provides the alternative to the language of utility. The speaker, we discover, is the language of the imagination, and its subject is itself; its object is to describe itself, to sing its own praises: "It is the only speech which fills the balloon of the whole man ... [it] can only come from one who is, at least while speaking, in the poet's habit, what we—what each of us—should somehow be: a complete particular man."

In the last section of the book, Gelvin has left, carrying "his seed safely away in a sack," and Babs speaks directly to us. The previous implicit analogy between her and language now becomes an explicitly stated equivalence: "My dears, my dears ... [if you love me] how I would brood upon you: you the world, and I, the language." Almost all the demonstrations of the various powers and delights of language, and all the explicit rhetoric about its nature are brought together in the concluding paragraph which Babs and language speak as one:

Then let us have a language worthy of our world, a democratic style where rich and well-born nouns can roister with some sluttish verb yet find themselves content and uncomplained of. We want a diction which contains the quaint, the rare, the technical, the obsolete, the old, the lent, the nonce, the local slang and argot of the street in neighborly confinement. Our tone should suit our time: uncommon quiet dashed with common thunder. It should be as young and quick and sweet and dangerous as we are. Experimental and expansive—venturesome enough to make the chemist envy and the physicist catch up—it will give new glasses to new eyes and put those plots and patterns down we find our modern lot in. Metaphor must be its god now gods are metaphors. It should not be too cowardly of song, but show its substance, sing its tunes so honestly and loud that even eyes can hear them, and continue to be a tongue that is its own intoxicant.... It's not the languid pissing prose we've got, we need; but poetry, the human muse, full up, erect, and on the charge, impetuous and hot and loud and wild like Messalina going to the stews or those damn rockets streaming headlong into stars.

Clearly, then, if we were to analyze our passage from the first part of the novel with an eye focused primarily on discovering what it reveals about Babs as a psychologically realistic character—her feelings about her early maturity, her relation to her father, her relation to Gelvin, and so on—we would be analyzing inappropriately. None of these matters is important in itself; each is subordinate to Gass's concern with demonstrating the rich and diverse properties of language. Eco's semiotic approach is far more appropriate.

But all these statements imply the kind of reasoning that underlies the theory of part one. Eco's approach is superior, but only because it yields results consistent with Gass's intention in the work as a whole. We can only decide it is superior after examining the whole and discovering that Gass's intention is to call for and to demonstrate a "language worthy of our world," a language, that is, of great range and depth in tone, vocabulary, and syntax, a language whose richness and diversity will be both recognized and celebrated by its users. In one sense, then, Eco's approach offers us new tools for discovering and understanding the role of language in fiction, but it is our principle of viewing that role in light of an intention which determines when we ought to employ those tools. To understand why this conclusion is valid we need to consider the relation between the theories in more detail.

In many respects, Eco's theory and ours do not compete with but complement each other. Although the terms each theory uses to describe language are different, and although Eco's theory is more elaborate, they do not essentially disagree about the nature of language. The theories do imply disagreements about literature, but not systematic ones. Eco's approach to aesthetic texts and the theory we have developed in part one have only some objects in common. That is, each theory attempts to account for phenomena that it identifies in its own way (in our theory, the class of works labeled fiction; in his, texts whose violations of existing codes enrich their content); the two sets intersect, but not every member of one is a member of the other. Eco's theory would not claim to apply to *The Ambassadors, Persuasion,* and *Sister Carrie* because these texts are not ambiguous and self-focusing in his sense of those terms. (Although Dreiser violates norms of the code and so writes an ambiguous text, his violations result in impoverishment rather than enrichment of the content.) And, despite Eco's implying in his defense of the value of aesthetic texts (see p. 192 above) that all such texts are fictional, there is nothing about his criteria which exclude nonfictional works from the class of aesthetic texts. Nonfictional texts can surely use the medium in an ambiguous and self-focusing manner that reveals new insights into the linguistic system; we can readily imagine, for example, an essay on semiotics that deliberately violated existing codes in order to exemplify some of the points about the medium it was trying to make.

Nevertheless, for some aesthetic texts, e.g., "I like Ike" and *Lolita,* the two theories do offer competing explanations. These different accounts result from the difference between our theory's assumption about the importance of intention for the way we understand any text, and Eco's assumption that in any aesthetic text the process of semiosis is always the focus of our attention. Just before he offers "I like Ike" as a simple example of an aesthetic text, Eco says that such texts direct "the attention of the addressee primarily to *its own shape*" (p. 264, his emphasis). Later he puts the point even more strongly: "If someone, whether consciously or unconsciously, follows the rule for making *mots-valise à la Joyce* he is not speaking 'ungrammatical' English so much as 'Finneganian.' What he is really saying is far less important than the underlying statement: *'I am joycing'* " (p. 272). With that second statement, Eco assumes a position rather close to Fish's belief in the primacy of deliberative acts. But our consideration of Fish—and of Lodge as well—allows us to see that "I am joycing" or a sentence's own shape will *not necessarily* be the most important aspect of a communication containing portmanteau words or other aesthetic elements. What is most important will depend on the sentence's use by a speaker with a specific intention in a certain context. In its original use as a campaign slogan "I like Ike" did not direct attention *primarily* to its own shape, but to the speaker's (or button-wearer's) support for Eisenhower's candidacy; the aspects of its expression form which direct attention to its shape are a *means* of making it a more effective slogan. Used by another speaker in another context, e.g., as an example text by a professor in a lecture on semiotics, "I like Ike" could direct attention primarily to its shape. And, of course, the same reasoning applies to the use of portmanteau words.

With *Lolita,* the contrast between the two theories is greater. Like the theorists we examined in part one, Eco assumes that everything in a fictional aesthetic text can be explained by reference to language; indeed, as we have seen in the remarks just quoted and in our analysis of *Willie Masters' Lonesome Wife,* denotation becomes devalued in his approach while the *process* of semiosis, the production of second and third level connotations, becomes the center of attention. With *Lolita,* then, Eco's approach would lead us to focus primarily on what Nabokov's manipulation of his medium reveals about the nature of language, the flexibility of the codes, and so on. As I have tried to argue in the previous chapter, if we view *Lolita* primarily as an opportunity for Nabokov to display his verbal artistry rather than as the representation of an action, we miss both much of the novel's pleasure and much of its value.

Nevertheless, Eco's approach to *Lolita* would not be as invalid as it would be incomplete; or rather it would be invalid only in that it would make a subordinate element of the work the dominant one. Although the approach entailed by our theory does not fully account for our experience of *Lolita,* Eco's would be more unsatisfactory. *Lolita,* in fact, is a work for which the two approaches would complement each other very well. Our theory leads us to discover the intention of the work and the crucial role language plays for the achievement of the intention; Eco's helps explain the additional pleasure offered by the style: at least part of the reason we marvel at Nabokov's skill is that his manipulation of the medium leads us to recognize new potentialities in our language.[5]

In summary, since authors will occasionally manipulate their medium so that segments of their texts become highly ambiguous and self-focusing, but since very few authors make such manipulation a controlling intention of an entire work, Eco's theory can offer us acute insight into some uses of language in fiction, but will rarely be able to account for our experience of whole works. *Willie Masters' Lonesome Wife* is the exception that proves the rule; the elements of Eco's theory that limit it—the assumption that the process of semiosis in aesthetic texts is always more important than other levels of content, the assumption that an aesthetic text is only language—are precisely the elements that enable his theory to give us the best insight into Gass's work. Gass, it seems, has made very similar assumptions in writing his own work. We can return now to our questions about what these assumptions imply for the fictional status of *Willie Masters' Lonesome Wife;* and as we answer those questions, we shall also implicitly show why Gass's work is an exception rather than an example of a common form, or a form that is likely to become common.

V

Each of our initial questions—is *Willie Masters' Lonesome Wife* really fiction? Is it worthwhile fiction?—involves us in some knotty problems that require some preliminary consideration. Our first question commits us to developing a working definition of the class of works we call "fiction." As the terms are generally understood, "novel" refers to a subset of works within the larger set "fiction"; thus, for a satisfactory definition, we must look beyond such identifying characteristics of the novel as character and story. At the same time, however, we would not call a set of utterances related *only* by a shared linguistic trait or property—for example, the use of the letter *a* exactly once in each word of the series—a fiction. Again as the terms are generally used, "nonfictional," or for the sake of clarity, "nonfictive" utterances are those which make or imply direct truth claims while "fictive" ones are those which do not. Following Barbara Herrnstein Smith, we can explain this very problematic distinction this way: in nonfictive utterances, the speaker is a historically determinate individual, while in fictive utterances, the speaker is created by such an individual.[6] As many examples, perhaps most obviously those in historical novels indicate, individual fictions may be comprised of both fictive and nonfictive utterances; yet, at the same time, fiction is involved in some essential way with the fictive. One important difference between the representation of a historical event in a historical novel and a historian's reconstruction of an historical event is that the novel has a created narrator and the history has a "real" one.

Keeping all these observations in mind, we can identify a work as a member of the class "fiction" if and only if it is comprised of a series of utterances which has some semantic coherence and which, as a whole, is understood to be spoken by a created speaker. This definition will be clarified as we continue, but now we must turn to some problems raised by our second question about *Willie Masters' Lonesome Wife,* i.e., is it valuable fiction.

This question leads us, not for the first time, into the very complex world of value judgments, and the complexity is compounded here because *Willie Masters' Lonesome Wife* is a contemporary work, one that has not yet faced the test of time. The value question is also more problematic because the issues we are concerned with in asking it to go beyond the particulars of Gass's work. We are concerned with *Willie Masters' Lonesome Wife* as an example of one *kind* of fiction and we cannot simply assume that whatever is true of Gass's work must inevitably be true of all works like it. For both these reasons, a conclusion such as *"Willie Master's Lonesome Wife* does not approach the achievement of *The Ambassadors, Sister Carrie, Persuasion,* and *Lolita"* is not a decisive judgment against fiction that makes language an end in itself.

In order to avoid such invidious comparisons, let us assume, first, that Eco's case for the value of aesthetic texts is convincing; he argues, as we have seen, that such texts are valuable because they develop in us an awareness of the way our cultural world is organized and they effectively train us in the ability to use one of the major sign systems which organize that world. Let us also assume that our fascination with language can be as endless as our fascination with characters in action. If it is ridiculous to say, "when you have read one tragedy you have read them all," it is equally ridiculous to say "when you have read one work like *Willie Masters' Lonesome Wife,* you have read them all." Although these positions may be debatable, they serve our purposes well because they give Gass's work the benefit of any doubt. These assumptions do not end our value inquiry but alter its direction by leading us to some formal questions that have implications for our evaluation of it as fiction: (1) Why is it so short—less than sixty pages, even counting the pages with photographs, the one that is virtually all asterisks, and the one that is a mirror-image of another? (2) Why does it become more and more essaylike as it progresses?

The first question has even greater force when we consider that

Gass's controlling intention allows him considerable freedom of choice in the selection, placement, and number of elements in the work. The basic movement of the work from the representation of a potentially realistic fictional situation to the expression of more and more statements explicitly about language, and virtually independent of Babs, is crucial to the successful achievement of the intention: the later statements gain their persuasive force from the earlier demonstrations of language's diverse powers and properties. Nevertheless, within that basic movement, Gass could replace many of the specific devices he employs without materially detracting from the effectiveness of the work. What are important in the progression are not the specific devices which reveal the inner life of language, but rather those revelations themselves. Gass might, for example, have chosen a different farcical one-act play as the occasion for the commentary in part two; he might have chosen different fragments from other narratives or placed them at different points in the work; he might even have chosen to explore different semantic fields in part one. He could not, however, leave out all farcical uses of language, all fragments from other narratives that suggest the continuity of the language of the imagination, or all exploration of semantic fields. By the end of the work Gass needs to include a full spectrum of devices that reveal the range of properties he wants to claim for language, but other than that he has considerable freedom.

From our point of view, the most interesting consequence of Gass's intention is that it apparently implies little or no limitation on how many times or through how many different devices the components of that style can be revealed. Gass, nevertheless, emphasizes variety rather than repetition: as we have seen, he employs different devices within each section of the work, and employs widely different strategies from one section to the next. The wisdom of this choice becomes obvious when we consider our experience of one of the more repetitive devices, or perhaps more accurately, one of the more common themes Gass plays variations on. By the time we reach the fourth or fifth typographical device designed to make us conscious of the conventions of reading, we pay little attention to it; in fact, if we react at all, we are less likely to treat it with the pleasure of discovery than with the indifference (or worse, contempt) of familiarity. The reason why indifference or tedium would result from the repeated revelations of the medium's properties is that the primary content of the work is the process of semiosis. Because the work progresses neither through the stages of a narrative nor through the steps of an argument but through the revelation of the major elements of the semiotic process in the linguistic sign-system, and because that system is so flexible, that revelation will be accomplished rather compactly. As we have seen in our analysis of the passage from the first section, when used by someone as inventive as Gass, language can reveal a multitude of its properties in a relatively short space, sometimes in even just a few well-chosen words. Thus, although Gass's intention allows him considerable freedom with the specific parts of his work, its success also depends on his restricting its length rather strictly.

This limitation of course does not constitute a strong objection against the value of *Willie Masters' Lonesome Wife:* a successful novella is more worthwhile than an unsuccessful novel. And, I think, *Willie Masters' Lonesome Wife* is quite successful; Gass's intention is worthwhile and his execution of it, for the most part, is very skillful.[7] Nevertheless, most people would agree that success with the longer form constitutes success of a higher order; we do not, for example, value any of James's novellas, exquisite as they are, as highly as we value *The Ambassadors.*

This restriction on length would be common to most works which made language an end in itself for much the same reason: since the medium is so flexible and rich, whatever property or properties of language an author wished to focus the reader's attention on would most likely be demonstrated concisely; after a point rather quickly arrived at, further demonstration would simply be repeating rather than expanding upon or completing the point. Nevertheless, this length limitation is not an absolute. If, for example, an author wanted to make *styles* rather than general properties of the linguistic system the focus of his work, the length limitation would not necessarily apply. An author who wanted to illustrate the pleasures and perils of the major literary styles of the last three centuries might write a work several times the length of *Willie Masters' Lonesome Wife:* not only would he have numerous styles to work with, but he could work with each one in numerous contexts. This author would encounter difficulties in making his work a fiction, but we can better understand those difficulties after considering why Gass's work has so much explicit commentary on language.

There are two especially significant features of this commentary. First, much of it does not seem fictive; indeed, it becomes less and less fictive as the work progresses. This effect is a direct consequence of Gass's success in destroying the traditional concept of character. By the time we reach the third section, Babs has been so fully exploded that we read the statements about language not as the utterances of a fictional character but as the statements of the nonfictional author. The second revealing feature of this commentary is that much of it does not exemplify the qualities it recommends. Consider, for example, the following passage from section three, which is also an example of a place where Gass seems to be speaking directly to us, and a paraphrase of it.

Again there is in every act of the imagination a disdain of utility, and a glorious, free show of human strength; for the man of imagination dares to make things for no better reason than they please him—because he *lives*. And everywhere, again, he seeks out unity: in the word he unifies both sound and sense; among many meanings, he discovers similarities, and creates new and singular organizations; between words and things he further makes a bond so that symbols seem to contain their objects. . . .

Paraphrase: Again the imagination acts with no regard for usefulness and every regard for a marvelous, unfettered display of human strength; for he who has imagination is not afraid to make things simply because they please him—because he is *alive*. And everywhere, again, he searches for oneness; in the word he brings together sound and meaning; among many meanings, he uncovers likenesses, and constructs different and unique arrangements; between words and things he creates a connection so that the words seem to embody their objects. . . .

Gass's version is fine prose, and no doubt superior to the paraphrase, but not that much is lost in my version. Gass does not "unite sound and sense" here nor does he create a "bond so that symbols seem to contain their objects," but uses language, as I do in the paraphrase, as a *means* to an *end* of expressing thoughts. This nonfictive, essaylike passage, nevertheless, plays an important role in creating the effectiveness of Gass's work; in some ways it is more important for our understanding of his intention than the passage we analyzed. To understand why Gass needs such passages and how they affect the fictional status of his work, let us imagine it as having no explicit rhetoric on the nature of language. Let us suppose, that is, that the whole work were like part one, an extended monologue by Babs on whatever came into her mind as she entertained Gelvin.

This hypothetical work would have one of two possible shapes. It might actualize a potential in the present part one and make such facts about Babs's character as her relationship to her father and the distance between her thought and actions important for their own sake. In this case, the role of language in the work would resemble the role it has in *Lolita;* it would offer us considerable pleasure in its own richness and ingenuity apart from its contribution to an intention, but it would also function as a crucial variable in the successful accomplishment of the intention, which most likely would be the representation of Babs as a character in her fixed fate as a lonesome wife.

The second possibility is that the experimentation with language would be so great, would take such precedence over the representation of Babs that we could not make sense of the work as a representation of a character or an action. In this case, Gass would again have created the potential for educating us about the powers of language by exemplifying those powers in the work. Because, however, we would have *only the demonstration* of language's rich inner life, the work as a whole would either be extremely confusing, or it would not be fiction. I can perhaps best explain this point by using Eco's terms.

In a passage such as the one we have analyzed, the information about the codes, the communication about the process of semiosis, or what we may call the metalinguistic communication, is in essence a communication by connotation. That information is mediated content; the passage makes us focus on the way individual sentences express their denotative (and indeed, first-level connotative meanings), and the expression and the denotation (or the expression, denotation, and connotation) unite to communicate the further connotative content about the nature of language. In our text with no explicit rhetoric on language, this content would still be present but it would remain in the background—just as it would in every other such passage in the work. Faced with a whole work in which we had no possibility of seeing individual sections as constituent parts of a representation of a character or an action, and in which we had no explicit statements about the nature of language and no implicit signals from the typography to point us to the importance of the metalinguistic communication, we would either be quite unable to reach any understanding of the whole, or would decide that it was not a fiction. Concluding that the work was primarily about its medium would also entail concluding that it was a series of linguistic exercises, and/or would entail settling on that interpretation only for lack of a better one, just as we could impose a thematic coherence on the work by looking for our theme at a high enough level of generality.

A concrete example will help demonstrate these points. There is a fairly well known language game which consists of a speaker giving his listener several sentences of the form "Molly and Polly like x but they don't like y" and then asking him to compose a sentence that fits the pattern. The listener is invariably baffled for a time; he can find no apparent pattern to a series of sentences such as "Molly and Polly like beer but they don't like wine. Molly and Polly like floors, but they don't like ceilings. Molly and Polly like rubber, but they don't like tires. Molly and Polly like books, but they don't like words." The trick is to figure out that what Molly and Polly like even more than books is letters, double letters—or more accurately, that what they like is anything referred to by a word containing a double letter. In the terms we have been using, the Molly and Polly game cannot be figured out until we focus on the process of semiosis.

Suppose that we do not know the game and are presented the above series as a text. That series is analogous to the postulated confusing or unfictional version of Gass's work. Like that text, this series is fictive; but even if we eventually discover its pattern, we would not consider it a fiction; it is too different from the texts we usually consider as belonging to that class—it lacks their common trait of semantic coherence.

Now suppose that again we do not know the Molly and Polly game and are presented with the following series as a text: "Molly and Polly like Daddy, but they don't like Mom. They like his looks, but not her face. They like Daddy's boots, but not Mom's shoes. They like his cigarettes but not her drinks. Molly and Polly like Daddy, but they don't like Mom." This text is analogous to our first postulated version of *Willie Masters' Lonesome Wife;* it is a fiction in which the process of semiosis remains as a background content. That is, although this text follows the pattern of the Molly and Polly game, it follows a more primary pattern at the level of denotative content (Molly and Polly like things associated with Dad but not with Mom). Thus, if asked to choose which of the following sentences would be more appropriate to add to the text, "Molly and Polly like Mommy but they don't like Dad," or "Molly and Polly like Dad's suits but not Mommy's dresses," we would unhesitatingly choose the second. The pattern created by the first-level denotative content is dominant and the double-letter pattern remains in the background.[8]

In Gass's version of *Willie Masters' Lonesome Wife*, the explicit statements about language—and the typographical experimentation as well—make the nature of language part of the denotation and first-level connotation of the text. As a result, they give us internal directions for interpreting the demonstrations of language's power; they bring the higher-level connotative content of those demonstrations from the background of the text into its foreground. But as we have seen, sometimes these devices convert the text from fiction to essay. There is, then, a curious paradox about Gass's work as metafiction: in order for us to read it as fiction that focuses our attention on the medium of fiction, a substantial segment of it must be nonfictive, must resemble an essay more than it does fiction. And parts of the work (such as the statement about the language of the imagination I have quoted and paraphrased above) must use language as a means in order to make us focus on it as an end.

Realizing this paradox will affect our evaluation of *Willie Masters' Lonesome Wife* in one respect: we cannot consider it as a highly successful example of a certain kind of fiction because its kind is not simply fiction; it is, instead, part essay, part fiction, or, as Gass calls it, an essay-novella.[9] Realizing the paradox will not of course affect the way we evaluate the work as an example of its own kind. That evaluation depends on such matters as how accurate and perceptive we judge Gass's statements about language, how important we feel it is to make such statements, how well we think he has demonstrated the powers he is claiming for language, how well we feel he has manipulated the conventions of traditional fiction, and so on.

The larger, more far-reaching question this analysis raises is whether all fictions which strive to make language their subject must become part essay as well.[10] The chief problem, we have seen, is to make the metalinguistic content move from the background of the text to the foreground. Gass's use of typography suggests one possible method for creating a fully fictional work whose subject is the process of semiosis. Again, Eco's terms provide an economical and accurate way to explain how the method works. In typographical manipulation, the lower level of the expression plane in the written medium (the typeface) contributes to the content plane. Gass's mirror-image page, for example, is a sign-function whose denotation is "left-to-right inverse of facing page"; its first-level connotation is "notice the left-to-right convention which governs reading and writing" and its second-level connotation is "examine the uses of the medium here."

In the more familiar terms we use to talk about fiction, such typographical manipulation is a signal from the author about where we should focus our attention in the text as a whole. Like any other signal, if it exists in isolation, we shall regard it as a deviation from the pattern organizing the foreground content of the text, but if we consistently receive such signals, as we do in *Willie Masters' Lonesome Wife,* and if the rest of the text rewards our close attention to the medium, we shall invert the normal means-ends relationship between the medium and its content.

Thus, we now have an answer to the basic question of this chapter: it is indeed possible to write fiction in which language becomes an end in itself. At the same time, we have also found a formal reason why such fiction is relatively uncommon: to demonstrate language's powers and properties is a necessary but not a sufficient condition for such fiction; an author must always use some other device, some other set of signals to make the metalinguistic content move from the background of the work to the foreground. Since an inventory of such devices would have a limited use—there is no invariant relationship between the use of a particular device and the creation of a particular effect—I shall not attempt to compile one here, but instead shall consider as a final example a possible fictional work which makes the medium its subject without using typographical experimentation to bring the metalinguistic content into the foreground.

The work is our hypothetical one demonstrating the pleasures and perils of major prose styles in the last three centuries. Suppose our author followed the sensible course of writing each chapter in a different style. He could then use the powerful system of signals formed by the title of the work and the titles of the chapters to focus our attention on the medium. Even if, however, the author imitated or echoed the various styles in the chapter titles (e.g., "A Single Woman of Large Talent in Want of Three or Four Couples in a Country Village" for the chapter on Austen's style), he would at those points be using language as a means. Furthermore, though such echoing or imitative titles could contribute to our understanding of the medium, they are more important for the effect they would have in common with straightforward one-word titles like "Austen," "Fielding," "Dickens," or "James": both tell us where to focus our attention as we read each chapter.

More difficult than making us focus on the language is the task of making the work a fiction rather than a casebook on style. The author would need some structure that would allow him to write a continuous, coherent narrative, yet would also allow that narrative to remain subordinate to the language in which it is told. One possible structure is the formula plot of the hard-boiled detective novel. The deliberate and extreme violations of the codes controlling the Hammet-Chandler style in such chapters as those on Fielding and James would help bring the metalinguistic content into the foreground. Furthermore, our author could keep the narrative subordinate to the medium by having the murderer leave clues in different styles, and by having his detective solve the mystery only after he learns to make the appropriate inferences from the *style* rather than from the content of the clues.

For such a work, which our author might call *The Stylish Eye*, to gain a place among the first rank of fiction would of course be difficult but by no means impossible. Indeed, it would be no more impossible than for any more traditional fiction to enter that rank. If our author's insight into those styles and his ear for capturing them were as acute as, say, James's insight into human psychology and his eye for literary craftsmanship, *The Stylish Eye* might approach the achievement of *The Ambassadors*. The pleasure and knowledge it would offer would be enormously different from the pleasure and knowledge offered by James's masterpiece, but it would not therefore be inferior in kind. Once we grant the author his subject, once we recognize that language, since it is so much a part of human life, is as legitimate a subject for fiction as human action, then our evaluation of works such as the hypothetical *The Stylish Eye* will depend on what it does for every other work of fiction: on how well the author creates and treats his subject.

In conclusion, then, our consideration of a particular work has once again led us to discover a limitation in the theory we developed in part one. Although fictional works which make language an end in itself are likely to remain relatively uncommon, they do represent a possibility that our theory did not anticipate. Determining what the limitations revealed in the last two chapters mean, first for our attempt to build a comprehensive theory, and second for our understanding of the relationship between our theory and the others we have examined here, is the task of the final chapter.

7

Multiple Questions, Multiple Answers, and the Status of Our Theory: Pluralism and the Language of Fiction

I

If this essay has taught us nothing else, it has taught us humility. It has shown that each of the carefully woven, apparently warm and comfortable blanket theories designed to cover the great body of fiction (or even of literature) either has several gaping holes or an area of such limited dimensions that some parts of the body are left out in the cold. If our discoveries were not so invariable, if they did not also apply to our own theory, we might be inclined to go on weaving, mending, and stitching until we had fashioned what we might now call the ultimate theoretical comforter, the single theory that could cover the immense body of relations between language and fiction. But we now know—and have the conviction of experience behind our knowledge—that such a theory is not possible. We know, in other words, that fully answering the central question of this essay—what is the role of the medium in the art of fiction—requires us to become pluralists. By considering just what kind of pluralism our investigation leads us to and by challenging our conclusions one last time, we can clarify the relation of our theory to the others we have considered, and consequently, can more precisely establish the claims we are making for its powers.

In the previous chapters we have discovered limits to our theory that are both genuine and serious. In concluding that language's role in fiction cannot always be satisfactorily explained in light of an intention and that the use of language in fiction could become an end in itself, we have in effect discovered that both our theory's fundamental methodological principle and its basic prediction about language's role in fiction are not universally valid. At the same time, however, each of the challenging texts has also reaffirmed the usefulness of the theory. Our approach to language in *Lolita* does illuminate a substantial part of its role, and Eco's semiotic approach to *Willie Masters' Lonesome Wife* is appropriate only because of Gass's intention in the whole work. These two conclusions together—the theory is limited, the theory is nevertheless useful—suggest, first, that our pluralism is one which must recognize the validity not merely of different questions about literature, but also of different answers to the same question; they suggest, second, that our theory needs to be supplemented rather than revised.

Revising the theory to account for the challenging cases will only weaken its explanatory power for other works. If *Lolita* leads us to stipulate that successful uses of language in fiction must be both intrinsically beautiful and subordinate to an intention, we shall then become unable to account for works such as *Sister Carrie*. If *Willie Masters' Lonesome Wife* leads us to adopt the assumptions and techniques of semiotic analysis for all fiction, we shall then become unable to account for language in works such as *The Ambassadors, Sister Carrie,* and *Persuasion,* and shall only be able to produce a more insufficient explanation of language's role in *Lolita*. If, however, we recognize that our approach to works like Nabokov's and Gass's is valid but insufficient, we shall retain the theory's considerable explanatory power even as we search for the necessary supplements to answer our questions about language in those works.

As for those supplements, Eco's approach, we have seen, is excellent for *Willie Masters' Lonesome Wife,* and helpful for *Lolita* as well. With Nabokov's novel, however, we seem to need a more general theory of value or artistic pleasure that would encompass elements of both Eco's approach and ours, and would explain the relation between the intrinsic power and beauty of any subordinate part or element of a work and its function in the whole. Developing such a theory would be an interesting and challenging task, but the more important point for our purposes here is the general one: our question about language in fiction ultimately requires more than one answer.

II

As described thus far, our pluralism is one with numerous limits; these limits become especially obvious when we compare our position with the kind of pluralism adopted by Wayne Booth in his extended and impressive treatment of the subject, *Critical Understanding.*[1] Booth's pluralism does have limits, but in welcoming New Critics, reader critics, structuralists, deconstructionists, and others into his critical universe (all under certain conditions, perhaps the most important of which is that each practitioner must be able to get out of his own system long enough to understand what someone in another system is doing), Booth appears to be far more genuinely pluralistic than we are. Though we are willing to admit that no one theory can be comprehensive, we remain committed to searching for the "best" account of language's role in any one work. Though the theory is not sufficient by itself, we are claiming that it is superior to each of the other five we have considered. Furthermore, we are claiming that our approach not merely supersedes but repudiates the alternative theories of part one. Even what we might offer as the most pluralistic aspect of our approach, the ability to benefit from the insights and techniques of the other theories, ultimately betrays a bias. We do not use these insights and techniques as reasons for reevaluating the repudiated theories, but appear to seize upon them as happy accidents (even a broken clock tells the right time twice a day) and appropriate them for our superior theory. Thus, for example, we apply some elements of Fish's experiential analysis to linguistic units controlled by grammar rather than defined by deliberative acts; we see Lodge's realization technique as a means to an end rather than an end in itself; and in our semiotic analysis of *Willie Masters' Lonesome Wife,* we adopt some of Miller's strategies for deconstruction but stop short of opening the text up to complete free play. The longer we look at our alleged pluralism, the more it appears to be actually a disguised monism.

Booth gives good reasons why we should find this conclusion, if substantiated by further analysis, very troubling. Monisms, though not without their uses, ultimately impoverish rather than enrich the life of criticism. Once we adopt the view that there is a single right approach to any text (though, in our case, we would not see that approach as identical for all texts, and indeed for some few we would want to combine two approaches), we seek as a matter of course to reduce the variety of critical questions that might be asked of it. Furthermore, once we become convinced of a monism, we are likely to judge everyone else's work according to how well it supports that position; this procedure, as anyone who has had his work reviewed by a monist knows, leads to misunderstanding and meaningless critical conflict.

Of course these negative practical consequences would not be decisive reasons against seeking a single right view, if someone could show that literature was a single entity about which only one kind of knowledge is possible, desirable, or "best." But such a demonstration seems impossible because different conceptions of literature emerge out of critics choosing different first principles for their criticism, and these principles, like the postulates of a geometry, seem beyond dispute. Building on the work of W. B. Gallie, Booth maintains that literature is "an essentially contested concept," one for which no single definition proves superior.[2] Just as an economist and a psychologist may explain an event such as a man's taking his wife out to dinner in very different but equally compelling ways, so a critic who locates literature in the reader may offer an account of a text's meaning that is very different from but as persuasive in its way as one offered by a critic who locates literature in the text. Because the first principles and ensuing general conceptions of each analyst are so different, their explanations can all be valued, for they yield different knowledge about the phenomena they seek to explain.

To go even this far toward a more genuine pluralism is to cast doubt on the major work of the previous chapters; at the same time, however, that work seems to cast doubt on this pluralism. If we drop the apparently monistic assumption that a single comprehensive theory of language in fiction is possible, we must ask the troublesome question of whether we have pitted different theories against each other when they are not in fact opponents, or not opponents among whom we can absolutely choose. If Fish's view that a text is the series of mental operations readers perform as they read it, Lodge's view that a text is the series of sentences its author composed, Miller's view that a text is a centerless system of signs, Eco's that a text is an ordered system of signs, and Olson's and ours (at least in part one) that a text is a linguistic representation of some aspect of human experience are all equally valid, then we must retract all claims for the superiority of our theory and offer it as just one more alternative. But to say at this stage of the essay that Fish, Lodge, and Miller offer ways of talking about language in fiction that are as valid as the one offered by our theory seems to be soft-headed. Have we not scrupulously tried to avoid prejudging these other theories, have we not put them to the test of doing what they claimed they can do, and have we not found them wanting? If our alternatives are a monism that sees our theory as superior and a pluralism that sees all four theories as equally valid, then, for heaven's sake, we might think, let us be monists and stop trying to apologize for it.

The general problem we are facing here is how to develop a pluralism with appropriate limits. To set too many is to adopt a disguised monism which would slowly destroy the life of criticism by depriving it of the variety of nutrients it needs, while to set too few is to adopt a relativism which would slowly destroy that life by giving it too many stimulants and not enough sustenance. The specific problem we are facing is whether the six apparently competing theories of language in fiction actually do compete, and if so, whether we have sufficient grounds for choosing among them.

The most immediately appealing way to establish appropriate limits is to identify some irreducible core of a text that all approaches must respect. But to follow this strategy is to be led into error because establishing such a core would only provide the basis for a new monism: we could judge all approaches according to how well they illuminated that core. Furthermore, identifying such a core is an impossible task because different approaches will construe texts in radically different ways: Miller's *Persuasion* has very little in common with our *Persuasion,* and what it does have in common with ours, it would not share with Fish's. To say that Miller must respect a core of determinate meaning in the text is only to impose our monistic assumptions on him.

The better way to solve our problem, the more workable method of founding a settlement between the rocks of monism and the swamps of relativism is to look harder at the different questions critics ask, to try to make some worthwhile distinctions among them, and thus to understand the implied relations among the answers to each kind of question. Very specific questions such as what is the narrator's tone in the first sentence of *Pride and Prejudice* ("It is a truth universally acknowledged that a single man in possession of a good fortune must be in want of a wife") have determinate answers because there is some clearly established, generally agreed upon phenomenon that exists independently of the question (the sentence itself). Different answers to these kinds of questions will compete with each other and can be judged as more or less adequate by reference to the phenomena they purport to explain. General questions such as what is literature, what is language, or what is meaning do *not* have single right answers because they are not about clearly defined, generally agreed upon phenomena (hence, the reason for the questions), and so different answers, in a sense, partially "create" the phenomena. More precisely, they construe independent phenomena as being one thing rather than another. Since there is no generally agreed upon way to identify the nature of the phenomena apart from their construal, the different answers are not so much competing explanations as different first principles. These principles, in turn, lead to the construction of different theories capable of different kinds of explanation. Intermediately specific questions such as what is the meaning of *The Ambassadors* have determinate answers within each postulated conception of meaning, but multiple answers across conceptions. The answers are determinate within conceptions because *The Ambassadors* exists as an independent, generally agreed upon phenomenon to be explained. The answers are multiple across conceptions because they are the consequence of different first principles; although, in one sense, the answers do compete (they all seek to give comprehensive accounts of the independent phenomenon, *The Ambassadors*), the competition cannot be resolved because we cannot choose among the first principles upon which the different answers are based. We can distinguish between the competition of answers to the specific questions and that of answers to the intermediately general ones by calling the first resolvable and the second nonresolvable.

Questions such as the one we have addressed here (what is the role of the medium in the art of fiction), which ask for specific explanations of such general entities as language and fiction, have answers whose relationships are most complex. The complexity arises because the answers both do and do not compete in resolvable ways, as we can see by examining the most knotty relationship in this essay, that between our theory and those of Fish, Lodge, and Miller. Since these theorists postulate a different view of literature from the one we do, their particular interpretations of individual texts would not be in a resolvable competition with ours; these interpretations, in one sense, are answers to essentially different questions. However, since these critics use their different first principles to construct theories that claim to explain phenomena which exist independently of their theories' postulated conceptions of literature, and since our theory makes the same claim, the different interpretations, in another important sense, do compete in resolvable ways. These independent phenomena are our intuitive knowledge of language and our experience with it. And although language itself, like literature, may be defined in many ways, there is a clearly established, generally agreed upon concept used to describe these phenomena: linguistic competence—though perhaps since we emphasize language in use more than Chomsky did when he coined the term we might amend it to "discourse competence," a term which would cover both knowledge and experience. Our case for the superiority of grammatical closure over deliberative acts, for the possibility of paraphrase in fiction, for the necessity of seeking to understand intentions, and for the determinacy of language in use all ultimately depend on appeals to what we know about language and what our experiences with it are. We are claiming, then, that interpretations based on the theories of Fish, Lodge, and Miller would not be invalid, but rather that they would be deficient as interpretations which purport to take discourse competence into account. More generally, we are claiming not that these theorists are wrong to define literature as they do, but that to define it in those ways fails to do justice to certain aspects of our discourse competence, and consequently hinders rather than advances the attempt to explain our experience of language in fiction.

Again, by reference to discourse competence, we are claiming that our theory is more appropriately flexible than Olson's and more widely applicable than Eco's. Similarly, we find our own conception of literature as the linguistic representation of human action unable to account fully for our experience of every work, and must therefore acknowledge its limits.

This explanation of the relation between our theory and the other five we have examined casts new light on the "benevolent imperialism" of our investigation, on, that is, our willingness to seize upon an insight from another approach and appropriate it for our own purposes. This imperialism, in effect, results from our remaining committed to a general pluralism even while pursuing a question which we believe has a best answer. As pluralists we recognize that the different approaches are likely to produce different worthwhile insights because they will open up different aspects of the same question. At the same time, in pursuing the most compelling answer to our question and finding some approaches deficient, we generally also find a flaw in the way these insights are used within each theory; consequently, we modify them for more effective use. Thus, as mentioned above, Fish's analysis of deliberative acts gets applied to grammatical units, Lodge's concept of realization becomes a useful way of explaining some uses of language in service of an intention, and Miller's deconstructive method provides an excellent beginning for our understanding the semiotics of *Willie Masters' Lonesome Wife*. Most dramatically, Eco's approach is adopted wholesale for Gass's work. In short, even as we discover the shortcomings of the competing explanations, as pluralists we welcome their existence. Encountering them not only requires us to reexamine our conclusions, but also to strengthen our theory, to make it more capacious and flexible.

Our pluralism, then, has different limits for different questions, and some relatively strict ones for our central question. If someone can show that discourse competence is a misleading or erroneous concept, we must give up all claims to the superiority of our theory; if someone can show that this concept, like the assertion that language plays different roles in different works, is a product of the theory rather than an independent foundation of it, we must also give up those claims. Until then, however, because our theory incorporates a superior account of our intuitive knowledge and general experience with language, we are justified in claiming that our theory gives not just a different but a better explanation of the role language plays in the competent reader's experience of successful fiction.

At the same time, we must recognize that not every critical question requires an answer which takes discourse competence into account. Indeed, certain kinds of knowledge about, certain valuable uses of, literature are possible only if we neglect this concept, or at least subordinate it to other phenomena. One might, for example, assume with Fish that literature is in the reader, and then study how readers from different social, economic, and educational backgrounds actually process a text in order to see how these variables affect the interpretation and evaluation of literature. One might adopt the literature-as-sentences view of Lodge and try to extract the complex essentially nonparaphrasable thematic meanings of a text. One might assume with Miller that the text is a system of signs and concentrate on the relationships between signifiers in it, and so heighten our awareness of the rich and delightful arbitrariness of language. One might also conceive of literature as essentially a product of history, and so focus on how it is shaped by and gives a critical perspective on historical forces. Or one may view literature as a revelation of an author's personality, or the transformation of his life experiences, or numerous other things, all of which can lead to important knowledge about literature, especially about its functions in and connections to that human activity we call culture.

As a result of this pluralism, we must acknowledge another way in which our theory is not truly comprehensive. Although it emerges as the approach that is best able to explain the fully competent (and perhaps ideal) reader's experience of fiction, and although it is capable of offering for most works an account that will explain the importance or unimportance of all an author's linguistic choices, it does not render obsolete every other theory of language's role in fiction. After our theory does its work, numerous other interesting and significant questions about language of fiction remain to be answered.

III

This reasoning about pluralism also clarifies what our theory is claiming about the nature of fiction. Since fiction is a phenomenon whose nature is not clearly defined and generally agreed upon (though most of us are confident that we can recognize it when we see it), our assertions about its nature are in large part the products of our theory rather than the foundations of it; thus we cannot claim that other approaches must agree with them. Nevertheless, these claims are not totally immune from confirmation or refutation because the class we call fiction exists independently of our theory. The classification of both *Sister Carrie* and *Willie Masters' Lonesome Wife* as fictions is established not by our theory, but by other agreements about the difference between fictional and nonfictional discourse. Consequently, the reach of our conclusions about the essentially nonlinguistic nature of fiction can be tested by examining whether they apply to works as different as Gass's and Dreiser's. Our conclusion that language need not but most often will be a subordinate element suggests that their reach is long though not unlimited.

Furthermore, the finding that our conclusions about the novels of part one do not apply with equal force to those of part two suggests that even within a conception of fiction built on discourse competence there is no single essence which all fictions share. When the relation among the basic elements of fiction can vary as greatly as it does between Dreiser's work and Gass's, when, that is, the more common relationship between language, on the one hand, and action, thought, and character on the other is inverted as it is in *Willie Masters' Lonesome Wife,* we cannot explain our experience of the two works with the same theory. We can, of course, conceive of the nature of fiction in other ways, and we can make further discriminations of kind within the two main classes we have found. But even our inability to find a single formulation of the essential nature of fiction within a single conception of literature leads to some important, though perhaps not totally surprising, consequences for critical discourse about it.

The limits of our theory suggest that we ought to be extremely wary of making—or crediting—blanket assertions about what fiction is or should be. To say that all fiction must imitate life, that all must subordinate ideas to action, that all must criticize existing social conditions, revive our dying language, or any of the other things we frequently hear fiction called on to do is to reveal less about the nature of good fiction than about the nature of one's critical monism. Despite our best intentions to improve the state of the art, critics who issue such calls (and their name is legion) may unwillingly contribute to its impoverishment. In trying to make fiction the best possible (single) thing it can be, they enjoin certain kinds of fiction and so in effect seek to reduce the variety of experience, and the resulting variety of knowledge and pleasure, the art of fiction offers us.

The danger of any pluralism, as Booth points out, is that it will become a sophisticated monism by insisting that its way of relating different explanations to each other is the best way.[3] But even without addressing the complex problems of constructing a pluralism of pluralisms, we can, I think, recognize that a commitment to pluralism does affect the status of all our conclusions, including the ones about pluralism. This commitment means that we must continue to invite opposing views, that although we are willing to take definite stands on the various questions we have rased here, we want the dialogue about them to remain open. Indeed, the commitment to pluralism means that we should not only be willing to face but should actually welcome someone treating us as we have tried to treat the other theorists here, i.e., with respect for what we have attempted to do and with rigorous scrutiny of our results. If the results are found wanting but prove to be the occasion for better insight into the relation between language and fiction (or the relation between different approaches to that question), then we should be satisfied. Limited as we all are in time, knowledge, and talent, no one of us working alone is ever likely to answer completely any of our major questions about art. Yet one critic's attempt, if done well enough, can make it more likely that the next will succeed. It is through the dialogue between critics, through the testing and modification of different conclusions, that we collectively overcome our individual limitations and advance our knowledge.

These reflections bring us to contemplate once again the rich and multiple pleasures of literary art, especially the art of fiction. Fictional worlds from—and of—words, worlds peopled by characters as different as Lambert Strether and Babs Masters, built upon actions as small and quiet as Anne Elliot's kindness and as large and splashy as Carrie Meeber's success, created by stylists as lumbering as Dreiser and as graceful as Nabokov, are not only, as Humbert Humbert realizes, worlds with potential immortality, but also, as we are beginning to realize, worlds with potentially inexhaustible resources. Creating a world both immortal and inexhaustible is perhaps the novelist's greatest achievement. That such creation is possible is not only eloquent testimony to the value of fiction; it is also perhaps the greatest wonder of language.

Notes

Chapter 1

1. See especially Murry Krieger, *A Window to Criticism: Shakespeare's Sonnets and Modern Poetics* (Princeton, 1964), and *The Play and Place of Criticism* (Baltimore, 1967); William K. Wimsatt and Monroe Beardsley *The Verbal Icon: Studies in the Meaning of Poetry* (Lexington, Kentucky, 1954); David Lodge, *Language of Fiction: Essays in Criticism and Verbal Analysis of the English Novel* (New York, 1966), and *The Novelist at the Crossroads and Other Essays on Fiction and Criticism* (Ithaca, New York, 1971); R. S. Crane, *The Languages of Criticism and the Structure of Poetry* (Toronto, 1953); Wayne C. Booth, *The Rhetoric of Fiction* (Chicago and London, 1961) and *A Rhetoric of Irony* (Chicago and London, 1974); and Elder Olson, "An Outline of Poetic Theory," *Critics and Criticism*, abridged ed. R. S. Crane (Chicago and London, 1957), pp. 3–23, and "William Empson, Contemporary Criticism, and Poetic Diction," *Critics and Criticism*, pp. 24–61.

2. Fish's most important works in this mode are *Surprised by Sin: The Reader in Paradise Lost* (New York, 1967), and *Self-Consuming Artifacts: The Experience of Seventeenth Century Literature* (Berkeley: University of California Press, 1972). An almost equally eminent reader response critic is Stephen Booth. See his *An Essay on Shakespeare's Sonnets* (New Haven, 1969) and *Shakespeare's Sonnets: Edited with Analytic Commentary* (New Haven, 1977).

3. See especially Jacques Derrida, *Of Grammatology*, trans. Gayatri Chakrovorty Spivak (Baltimore, 1977), and *Writing and Difference*, trans. Alan Bass (Chicago and London, 1978; Paul de Man, *Blindness and Insight* (New York, 1971) and *Allegories of Reading: Figural Language in Rousseau, Nietzsche, Rilke, and Proust* (New Haven, 1979); J. Hillis Miller, "Ariadne's Thread: Repetition and the Narrative Line," *Critical Inquiry* 3 (1976):57–77, "Stevens' Rock and Criticism as Cure, I," *Georgia Review* 20 (1976):5–31, and "The Critic as Host," *Critical Inquiry* 3 (1977):439–47; and Harold Bloom, de Man, Derrida, Geoffrey Hartman, and Miller, *Deconstruction and Criticism* (New York, 1979).

4. See especially Roland Barthes, *Elements of Semiology*, trans. Anette Lavers and Colin Smith (New York, 1968), and *S/Z*, trans. Richard Miller (New York, 1974); and Umberto Eco, *A Theory of Semiotics* (Bloomington, 1976), and *The Role of the Reader: Explorations in the Semiotics of Texts* (Bloomington, 1979).

Chapter 2

1. Stanley Fish, *Self-Consuming Artifacts* (Berkeley, 1972), p. 409. Hereafter cited as *SCA*.

2. Ibid., p. 426.

3. Ibid., p. 387.

4. Ibid., pp. 387–88.

5. Ibid., p. 388.

6. Ibid., p. 393.

7. Ibid.

8. Stanley Fish, "Facts and Fictions: A Reply to Ralph Rader," *Critical Inquiry* 1 (1975):889.

9. Ibid., pp. 888–89.

10. Recently Fish has modified this position by arguing that there is only uniformity of response within "interpretive communities," by which he means groups of people who share the same critical assumptions. See Stanley Fish, "Interpreting the *Variorum*," *Critical Inquiry* 2 (1976):465–85. He has further extended this position by arguing that the different assumptions of different readers cause them, while reading the same work, to create different texts. See "Normal Circumstances, Literal Language, Direct Speech Acts, the Ordinary, the Everyday, the Obvious, What Goes Without Saying, and Other Special Cases," *Critical Inquiry* 4 (1978):625–44. I consider this position in some detail in chapter 3 where I take up the question of authorial intention and textual meaning.

11. *SCA*, p. 406. Fish himself does not single out "historical knowledge" as one of the criteria for determining informed readers, but his discussion makes it clear that by semantic knowledge he also means historical knowledge.

12. Ibid., pp. 393–94.

13. Ibid., p. 393.

14. Ibid., pp. 394–95.

15. Ibid., p. 395.

16. Ralph Rader, "Fact, Theory, and Literary Explanation," *Critical Inquiry* 1 (1974):270.

17. "Facts and Fictions," p. 889n.

18. Ibid.

19. For Fish's reading of Donne's sermon, see *SCA*, pp. 43–77.

20. Ibid., p. 398.

21. Ibid., p. 399.

22. Ibid.

23. Henry James, *The Ambassadors*, ed. S. P. Rosenbaum (New York: Norton, 1964), p. 217. All quotations from the novel are taken from this edition, which is a corrected reprint of the New York Edition.

24. Quoted from William Veeder, *Henry James—The Lessons of the Master* (Chicago, 1975), p. 2.

25. Stanley Fish, *Surprised by Sin* (Berkeley, 1971), pp. 24–25. This book was originally published by Macmillan and St. Martin's Press, 1967.

26. "Fact, Theory, and Literary Explanation," p. 263.

27. *Surprised by Sin*, p. 28.

28. "Fact, Theory, and Literary Explanation," p. 264.

29. *Surprised by Sin*, p. 23, also quoted by Rader, p. 263.

30. "Fact, Theory, and Literary Explanation," p. 263.

31. The work of T. G. Bever presents some results of psycholinguistic approaches to sentence processing. See his "Perception, Thought, and Lan-

guage," in *Language Comprehension and the Acquisition of Knowledge*, ed. Roy O. Freedle and John B. Carroll (New York, 1972), pp. 99–112.

32. We have already seen that for Rader this description is its meaning. Fish finally argues that "the logic of the reading experience ... says to us that if one were to compare Satan's spear with the tallest pine the comparison would be inadequate," *Surprised by Sin*, p. 27, but the impact of the "inadequate comparison" depends on our first realizing that the spear is much, though indefinitely, larger than the pine.

33. Noam Chomsky defines competence as "the ability of the idealized speaker-hearer to associate sounds and meanings strictly in accordance with the rules of his language." *Language and Mind* (New York, 1972), p. 116.

34. This is not to deny that language changes; but here we are looking at language from a synchronic viewpoint.

35. Of course in ambiguous sentences we can see that more than one relationship is possible even after we have grammatical closure.

36. For an argument that there is occasionally perfect synonymy, see E. D. Hirsch, Jr., "Stylistics and Synonymity," *Critical Inquiry* 1 (1975):559–79.

37. *SCA*, p. 394.

38. This example also indicates the dangers implicit in Fish's system of comparing complexity of thought against complexity of expression in order to determine the appropriateness of the expression. How do we determine complexity of thought? "2 is greater than 1" may be enormously complex. How complex is "$E = mc^2$" or "I love you"?

39. "Interpreting the *Variorum*," p. 468.

40. For a more extended discussion of this relationship between parts and wholes, see chapter 3, pp. 81–96.

41. Thought as an element of fiction is more closely tied to language than either character or action but its essence is still nonlinguistic. A particular element of thought is not tied to a particular linguistic expression (synonymy is possible); more importantly, a particular thought can be expressed very clearly through means other than its direct articulation. In *Lord of the Flies*, for example, Golding vividly expresses his thought that humans are inherently evil as much or more through the *sequence of actions* representing the degeneration of the boys' island from paradise to inferno, than through the Lord of the Flies' statement to Simon asserting that the beast the boys fear is within them. A glance at another art form, the movies, also indicates that thought has a nonlinguistic essence. A sequence of camera shots with no corresponding dialogue on the sound track can quite clearly express elements of thought that function as part of a work; to take a simple example, a director may alternate shots of an unscrupulous rich man enjoying a sumptuous banquet with shots of a virtuous poor man, a former rival of the rich one, unsuccessfully begging for his dinner, in order to express his thought about the relation between virtue and material success. But cf. Ferdinand de Saussure, *Course in General Linguistics*, trans. Wade Baskin (New York, 1959), pp. 111–13.

For a subtle treatment of how we can deduce novelists' ethical beliefs from their novels, see Sheldon Sacks, *Fiction and the Shape of Belief* (Berkeley, 1964).

42. For a somewhat different critique of Fish's position, see Edward Regis, Jr., "Literature *by* the Reader: The 'Affective' Stylistics of Stanley Fish," *College English* 38 (1976):263–80.

43. F. O. Matthiessen, *Henry James: The Major Phase* (New York, 1944), p. 39.

44. Robert Marks, *James's Later Novels* (New York, 1960), p. 103.

45. Frederick Crews, *The Tragedy of Manners* (New Haven, 1957), pp. 55–56; and Ronald Wallace, *Henry James and the Comic Form* (Ann Arbor, 1975), p. 131.

46. Both Crews and Wallace quote this passage from *The Notebooks of Henry James,* ed. F. O. Matthiessen and Kenneth B. Murdock (New York, 1955), p. 415.

47. *The Ambassadors,* pp. 344–45.

Chapter 3

1. David Lodge, *Language of Fiction: Essays in Criticism and Verbal Analysis of the English Novel* (New York, 1966), p. 74. Hereafter referred to by page numbers in parentheses in the text.

2. Quoted from John J. MacAleer, *Theodore Dreiser: An Introduction and Interpretation* (New York, 1968), p. vii.

3. There is also a sense in which Lodge is not totally consistent within his theory; for example, after he speaks of the writer's choice as unlimited, he qualifies his claim by saying that nothing limits the writer but "his sense of the aesthetic logic and aesthetic possibilities of his literary structure." Again, because I am not so much interested in Lodge as in the language-is-all position, I have ignored these inconsistencies.

4. W. K. Wimsatt and Monroe C. Beardsley, *The Verbal Icon: Studies in the Meaning of Poetry* (Lexington, Kentucky, 1954), p. x.

5. Nelson Goodman, "The Status of Style," *Critical Inquiry* 1 (June 1975):799–811. Interestingly, however, Goodman believes it can be useful to study style—but of course he defines it in a different way from most theorists. For him style is the characteristic way one creates his art work; with an author or a period, he would study everything from characteristic diction and syntax to characteristic organization of material. For him sentences such as "The boy ate his dinner" and "The mouse ate cheese" would be stylistically related to "The lion ate the lion-tamer," while "The lion-tamer was eaten by the lion" would not.

6. E. D. Hirsch, Jr., "Stylistics and Synonymity," *Critical Inquiry* 1 (March 1975):559–79.

7. This characterization of "speech-events" has some obvious similarity to points made by "speech act" theorists like J. L. Austin and John Searle, especially that the meaning of sentences depends upon conditions governing their *use.* See especially Austin, *How to Do Things with Words* (Cambridge, Massachusetts, 1962) and Searle, *Speech Acts* (London, 1969); for a speech-act approach to literature building on the work of H. P. Grice with the Cooperative Principle governing all discourse, see Mary Louise Pratt, *Toward a Speech Act Theory of Literary Discourse* (Bloomington, Indiana, 1976). My work in this book is far more compatible with the work of these theorists than it is competitive. But it is also significantly different. The most important difference is between my controlling concept of intention and their controlling concept of illocutionary act. Illocutionary acts are the uses to which language can be put in sentences, e.g., promising, requesting, asserting, and so on; intentions are the various purposes of either

sentences or larger discourses. In speech act terms, intentions unite illocutionary acts with possible perlocutionary effects, e.g., promising in order to persuade and the like. As a result of these differences, I believe speaking about intentions offers a better way of speaking about style than does speaking about illocutionary acts. First, it allows us to understand a more flexible relation between the linguistic and nonlinguistic aspects of an utterance. In speech act theory, the particular style of any illocutionary act (i.e., a locutionary act) is important only to the extent that it reveals conditions governing the illocutionary act. With intention as our controlling concept, as we shall see in more detail later in this chapter, style can be more or less important for the successful accomplishment of a communication on different occasions. Second, the concept of intention, not surprisingly, is more useful for discourses larger than the sentence. In Lodge's discourse on Brown-Green-Grey, for example, the speech act theorist must consider two assertions and a report of a third, while we can consider a single, unified creation of a character. Again, we can be more flexible in considering the effect of style. We might, for example, want to consider the effect of a stylistic alteration which would also alter the illocutionary force of a single sentence (and thus from the speech act point of view make it not a paraphrase) but would not change our understanding of the general intention of the whole discourse (and thus, from our point of view would leave it as a paraphrase, e.g., "As a friend of his queried, 'Isn't Grey a difficult man to pin down?'") Pratt's book does suggest ways of overcoming this limitation of speech act analysis, but these ways are more appropriate for her project (identifying and explaining the importance of underlying similarities in the conventions controlling literary and nonliterary discourse) than for mine.

8. For the sake of simplicity I leave out some of the other things I would need to know to make this interpretation—things about the athletic contest, and about my friend's way of speaking. The amount of knowledge shared or assumed between speakers in any situation is quite extensive, and might be impossible to make a full inventory of.

9. For an insightful discussion of the distinction between literary and nonliterary uses of language, see Barbara Herrnstein Smith, "Poetry as Fiction," *New Literary History* 2 (1971):259–82; reprinted in *New Directions in Literary History*, ed. Ralph Cohen (Baltimore and London, 1974). Smith distinguishes between natural utterances, which have a historically determinate speaker, and fictive utterances, which do not, and considers some of the consequences of the distinction for the way we understand language in literature. Unfortunately, I did not encounter her further elaboration of those consequences in *On the Margins of Discourse* (Chicago, 1978) (which also reprints "Poetry as Fiction") until after this essay was essentially complete, and as a result, I do not try to indicate how her ideas anticipate, complement, or conflict with the ones advanced here. For a direct discussion of her work see my review of *Margins* in *Modern Philology* 78 (1981) (in Press).

10. Though developed independently, this analysis of the relation between part and whole is similar to the one underlying Barbara Herrnstein Smith's discussion of "retrospective patterning" in *Poetic Closure* (Chicago, 1968), pp. 10–14 and *passim*, and to the one underlying E. D. Hirsch's discussion of "corrigible schemata" in *The Aims of Interpretation* (Chicago, 1976), pp. 33–34.

11. See "Interpreting the *Variorum*," *Critical Inquiry* 2 (1976):465–85, and

"Normal Circumstances, Literal Language, Direct Speech Acts, the Ordinary, the Everyday, the Obvious, What Goes Without Saying, and Other Special Cases," *Critical Inquiry* 4 (1978):625–44. My discussion here refers to the later article which is a full development of the position Fish is arguing for in the earlier one. Hereafter I shall cite it by the initials NC and page numbers in parentheses in the text.

12. The dispute over when Milton actually wrote the play complicates but does not repudiate this point. We simply need to investigate what consequences, if any, the early (1647) or late (1667–70) composition has for the meaning of the poem (would Milton have been more likely to write a typological work at one point than the other?), and take those consequences into account as one factor in our interpretation.

13. Brooks's and Bateson's remarks are quoted by Hirsch in appendix 1 to *Validity in Interpretation,* (New Haven, 1967), "Objective Interpretation," p. 228. For the original sources, see Cleanth Brooks, "Irony as a Principle of Structure," in *Literary Opinion in America,* ed. M. D. Zabel (2nd ed., New York, 1951), p. 736, and F. W. Bateson, *English Poetry: An Introduction* (rev. ed. New York, 1966), pp. 29–30, 59. Hirsch's appendix originally appeared as an article in *PMLA* 75 (1960):463–79. (Bateson's remarks on "A slumber" are identical to those in the 1950 first edition.) References to Hirsch's work will hereafter be cited by the initials VI and page numbers in parentheses in the text.

14. In writing *Validity in Interpretation,* Hirsch refuses either to defend or repudiate his choice of Bateson over Brooks, saying that his treatment of the dispute is not extensive enough. He does, however, defend his basic procedure for adjudicating the dispute.

15. Norman Holland, "Literary Interpretation and Three Phases of Psychoanalysis," *Critical Inquiry* 3 (1977):229.

16. David Ferry, *The Limits of Mortality* (Middletown, Conn., 1959), pp. 77–78.

17. Spencer Hall, "Wordsworth's Lucy Poems: Context and Meaning," *Studies in Romanticism* 10 (1971):168 makes a similar point about the poem as a whole.

18. For a fuller treatment of the poem and of Brooks and Bateson, see my "Validity *Redux:* The Relation of Author, Reader and Text in the Act of Interpretation" (forthcoming).

19. Some readers may perhaps wonder why I do not substitute the term "form" for "intention" since my characterization of intention resembles the way some theorists, most notably neo-Aristotelian ones, would characterize form. Although the concept is far more important than the term that identifies it, I believe that "intention" has several advantages over "form." It ties the work and the meaning of its language more directly and more obviously to its author. "Intention" also allows us to see and to emphasize the similarity between the way we understand literature and the way we understand everyday speech. Finally, and perhaps most importantly, "intention" allows us to stress the *a posteriori* nature of understanding better than "form," since the latter term often quickly leads us to the categories of "comedy," "tragedy," etc., and from there to the barbarous practice of fitting works into the molds created by those types. With "intention," I believe, we shall be better able to respect the unique individuality of each text. For an excellent discussion of the concept of form, its importance in understanding texts, and the relationships between theories of form when they offer compet-

ing interpretations of texts, see Walter Davis, *The Act of Interpretation: A Critique of Literary Reason* (Chicago, 1978). The theories Davis discusses are R. S. Crane's, Kenneth Burke's, and a dialectical one he has synthesized from the work of Hegel and Heidegger; the literary text he works with is Faulkner's "The Bear."

20. John Flanagan, "Dreiser's Style in *An American Tragedy*," *Texas Studies in Language and Literature* 7 (Autumn 1965):287.

21. Theodore Dreiser, *Sister Carrie*, ed. Claude Simpson (Boston, 1959), p. 232. Hereafter references will be made by page numbers in parentheses in the text.

22. Vern Wagner, "The Maligned Style of Theodore Dreiser," *Western Humanities Review* 19 (Spring 1966):177.

23. Walter Blackstock, "Theodore Dreiser's Literary Style," *Florida State University Studies*, ed. Weymouth Jordan (Tallahassee, 1953), p. 98.

24. For simplicity's sake, I shall call the speaker of this passage "Dreiser" rather than "the narrator." The usage is a justifiable shorthand because there is virtually no distance between Dreiser and his narrator here.

Chapter 4

1. The basic statement on the notion of decentering is Derrida's "Structure, Sign, Play in the Discourse of the Human Sciences," in *The Structuralist Controversy*, ed. Richard Macksey and Eugenio Donato (Baltimore, 1972), pp. 247–64.

2. Although deconstructionist critics generally share these assumptions, there is considerable diversity among them. Perhaps the best overview is J. Hillis Miller's "Stevens' Rock and Criticism as Cure, II," The *Georgia Review* 30 (Summer 1976):330–48.

3. Jacques Derrida, *Of Grammatology*, trans. Gayatri Chakrovorty Spivak (Baltimore, 1977), pp. 10–18.

4. Ferdinand de Saussure, *Course in General Linguistics*, trans. Wade Baskin (New York, 1959), pp. 115–17.

5. Ibid., p. 118.

6. Louis Hjelmslev, *Principles de Grammaire General* (Copenhagen, 1928).

7. *Of Grammatology*, p. 62.

8. Ibid., p. 63.

9. Ibid.

10. Ibid.

11. Ibid., p. 65.

12. See Derrida's essay, "Difference," in *Speech and Phenomena*, trans. David Allison (Evanston, Illinois, 1973), pp. 129–60.

13. *Of Grammatology*, p. 69.

14. Booth made the charge in his evaluation of the work of M. H. Abrams, "M. H. Abrams: Historian as Critic, Critic as Pluralist," *Critical Inquiry* 2 (1976):441. Miller's reply was given in a symposium at the December 1976 MLA meeting under the title "The Critic as Host." Miller's talk, along with a reply from Abrams, "The Deconstructive Angel," and an overview presented by Booth, "'Preserving the Exemplar': Or, How Not to Dig Our Own Graves" has since been published in *Critical Inquiry* 3 (1977):407–47.

15. "The Critic as Host," p. 443.

16. Ibid.

17. Ibid.

18. J. Hillis Miller, "Ariadne's Thread: Repetition and the Narrative Line," *Critical Inquiry* 3 (1976):72.

19. Miller demonstrates the indeterminacies of this figure in "Ariadne's Thread."

20. In the summary—and in several of my later remarks about the novel—I am indebted to Stuart Tave, *Some Words of Jane Austen* (Chicago, 1973), pp. 256–87.

21. I have never seen Miller use these terms from generative grammar; I use them simply to introduce the usual meanings of the word to be deconstructed, and in this sense I am following his practice.

22. Jane Austen, *Persuasion,* ed. R. W. Chapman (New York, 1958), p. 103. Hereafter cited by page numbers in parentheses in the text.

23. "The Deconstructive Angel," p. 428.

24. Ibid., pp. 437, 435.

25. Ibid., p. 437.

26. J. Hillis Miller, "Deconstructing the Deconstructors," *Diacritics* 5 (Summer 1975):30.

27. "The Critic as Host," p. 444.

28. The somewhat paradoxical relation between speakers and their language is illustrated in part by my use of "man" here. I intend it in the generic sense, but for many readers (myself included) the word is now tainted with sexist overtones. I use it because we have not yet found a better substitute. But if enough speakers feel the need for a new, untainted word, one shall be found (perhaps "person-kind" will catch on, or a blended word like "wankind," pronounced "one-kind," will emerge from the play of difference).

29. *Course in General Linguistics,* p. 113.

30. "The Critic as Host," p. 442.

31. For an attempt to develop a formal semantic theory, see Jerrold J. Katz and Jerry A. Fodor, "The Structure of a Semantic Theory," *Language* 39 (1963):170–210. Reprinted in *The Structure of Language,* eds. Fodor and Katz (Englewood Cliffs, N.J., 1964), pp. 479–518. But see also Umberto Eco's critique of this model in *A Theory of Semiotics* (Bloomington, 1976), pp. 96–105.

32. This characterization of the intention depends in part on the work of Sheldon Sacks. See his "Golden Birds and Dying Generations," *Comparative Literature Studies* 6 (1969):274–91 and "Novelists as Storytellers," *Modern Philology* 73 (1976):S97–S109.

33. See Sacks, "Novelists as Storytellers," for a similar point about another scene in this section of the novel.

Chapter 5

1. The quoted phrase is from Alfred Appel, Jr., "*Lolita:* The Springboard of Parody," *Wisconsin Studies in Contemporary Literature* 7 (Spring 1967):241, but he completes it differently; he says Nabokov's vision "overrides the circumscribing sadness, absurdity and terror of everyday life." My sentence is close in spirit to the argument of Page Stegner, *Escape into Aesthetics: The Art of Vladimir Nabokov* (New York, 1966), pp. 102–15.

2. Donald E. Morton, *Vladimir Nabokov* (New York, 1974), p. 70.

3. "William Empson, Contemporary Criticism, and Poetic Diction," *Critics and Criticism,* abridged ed., R. S. Crane (Chicago, 1957), p. 34.

4. Ibid., p. 33.

5. Ibid., p. 34.

6. Ibid., p. 50.

7. Ibid., p. 51.

8. For another discussion of what Olson means by refinements see his remarks on Macbeth's "Tomorrow and tomorrow and tomorrow" soliloquy in *Tragedy and the Theory of Drama* (Detroit, 1964), pp. 113–25.

9. Vladimir Nabokov, *Lolita* (New York, 1957), p. 227. Hereafter references will be made by page numbers in parentheses in the text.

10. "Life," of course, as Humbert uses it here means sex organ.

11. See for example Carl Proffer, *Keys to Lolita* (Bloomington, 1968), pp. 104–5.

12. For evidence about this remark concerning "My Last Duchess" see Ralph Rader, "The Dramatic Monologue and Related Lyric Forms," *Critical Inquiry* 3 (Autumn 1976):131–52.

13. Perhaps the most prominent differing interpretation is Alfred Appel's: see his "Introduction" to *The Annotated Lolita* (New York, 1970). Appel argues that *Lolita,* like *Pale Fire,* is "involuted," i.e., is largely about its own artifice. To explain why I find this account finally unsatisfactory would require a separate argument, but the more important point is that even if Appel's interpretation is better than the one offered here, we still cannot fully explain the role of the medium as subordinate to a larger end. Appel's interpretation at best offers a general account—the style calls attention to itself and its ultimate artificer Nabokov; it does not enable us to account for the particular pleasures of particular passages.

Chapter 6

1. Larry McCaffery, "The Art of Metafiction: William Gass's *Willie Masters' Lonesome Wife, Critique* 18 (1976):23. Gass's own beliefs about the importance of the medium also make him an interesting author to study here. He explicitly states his belief that everything in fiction is language in his chapter "The Medium of Fiction" in *Fiction and the Figures of Life* (New York, 1972). More generally, he has commented; "I think of myself as a writer of prose rather than a novelist, critic, or story-teller, and I am principally interested in problems of style." *Contemporary Novelists* ed. James Vinson (London, 1976), p. 503.

2. Umberto Eco, *A Theory of Semiotics* (Bloomington, 1976), p. 16, his emphasis. I shall hereafter cite this work by page numbers in parentheses in the text. Needless to say, my use of Eco's semiotics in this chapter is not designed to be an account of the only way semiotics can be applied to literary criticism; I am concerned only with the narrower issues of what semiotics can contribute to our understanding of style in a metafictional text such as *Willie Masters' Lonesome Wife* and of how such contributions are related to the theory of part one. For a broader understanding of how semiotics can be applied to the interpretation of literature, see among other works Eco's *The Role of the Reader: Explorations in the Semiotics of Texts* (Bloomington, 1979).

3. *Willie Masters' Lonesome Wife* (New York, 1971). The pages are not numbered, but this passage is from the second and third pages of written text. Gass's work was first published as *Triquarterly Supplement Number Two* (1968). The appearance of the two editions is somewhat different, e.g., different sections of the work are printed on different colored paper in the *Triquarterly* edition. McCaffery discusses some of these differences further in "The Art of Metafiction."

4. McCaffery discusses this analogy as well; see "The Art of Metafiction," pp. 21–34. Tony Tanner also perceptively discusses the relation between sex and language in the book, "Games American Writers Play," *Salmagundi* 35 (Fall 1976):117–21.

5. I would hesitate, however, to say that Eco's approach would *fully* explain our pleasure in the style; its source, I think, is finally not what it reveals about our language, but what it reveals about Nabokov as an artist. A sentence like the one describing "the trip of the tongue" Lolita's name leads us to take is so marvelous because it demonstrates a man masterfully in control of his medium, a control that is reflected in both the violation and observance of the codes, and a control that is wonderfully exercised even while the primary focus of the communication is away from the medium.

6. See "Poetry as Fiction," *New Literary History* 2 (1971):259–2; reprinted as chapter 2 of *On the Margins of Discourse* (Chicago, 1978).

7. These remarks are purposefully brief, general, and limited by the concerns discussed above. A full discussion of the value of Gass's work would have to grapple with the complex question of its possible sexism. Is the implied metaphor of language as a woman to be *used* by others, albeit in a reverent way, finally sexist? Or does the value placed on the rich inner life of language enable Gass's metaphor to transcend sexist attitudes?

8. I do not mean to argue here that the sentence "Molly and Polly like Mommy, but they don't like Dad" could not be used by the original author to conclude his series. It could, but it would have two results: it would make the double-letter pattern dominant, and it would remove the text from the class we call "fiction." The question as I put it here is: Which of the two sentences is more probably consistent with the author's intention as revealed in the text as we have it?

9. *Contemporary Novelists,* ed. James Vinson (London, 1976), p. 502. In her brief evaluation of Gass's work, Paula Hart confirms that the label "essay-novella" after *Willie Masters' Lonesome Wife* (which is listed under the heading "Novels") was given by Gass (p. 503).

10. This question is not meant to imply that Gass really wanted to write fiction, but was unable to. It makes far more sense to assume that he sought to write an essay-novella and succeeded. The question we are asking now is "Suppose Gass did really want to write fiction—would he have been able to while also keeping the medium itself as the primary focus of the work?"

Chapter 7

1. Wayne Booth, *Critical Understanding: The Powers and Limits of Pluralism* (Chicago and London, 1979). Although I shall treat Booth only briefly here, his work has had a pervasive influence on my thinking about pluralism. Nevertheless,

I am by no means sure he would agree with everything I say here; indeed, I suspect that he would find my final pluralistic position one which still has too many limits.

For a different but also impressive treatment of some problems of pluralism, see Walter Davis, *The Act of Interpretation: A Critique of Literary Reason* (Chicago and London, 1978).

2. *Critical Understanding*, pp. 211–15.

3. Ibid., p. 5 and *passim*.

Selected Bibliography

This bibliography primarily contains works cited in the foregoing pages, but also includes a few closely related ones. For a virtually comprehensive list of works on language and literature see David Bleich, Eugene R. Kintgen, Bruce Smith, and Sandor J. Vargyai, "The Psychological Study of Language and Literature: A Selected Annotated Bibliography," *Style* 12 (Spring 1978):113–210. Umberto Eco's bibliography in *A Theory of Semiotics* (Bloomington, 1976) is also useful and extensive; it includes some philosophical and linguistic works not mentioned by Bleich et al.

Abrams, M. H. "The Deconstructive Angel." *Critical Inquiry* 3 (1977):425–38.
Altieri, Charles. "The Hermeneutics of Literary Indeterminacy: A Dissent from the New Orthodoxy." *New Literary History* 10 (1978):71–99.
———. "Presence and Reference in a Literary Text: The Example of Williams' 'This is Just to Say.'" *Critical Inquiry* 5 (1979);489–510.
Appel, Alfred, Jr. *The Annotated Lolita*. New York: McGraw-Hill, 1970.
———. "The Art of Nabokov's Artifice." *Denver Quarterly* 3 (Summer 1968):25–37.
———. "*Lolita:* The Springboard of Parody." *Wisconsin Studies in Contemporary Literature* 8 (1967):204–41.
Austen, Jane. *Persuasion*. Edited by R. W. Chapman. New York: Norton, 1958.
Austin, J. L. *How to Do Things with Words*. Cambridge, Massachusetts: Harvard University Press, 1962.
Bader, Julia. *Crystal Land: Artifice in Nabokov's Novels*. Berkeley: University of California Press, 1972.
Barthes, Roland. *Elements of Semiology*. Translated by Annette Lavers and Colin Smith. New York: Hill and Wang, 1968.

————. *S/Z*. Translated by Richard Miller. New York: Hill and Wang, 1974.

Bateson, Frederick W. *English Poetry: An Introduction*. New York: Barnes and Noble, 1966.

Blackstock, Walter. "Theodore Dreiser's Literary Style." *Florida State University Studies*. Edited by Weymouth Jordan. Tallahassee: University of Florida Press, 1952.

Bloom, Harold; de Man, Paul; Derrida, Jacques; Hartman, Geoffrey; and Miller, J. Hillis. *Deconstruction and Criticism*. New York: Seabury Press, 1979.

Booth, Stephen. *An Essay on Shakespeare's Sonnets*. New Haven, Yale University Press, 1969.

————, ed. *Shakespeare's Sonnets: Edited with Analytic Commentary*. New Haven: Yale University Press, 1977.

Booth, Wayne C. *Critical Understanding: The Powers and Limits of Pluralism*. Chicago: University of Chicago Press, 1979.

————. "M.H. Abrams: Historian as Critic, Critic as Pluralist." *Critical Inquiry* 2 (1976):411–45.

————. "Preserving the Examplar: Or, How Not to Dig Our Own Graves," *Critical Inquiry* 3 (1977):407–23.

————. *The Rhetoric of Fiction*. Chicago: University of Chicago Press, 1961.

————. *A Rhetoric of Irony*. Chicago: University of Chicago Press, 1974.

Brooks, Cleanth. "Irony as a Principle of Structure." *Literary Opinion in America*. Edited by M. D. Zabel. New York: Harper and Row, 1951.

Chomsky, Noam. *Aspects of the Theory of Syntax*. Cambridge: M.I.T. Press, 1965.

————. *Language and Mind*. New York: Harcourt, Brace, Jovanovich, 1972.

Contemporary Novelists. Edited by James Vinson. London: St. James Press, 1976.

Crane, R. S. *The Languages of Criticism and the Structure of Poetry*. Toronto: University of Toronto Press, 1953.

Crews, Frederick. *The Tragedy of Manners*. New Haven: Yale University Press, 1957.

Culler, Jonathan. *Structuralist Poetics: Structuralism, Linguistics and the Study of Literature*. Ithaca, N.Y.: Cornell University Press, 1975.

Davis, Walter A. *The Act of Interpretation: A Critique of Literary Reason*. Chicago: University of Chicago Press, 1978.

de Man, Paul. *Allegories of Reading: Figural Language in Rousseau, Nietzsche, Rilke, and Proust.* New Haven: Yale University Press, 1979.

———. *Blindness and Insight.* New York: Oxford University Press, 1971.

Derrida, Jacques. *Of Grammatology.* Translated by Gayatri Chakrovorty Spivak. Baltimore: The Johns Hopkins University Press, 1977.

———. "Signature Event Context." *Glyph* 1 (1977):172–97.

———. *Speech and Phenomena and Other Essays on Husserl's Theory of Signs.* Translated by David Allison. Evanston, Illinois: Northwestern University Press, 1973.

———. "Structure, Sign, Play in the Discourse of the Human Sciences." *The Structuralist Controversy.* Edited by Richard Macksey and Eugenio Donato. Baltimore: The Johns Hopkins University Press, 1972.

———. *Writing and Difference.* Translated by Alan Bass. Chicago: University of Chicago Press, 1978.

Dreiser, Theodore. *Sister Carrie.* Edited by Claude Simpson. Boston: Houghton Mifflin, 1959.

Dupee, F. W. "A Preface to *Lolita.*" *Anchor Review* 2 (1957):1–13.

Eco, Umberto. *The Role of the Reader: Explorations in the Semiotics of Texts.* Bloomington: Indiana University Press, 1979.

———. *A Theory of Semiotics.* Bloomington: Indiana University Press, 1976.

Elias, Robert H. *Theodore Dreiser, Apostle of Nature.* New York: Knopf, 1948.

Ferry, David. *The Limits of Mortality: An Essay on Wordsworth's Major Poems.* Middletown, Conn.: Wesleyan University Press, 1959.

Field, Andrew. *Nabokov: His Life in Art.* Boston: Little, Brown. 1967.

Fish, Stanley. "Facts and Fictions: A Reply to Ralph Rader." *Critical Inquiry* 1 (1975):883–91.

———. "Interpreting the *Variorum.*" *Critical Inquiry* 2 (1976):465–85.

———. "Normal Circumstances, Literal Language, Direct Speech Acts, the Ordinary, The Everyday, the Obvious, What Goes Without Saying, and Other Special Cases." *Critical Inquiry* 4 (1978):625–44.

————. *Self-Consuming Artifacts: The Experience of Seventeenth Century Literature*. Berkeley: University of California Press, 1972.

————. *Surprised by Sin: The Reader in Paradise Lost*. Berkeley: University of California Press, 1971.

————. "What is Stylistics and Why Are They Saying Such Terrible Things About It?" *Approaches to Poetics: Selected Papers from the English Institute*. Edited by Seymour Chatman. New York: Columbia University Press, 1973.

Flanagan, John. "Dreiser's Style in *An American Tragedy*." *Texas Studies in Language and Literature* 7 (1965):285–94.

Fowler, Douglas. *Reading Nabokov*. Ithaca, N. Y.: Cornell University Press, 1973.

Gass, William. *Fiction and the Figures of Life*. New York: Knopf, 1970.

————. *Willie Masters' Lonesome Wife*. New York: Knopf, 1971.

————. *The World Within the Word*. New York: Knopf, 1978.

Goodman, Nelson. *Languages of Art: An Approach to a Theory of Symbols*. New York: Bobbs-Merrill, 1968.

————. "The Status of Style." *Critical Inquiry* 1 (1975):799–811.

Hall, Spencer. "Wordsworth's Lucy Poems: Context and Meaning." *Studies in Romanticism* 10 (1971):159–75.

Hemingway, Ernest. *A Farewell to Arms*. New York: Scribners, 1929.

Hirsch, E. D., Jr. *The Aims of Interpretation*. Chicago: University of Chicago Press, 1976.

————. "Stylistics and Synonymity." *Critical Inquiry* 1 (1975):559–79. Reprinted in *The Aims of Interpretation*.

————. *Validity in Interpretation*. New Haven: Yale University Press, 1967.

Hjelmslev, Louis. *Principes du Grammaire Generale*. Copenhagen: KDVS Hist.-filol. Medd. XVI, I, 1928.

Holland, Norman. "Literary Interpretation and Three Phases of Psychoanalysis." *Critical Inquiry* 3 (1977):221–34.

James, Henry. *The Ambassadors*. Edited by S. P. Rosenbaum. New York: Norton, 1964.

Katz, Jerrold J., and Fodor, Jerry A. "The Structure of a Semantic Theory." *Language* 39 (1963):170–210. Reprinted in *The Structure of Language*. Edited by Fodor and Katz. Englewood Cliffs, N. J.: Prentice Hall, 1964.

Krieger, Murray. *The Play and Place of Criticism*. Baltimore, Johns Hopkins University Press, 1967.

————. *A Window to Criticism: Shakespeare's Sonnets and Modern Poetics*. Princeton: Princeton University Press, 1964.

Language Comprehension and the Acquisition of Knowledge. Edited by R. O. Freedle and John B. Carroll. New York: Halstead Press, 1972.

Leyburn, Ellen Douglas. *Strange Alloy: The Relation of Comedy to Tragedy in the Fiction of Henry James*. Chapel Hill: University of North Carolina Press, 1968.

Lodge, David. *Language of Fiction: Essays in Criticism and Verbal Analysis of the English Novel*. New York: Columbia University Press, 1966.

————. *The Novelist at the Crossroads and Other Essays on Fiction and Criticism*. Ithaca, N. Y.: Cornell University Press, 1971.

————. "Towards a Poetics of Fiction: An Approach through Language." *Towards a Poetics of Fiction*. Edited by Mark Spilka. Bloomington: Indiana University Press.

MacAleer, John J. *Theodore Dreiser: An Introduction and Interpretation*. New York: Holt, Rhinehart, and Winston, 1968.

Marks, Robert. *James's Later Novels*. New York: William Frederick Press, 1960.

Matthiessen, F. O. *Henry James: The Major Phase*. New York: Oxford University Press, 1944.

McCaffery, Larry. "The Art of Metafiction: Gass's *Willie Masters' Lonesome Wife*." *Critique* 18 (1976):21–35.

Miller, J. Hillis. "Ariadne's Thread: Repetition and the Narrative Line." *Critical Inquiry* 3 (1976):57–77.

————. "The Critic as Host." *Critical Inquiry* 3 (1977):439–47.

————. "Deconstructing the Deconstructors." *Diacritics* 5 (Summer 1975):24–31.

————. "*Spring and All* and the Progress of Poetry." *Daedalus* 99 (1970):405–34.

————. "Stevens' Rock and Criticism as Cure, I." *Georgia Review* 30 (1976):5–31.

————. "Stevens' Rock and Criticism as Cure, II." *Georgia Review* 30 (1976):330–48.

————. "Walter Pater: A Partial Portrait." *Daedalus* 105 (1976):97–114.

Mitchell, Charles. "Mythic Seriousness in *Lolita*." *Texas Studies in Literature and Language* 5 (1963):329–43.

Morton, Donald. *Valdimir Nabokov*. New York: Frederick Unger, 1974.

Nabokov, Vladimir. *Lolita.* New York: Fawcett Publishing Co., 1957.

The Notebooks of Henry James. Edited by F. O. Mathiessen and Kenneth B. Murdock. New York: George Braziller, 1955.

Olson, Elder. "An Outline of Poetic Theory." *Critics and Criticism.* Abridged edition. Edited by R. S. Crane. Chicago: University of Chicago Press, 1957.

———. *Tragedy and the Theory of Drama.* Detroit: Wayne State University Press, 1954.

———. "William Empson, Contemporary Criticism, and Poetic Diction." *Critics and Criticism,* 1957.

Poirier, Richard. *A World Elsewhere: The Place of Style in American Literature.* New York: Oxford University Press, 1966.

Pratt, Mary Louise. *Toward a Speech Act Theory of Literary Discourse.* Bloomington: Indiana University Press, 1976.

Proffer, Carl. *Keys to Lolita.* Bloomington: Indiana University Press, 1968.

Rader, Ralph. "The Concept of Genre and Eighteenth Century Studies." *New Approaches to Eighteenth Century Literature: Selected Papers from the English Institute.* Edited by Phillip Harth. New York: Columbia University Press, 1974.

———. "The Dramatic Monologue and Related Lyric Forms." *Critical Inquiry* 3 (1976):131–52.

———. "Explaining Our Literary Understanding: A Reply to Jay Schleusener and Stanley Fish." *Critical Inquiry* 1 (1975):901–11.

———. "Fact, Theory, and Literary Explanation." *Critical Inquiry* 1 (1974):245–72.

Regis, Edward, Jr. "Literature *by* the Reader: The 'Affective' Stylistics of Stanley Fish." *College English* 28 (1976):263–81.

Sacks, Sheldon. *Fiction and the Shape of Belief: A Study of Henry Fielding, with Glances at Swift, Johnson, and Richardson.* Berkeley: University of California Press, 1964.

———. "Golden Birds and Dying Generations." *Comparative Literature Studies* 6 (1969):274–91.

———. "Novelists as Storytellers." *Modern Philology* 73 (1976):S97–S109.

Saussure, Ferdinand de. *Course in General Linguistics.* Translated by Wade Baskin. New York: McGraw-Hill, 1959.

Scott, Sir Walter. *The Heart of Midlothian.* Boston: Houghton Mifflin, 1966.

Searle, John R. "Reiterating the Differences: A Reply to Derrida." *Glyph* 1 (1977):198–208.

————. *Speech Acts: An Essay in the Philosophy of Language.* London: Cambridge University Press, 1969.

Smith, Barbara Herrnstein: *On the Margins of Discourse.* Chicago: University of Chicago Press, 1978.

————. *Poetic Closure.* Chicago: University of Chicago Press, 1968.

The Stature of Theodore Dreiser. Edited by Alfred Kazin. Bloomington: Indiana University Press, 1955.

Stegner, Page. *Escape into Aesthetics: The Art of Vladimir Nabokov.* New York: Dial Press, 1966.

The Structure of Language. Edited by Jerry A. Fodor and Jerrold J. Katz. Englewood Cliffs, N.J.: Prentice-Hall, 1964.

Tanner, Tony. *City of Words: American Fiction, 1950–1970.* New York: Harper and Row, 1971.

————. "Games American Writers Play." *Salmagundi* 35 (Fall 1976):110–40.

Tave, Stuart. *Some Words of Jane Austen.* Chicago: University of Chicago Press, 1974.

Trilling, Lionel, "The Last Lover—Vladimir Nabokov's *Lolita.*" *Griffin* 7 (August 1958):4–21.

Veeder, William. *Henry James—The Lessons of the Master: Popular Fiction and Personal Style in the Nineteenth Century.* Chicago: University of Chicago Press, 1975.

Wagner, Vern. "The Maligned Style of Theodore Dreiser." *Western Humanities Review* 19 (1965):175–84.

Wallace, Ronald. *Henry James and the Comic Form.* Ann Arbor: University of Michigan Press, 1975.

Wimsatt, W. K., and Beardsley, Monroe C. *The Verbal Icon: Studies in the Meaning of Poetry.* Lexington, Kentucky: University of Kentucky Press, 1954.

Index

Abrams, M. H., 128–29, 130, 131, 134
Action: within neo-Aristotelian theory,
8, 156–60; as nonlinguistic element
of fiction, 4, 42, 43, 75, 115–16, 149;
within organicist criticism, 8, 71,
72; and thought, 235 n.41; in *Willie
Masters' Lonesome Wife*, 201–2,
207
Aesthetic texts, 12, 190–92; *Willie
Masters' Lonesome Wife* as example of, 193–202, 207–10
Ambassadors, The (James), 14, 185,
208, 211, 213, 219, 222; analyzed by
Fish's principles, 20–28, 41; conclusions about related to other
novels, 149–51; critique of Olson's
perspective on, 160–61; deconstructionist perspective on, 130;
importance of style in, 43–66; intention of, 44–45, 56–58; material
action of; 57; in method of this
book, 10, 13, 15; style compared
with that of *Persuasion*, 147–48;
style compared with that of *Sister
Carrie*, 114–15; style of conclusion
analyzed, 58–66; style of passage
from book 8 analyzed, 46–56; style
of conclusion from Olson's perspective, 157–58
Ambiguity: in aesthetic texts, 190–92,
209; in *The Ambassadors, Lolita,*
and *Sister Carrie*, 208–9; and
grammatical closure, 235 n.35; potential for emphasized by Miller,
134; of sentences out of context, 86;
in *Willie Masters' Lonesome Wife*,
193–201

Aporia, 124, 128, 130, 133
Appel, Alfred Jr., 240 n.1, 241 n.13
Argument from bad writing, 67, 70. *See
also* Lodge, David
Argument from translation, 67, 69. *See
also* Lodge, David
Artistic success and stylistic felicity,
149–50
"A Slumber Did My Spirit Seal"
(Wordsworth), 92–97
Audience as part of context, 35, 39, 78,
81. *See also* Reader; Reader-
response criticism
Austen, Jane, 219, 225–26. *See also
Persuasion*
Austin, J. L., 236 n.7
Author: in aesthetic texts, 191–92; as
maker of meaning, 86–97; in
pluralistic approach to criticism,
229. *See also* Intention

Barth, John, 12,
Barthelme, Donald, 12
Barthes, Roland, 12
Bateson, Frederick, 92, 94–95
Beardsley, Monroe, 17, 80
Bever, T. G., 234 n.31
Blackstock, Walter, 98
Booth, Stephen, 232 n.2
Booth, Wayne, 8, 122–23, 222–24, 231,
242 n.1
Brooks, Cleanth, 92, 94–95
Bunyan, John, *(The Pilgrim's Prog-
ress),* 20, 40
Burke, Kenneth, 239 n.19

Cameron, J. M., 70

Chandler, Raymond, 219
Character: within neo-Aristotelian criticism, 8, 156–60; as nonlinguistic element of fiction, 4, 42, 43, 82–83, 115–16, 149; within organicist criticism, 8, 71, 72; in *Willie Masters' Lonesome Wife*, 201–2, 207
Chomsky, Noam, 31, 227
Circumstance, 189
Codes, Eco's theory of, 186–92
Communication, failures in, 87–88
Competing explanations, 224–29
Connotation: in aesthetic texts, 215–16, 217, 218; in Eco's compositional analysis, 189; defined, 186–87, in *Willie Masters' Lonesome Wife*, 193–201, 209. *See also* Eco, Umberto
Conrad, Joseph, 11
Content as inseparable from form, 67–68, 70, 78–81. *See also* Content plane; Synonymy
Content plane: in aesthetic texts, 190–92; in Eco's semiotics, 186–92; in *Willie Masters' Lonesome Wife*, 193–201, 218. *See also* Expression plane
Context: in Eco's Semiotics, 189; importance of, 134–35; inevitability of, 91; relation to meaning, 35, 36, 41, 42, 78–81, 86. *See also* Speech-event
Continuum as model for roles of style in fiction, 150–52
Coover, Robert, 12
Crane, R. S., 8, 155, 239 n.19
Crews, Frederick, 58

Davis, Walter, 237 n.19, 243 n.1
Death's Duell (Donne), 20, 40
Deconstruction. *See* Derrida, Jacques; Miller, J. Hillis
Deliberative Acts. *See* Fish, Stanley
de Man, Paul, 11, 117
Denotation: in aesthetic texts, 215–!6, 217, 218; in Eco's compositional analysis, 189; defined, 186–87; in

Willie Masters' Lonesome Wife, 193–201, 209. *See also* Eco, Umberto
Derrida, Jacques: model of origin of meaning of questioned, 131; position of as basis for Hillis Miller's, 118–22; as representative deconstructionist, 11, 117, 118
Discourse competence, 227–29, 230. *See also* Linguistic competence
Donne, John, 20, 40
Dickens, Charles, 151, 219
Dreiser, Theodore. *See Sister Carrie*

Eco, Umberto, 13, 240 n.31; and compositional analysis of signs, 189; on connotative and denotative meaning, 186–87; and language of *Lolita*, 209, 222; and pluralism, 222, 224, 227, 228; as representative semiotician, 12; semiotic theory of described, 185–92; semiotic theory of applied to *Willie Masters' Lonesome Wife*, 193–201; theory of aesthetic texts of, 190–92; theory of codes of, 186–90; on value of aesthetic texts, 191–92
Eliot, George, 151
Encyclopedic knowledge, 79–82
Essentially contested concepts, 224
Expression plane: in aesthetic texts, 190–92; in Eco's semiotics, 186–92; in *Willie Masters' Lonesome Wife*, 193–201, 218. *See also* Content plane

Farewell to Arms, A (Ernest Hemingway), 72–75, 98
Faulkner, William, 10, 239 n.19
Ferry, David, 95
Fiction: identifying characteristics of, 210–11; nature of, 229–30; and pluralism, 229–31; as worlds from words, 115–16, 149; as world of words, 218–20. *See also* Fictive discourse; Literary discourse
Fictive discourse, 210, 214–17
Fielding, Henry, 11, 28, 151

First principles in criticism, 224–29
Fish, Stanley: approach applied to *The Ambassadors* of, 20–28; approach of described, 15–20; approach of critiqued 28–34, 38–43; from deconstructionist perspective, 117; and importance of deliberative acts, 17, 28–34, 38–43; and importance of interpretive assumptions, 87, 89–91; notion of informed reader of, 18, 22, 32–33; and pluralism, 223–29; as representative reader-response critic, 9–10, 12, 13
Flanagan, John, 97
Fodor, Jerry A., 240 n.31
Form: and intention 41, 237 n.19; and content, 67–68, 70
Frege, Gottlob, 37

Gallie, W. B., 224
Gass, William. *See Willie Masters' Lonesome Wife*
Goodman, Nelson, 75–76
Golding, William (*Lord of the Flies*), 235 n.41
Grammar: in reader-response criticism, 9, 17–20; in theory of part one, 28–35. *See also* Semantics; Syntax
Grammatical closure, 28–34, 35, 43

Hall, Spencer, 238 n.17
Hammet, Dashiell, 219
Hardy, Thomas, 9, 151, 204
Hartman, Geoffrey, 11, 117
Heart of Midlothian, The (Scott), 41–42, 151
Hegel, Friedrich, 129, 134
Hemingway, Ernest, 11, 72–75, 98
Hirsch, E. D., Jr.: on synonymy, 75–76, 235 n.36; on intention, 87–89, 92–94, 237 n.10
History: in criticism, 229; in fiction, 77
Hjelmslev, Louis, 120
Holland, Norman, 95

Indeterminacy. *See* Derrida, Jacques; Miller, J. Hillis

Intention: of *The Ambassadors*, 44–45, 56–58; and discourse competence, 227; distinguished from meaning, 84, 86–97; and Eco's semiotics, 207; and importance of style in *The Ambassadors*, 46–66; and importance of style in *Lolita*, 165–82; and importance of style in *Persuasion*, 137–48; and importance of style in *Sister Carrie*, 101–15; and importance of style in *Willie Masters' Lonesome Wife*, 193–207; initial assumption about, 7; and limits of theory of part one, 221–22; of *Lolita*, 161–65; as nonlinguistic aspect of speech event, 35, 78, 81–97; of *Persuasion*, 135–36; in Rader's view, 30, 41; relation to language of a text of, 84–86; of *Sister Carrie*, 98–101; and stylistic felicity, 149–50; of *Willie Masters' Lonesome Wife*, 202–7, 212
Interpretant, 118

Jakobson, Roman, 190, 191
James, Henry. *See Ambassadors, The*
Joyce, James, 9, 155, 208

Katz, Jerrold, J., 240 n.31
King Lear, 40, 46, 130, 159–60
Krieger, Murray, 8

Language: distinguished from style, 6; as explanatory principle of literary response, 7; relation to intention, 81–97; relation of to its users, 131–35; role of in *The Ambassadors*, summarized, 65–66; role of in Eco's theory of aesthetic texts, 190–92; role of in Fish's theory, 67–71; role of in *Lolita* summarized, 182–83; role of in Miller's theory, 118–24; role of in Olson's theory, 156–60; role of in *Persuasion* summarized, 147–48; role of in *Sister Carrie* summarized, 113–14; role of in *Willie Masters' Lonesome Wife* summarized, 206–7. *See also*

Grammatical closure; Linguistic competence; Style

Langue, 93

Limits of theory summarized, 221–22, 229

Linguistic competence: as ground for theoretical reasoning, 227; and relation of to Fish's theory, 31–34, 37; and relation of to Lodge's theory, 76–77; and relation of to notion of indeterminacy, 134. *See also* Intention

Literary discourse, 70–71, 75–78, 80–81

Lodge, David: approach of described, 67–71; approach of critiqued, 71–81; argument from bad writing of addressed, 70; argument from translation of addressed, 69; concept of realization of, 72–73, 148, 179, 223; philosophical basis of theory of, 70; and pluralism, 223–29; practical basis of theory of, 70–71; related to New Critics, 68; as representative idealist-organicist critic, 7–9, 12, 66; views on literary and nonliterary discourse of, 75–77

Logocentric tradition, 119–22

Lolita (Nabokov), 184, 185, 211, 215; and Eco's approach, 208–9, 242 n.5; as example of stylistic beauty, 3–4, 7; Humbert Humbert's narrative stance in, 162–63, 164, 179–82; implications for pluralism of, 222; intention of, 161–65; in method of this book, 9, 10, 13, 14, 152, 155, 156, 161; misuse of style in, 182; role of style in summarized, 182–83; seduction scene in, 164; style of davenport scene of analyzed, 172–76; style of opening invocation of analyzed, 165–71; style of paraphrased, 166, 174; variety of style in, 177–79

Lord of the Flies (William Golding), 235 n. 41

MacAleer, John J., 236 n.2

Marks, Robert, 58, 60

Matchmaker, The (Wilder), 36

Matthiessen, F, O., 58, 59

McCaffery, Larry, 241 n.1, 242 n.3

Meaning: and context, 35–38; 78–81; distinguished from intention, 84, 86–97; and grammar, 28–34. *See also* Intention; Pluralism; Speech event

Media in representational arts, 6–7

Meredith, George, 10

Metafiction, 12, 185, 210–20. *See also* *Willie Masters' Lonesome Wife*

Miller, J. Hillis: approach of applied to *Persuasion*, 124–28; approach of compared to Eco's, 192; approach of critiqued, 128–35; approach of described, 122–24; and pluralism, 223–29; as representative deconstructionist, 11, 12, 13, 117, 118; view of language and its users of, 131; and *Willie Masters' Lonesome Wife*, 223, 228

Milton, John, "Lawrence of Virtuous Father Virtuous Son," 40–41; *Paradise Lost*, 18, 20, 29–34, 40, 43; *Samson Agonistes*, 89, 90, 91, 238 n.12

Moncrieff, Scott, 69

Monism, 223–31

Morton, Donald E., 241 n.2

Nabokov, Vladimir. *See Lolita*

Narrative progression, 20, 40–41

Neo-Aristotelian criticism, 238 n.19. *See also* Olson, Elder

New Critics, 68, 223. *See also* Lodge, David

Nonfictive discourse, 210, 214–17

Nonliterary discourse, 70–71, 75–78, 80–81

Olson, Elder: approach of critiqued, 160–61; approach of described, 156–60; concept of speech as action of, 159–60; concept of speech as meaningful of, 159–60; in method of this book, 9, 13, 14, 152, 155; relation of to theory of part one,

156–61; as representative neo-Aristotelian, 8
Ordinary Discourse. *See* Nonliterary discourse
Organicist-idealist criticism. *See* Lodge, David

Pale Fire (Nabokov), 241 n.7
Paradise Lost, 18, 20, 29–34, 40, 43
Paraphrase: effect on *The Ambassadors* of, 57; effect on *Lolita* of, 166–74; effect on *Persuasion* of, 147; effect on *Sister Carrie* of, 114–15; in Lodge's theory, 69, 70, 75–80; of passage from *The Ambassadors*, 46; of passage from *Persuasion*, 137; of passage from *Sister Carrie*, 113; of passage from *Willie Masters' Lonesome Wife*, 214; of passages from *Lolita*, 166, 174; possibility of in literary language, 4. *See also* Synonymy
Parole, 93. *See also* Saussure, Ferdinand de
Pater, Walter, 17, 18, 19, 20, 38, 39
Peirce, C. S., 188
Persuasion (Austen), 185, 208, 211, 222; conclusions about related to other novels, 149–52; deconstructed, 124–28, 130; importance of style of summarized, 147–48; intention of 135–36; in method of this book, 11, 12, 13, 116, 118; style of analyzed, 137–48; style of compared with style of *The Ambassadors*, and of *Sister Carrie*, 147–48
Pilgrim's Progress, The (Bunyan), 20, 40
Plot: in Lodge's theory, 67; in *A Farewell to Arms*, 74
Pluralism, 221–31; and nature of fiction, 230–31; problem of limits to 225–29. *See also* Booth, Wayne; Davis, Walter
Pratt, Mary Louise, 236 n.7
Presence, metaphysics of, 119–22, 130
Pride and Prejudice (Austen), 225

Proffer, Carl, 241 n.11
Proust, Marcel, 69

Questions, kinds of, 225–29. *See also* Pluralism

Rader, Ralph, 19, 29–32, 41, 241 n.12
Reader: actual, 228–29; as ideal, 45–46, 229; informed, 17–18, 22, 32–33; as subordinate to authors and texts, 86–97
Reader-response criticism. *See* Fish, Stanley
Realization, 72–73, 148, 223, 228. *See also* Lodge, David
Reference, 37, 187, 188
Regis, Edward Jr., 235 n.42
Relativism, 225

Sacks, Sheldon, 235 n.41, 240 n.32, 240 n.33
Samson Agonistes (Milton), 89, 90, 91, 238 n.12
Saussure, Ferdinand de: distinction between *langue* and *parole* of, 93; as interpreted by Derrida, 118–22; on language and thought, 235 n.41; principle of value in difference of, 10, 132
Scott, Walter, 9, 41–42, 151
Searle, John, 90, 236 n.7
Semantic fields in *Willie Masters' Lonesome Wife*, 193–201
Semantics: in Eco's theory of codes, 188–92; as element of style, 3, 35–39; in Fish's theory, 17–20; as insufficient for meaning, 29–34; as necessary for meaning, 29–34; and paraphrase, 76; requirements for a theory of, 134–35
Sememe, 189
Semiosis, process of: as focus in aesthetic texts, 208, 108, 210, 216, 218; as metalinguistic content, 215–18; in *Willie Masters' Lonesome Wife*, 193–201
Semiotics. *See* Eco, Umberto
Sense, 37

Sexism, 240 n.28, 242 n.7
Shakespeare, 40, 46, 130, 159–60
Sign, 10, 117, 186. *See also* Eco, Umberto
Sign-function, 186–92
Sign-vehicle, 188, 189, 190
Signification: in Eco, 186–90; in Saussure, 119
Signified, 10, 118–22. *See also* Content plane
Signifier, 10, 118–22. *See also* Expression plane
Sister Carrie (Dreiser), 130, 185, 208, 211, 222; conclusions about related to other novels, 149–52; as example of deficient style, 3–4, 7; importance of Hurstwood plot in, 100–101; intention of, 90–101; in method of this book, 9, 10, 13, 14, 66–67; and nature of fiction, 230; seen from reader-response perspective, 9; style of analyzed, 101–11; style of compared with style of *The Ambassadors*, 114–15; style of compared with style of *Persuasion*, 147–48; style as component of success, 149–50; style of evaluated, 111–15; style of paraphrased, 113; typical defenses of style of, 97–98; typical stylistic flaws in, 97
Smith, Barbara Herrnstein, 210, 231 n.9, 231 n.10
Speech as understood by Derrida, 119–22
Speech act theory, 236 n.7
Speech event: importance of nonlinguistic knowledge in, 134–35; nonlinguistic aspects of, 35, 78–81, 160. *See also* Context; Intention
Stegner, Page, 240 n.1
Sterne, Laurence, 150, 151, 204
Structuralism, 15, 223
Style: as device in metafiction, 213, 218–20; distinguished from content, 37–38; distinguished from language, 6; importance of in *The Ambassadors*, 43–66; importance of in *Lo-lita*, 162–83; importance of in *Persuasion*, 137–48; importance of in *Sister Carrie*, 101–15; in Lodge's theory, 75–77; in Olson's theory, 156–60; questions about importance of, 4; relation of to intention, 81–86. *See also* Intention; Language; Paraphrase; Synonymy
Stylish Eye, The (hypothetical), 218–20
Supplements to theory of part one, 222
Synonymy: consequences of for study of style, 41, 43; criteria for, 77–80; plausible existence of, 35–38. *See also* Goodman, Nelson; Hirsch, E. D., Jr.; Lodge, David
Syntax: and complexity of *The Ambassadors*, 28; as element of style, 3, 35–39; in Fish's theory, 17–20; as insufficient for meaning, 35; as necessary for meaning, 29–34; and paraphrase, 76

Tanner, Tony, 242 n.4
Tave, Stuart, 240 n.20
Tess of the D'Urbervilles (Hardy), 151, 204
Text, role of in creating meaning, 86–97
Thought, 42, 235 n.41
Trace, the. *See* Derrida, Jacques
Tristram Shandy (Sterne), 150, 151, 204

Value: as produced in language from difference, 119–20; of aesthetic texts, 192, 210–20; theory of, 222
Veeder, William, 234 n.24

Wagner, Vern, 97
Wallace, Ronald, 58
Whitehead, Alfred North, 18, 38, 39
Wilder, Thornton, 36
Willie Masters' Lonesome Wife (Gass): intention of, 202–7; language of analyzed, 193–201; length of, 212–23; in method of this book, 13, 14, 152, 155, 156, 183–85; and Miler's approach, 223, 228; and nature

of fiction, 230; nonfictive discourse in, 214–18; passage from paraphrased, 214; and pluralism, 222; as representative metafiction, 12; success of, 210–18 and theory of part one of, 209; typography of, 184, 196, 202, 203, 204, 212–13, 217, 218; as uncommon type of fiction, 214–18
Wimsatt, William, 8, 17, 72, 80

Woolf, Virginia, 9, 155
Wordsworth, William ("A Slumber Did My Spirit Seal"), 92–97
Worlds of words, 218–20. *See also* Fiction; *Willie Masters' Lonesome Wife*
Worlds from words, 115–16, 149. *See also* Fiction
Writing as understood by Derrida, 119–22